OF RIVERS, BAGUETTES
& BILLABONGS

Published by Brolga Publishing Pty Ltd
PO Box 12544 A'Beckett St Melbourne Australia 8006
ABN 46 063 962 443
email: sales@brolgapublishing.com.au
web: www.brolgapublishing.com.au

Copyright © Reg Egan 2012
National Library of Australia Cataloguing-in-Publication entry
        Of Rivers, Baguettes and Billabongs
        Reg Egan
        ISBN 9781922036599
        Social history.
        cultural relations.
        Australians--Travel--France.
        France--Relations--Australia.
        Australia--Relations--France.
        Darling River (Qld. and N.S.W.)--Social conditions.
        Dodoigne River (France)--Social conditions.
Dewey Number: 306.42
Printed in China
Cover design by David Khan
Typeset by Wanissa Somsuphangsri

Of Rivers, Baguettes

& Billabongs

An exploration of the Dordogne
and east of the Darling

By Reg Egan

Every man has two countries —
his own and France.

Attributed to Thomas Jefferson

(1743 – 1826)

PREFACE

Writers are a curious mob: a few make a handsome living, some make enough to exist and thereby justify their occupation but the majority survive - somehow. So, why do they do it? Why do they stick at it?

The glib answer is: because they love it. But perhaps it is more than that; perhaps it is also a wish to share. They have come upon something or have discovered something which is too good to keep to themselves and so they want to share it with you; whether you like it or not. And while I hope that I do not sound too fervent, that is the principal reason for this book: a wish to share two great loves; one which began to manifest itself when I was as young as six or seven and the other which crept into my life when I was in my early thirties and burst like a grand fireworks display when I crossed the Rhine into France in 1972.

I lived the first nineteen or so years of my life in the bush. I do not mean the country, which is sometimes referred to as "the bush" by clever and disparaging media people, I actually mean the bush. It was a place called Tolmie and it was in the hills halfway between the towns of Mansfield and Whitfield in north-eastern Victoria.

Our farm had deep rich brown soil, a big rainfall and was cold and frosty and wet in winter with the occasional three or four inches (75 – 100 millimetres) of snow. In summer it could be hot but the nights were always cool to cold.

If you walked up to the back of our farm (and on to the neighbour's farm) you had a reasonably good view down towards Cheshunt and the valley of the King River; you were aware of the wonderfully scenic Powers Lookout a few miles away and of the Mt Buffalo park in the far distance; there was Mt Feathertop straight ahead but also very distant and Mt Hotham, wonderful, enigmatic Hotham and Dinner Plain near by; and finally as you turned to your right there was Mt Cobbler and Stirling and Buller.

Great country, great bush — with its elusive wild orchids, its startlingly clear creeks and their rocks, its rich hillsides blazing in the yellow wattles on a sunny afternoon in late winter, its serious gum trees in their unique greens, deep blue and grey-greens and its questioning native animals like its quick gliders, its ringtail possums, its mumbling, bumbling wombats, its clumsy wallabies and graceful grey kangaroos, and, and… Yes the list could be long.

Even as a boy I was in love with it all, and thanks to my parents and the majority of our schoolteachers, I was rather proud to be an Australian. Yet I had seen a tiny portion of this country. I did not so much as hear the roll of the sea and feel the sand beneath my feet until I was nineteen, and I knew nothing of the beauty of Tasmania, or of the glorious eastern coast of Australia. I had not been to the mountains of our Great Dividing Range nor had I felt the soft and deep warmth of our sub-tropical state of Queensland, and although I had heard about our cattle kings and our intrepid explorers, I had only read of the Outback and the glorious shapes and colours of the centre of this continent. But, ignorant though I was and am, I came to love it all. Then France arrived on the scene.

You can love two countries. Indeed you can love more than two, but let me, a real Aussie, explain to you about France.

Wine has taken me on a terrible, and a momentous journey. It was wine that led me to one of Melbourne's most honoured wine merchants Seabrook & Son adjoining the demolished Selbourne Chambers in Bourke Street. And it was Tom Seabrook ("old Tom", the father of Doug) who suggested that I should get a copy of the little Penguin paperback *The Generous Earth* by Philip Oyler, and it was Philip the lovesick Englishman who started my affair with France. Philip literally immersed himself in pre-World War Two France, but it was the valley of the Dordogne River which captured him heart and soul and held him a prisoner for the rest of his life.

Then came Freda White and her *Three Rivers of France* — Dordogne, Lot and Tarn, and then we went to France and finally we came upon the valley of the Dordogne. What more could a man ask?

Well, he could, as I have said, ask for a chance to share his love with you. Then comes the problem — how do you concentrate and condense your justification for the affection that you have for both these remarkable countries?

It seemed to me that you would choose a thing or an area that was involved in the history of each country and was to an extent at its geographical centre or near centre. At first therefore, I chose two rivers: the Dordogne in France and the Darling in Australia. Now in France I could have picked the Loire with its historical but perhaps too pretty and perfect châteaux; or I might have chosen the Seine rising in some quite beautiful country just to the north of the middle of France; or I might have written about the mighty

Rhone and its remarkable exit in the south of France; or I could have selected the Lot. But I finally concluded that it was the Dordogne originating in the Massif Central, that was most representative of the France that I had come to know and love, and especially villages and towns in its valley like Carennac and Sarlat.

The next task was to justify my Australian river — The Darling. The river which is in the eastern half of Australia marks, in its west, the start of the Outback. The Outback; what a word. But the more I researched and looked at the Darling River itself, the more I realised that it would not do. It is a boundary of sorts but it does not represent Australia in the way that the Dordogne Valley represents France. It is a river that seemed to gather together the highly adventurous squatters and nomads of the outback with their more conservative counterparts to the east of the river and it also encompassed many such squatters and station owners from over the border in Queensland.

But it was, even before the coming of the upstream irrigators and cotton magnates, an unreliable river, a stream that was as our historian C.E.W. Bean admitted in the early 1900s, "a river [which] will be navigable, on an average, for six or eight months in each year [and only] in the lower reaches". And even then we are speaking of navigable for relatively small steamers like his paddle steamer the *Dreadnought*.

No, the Darling and its valley and the valleys of its tributaries like the Bogan and the Culgoa and the Namoi and the rest of them, bear no resemblance to the Dordogne and its tributaries. Those Australian valleys are to a great extent uninhabitable, but the Darling does, as I have said, mark a boundary in Australia — it always has and it always will. It is the boundary that signals the beginning of the Outback and that Outback and its interpretation by writers and poets and painters and their like (living principally to the east and in the large towns and cities) describes and fixes many of the characteristics for which Australians are known and admired. And so, I could and I have, therefore, written about the actual valley and the people of the Dordogne but the spirit of the Darling and its influence, its disproportionate influence on the creation of the Australian character as we have come to know it.

I ask you to bear in mind, when reading this account of part of the geography and history of France and Australia, that it does not claim to be a complete or an exhaustive account. I hope it will simply whet your appetite and that you will now begin to explore the two countries and their architecture, their countryside, their writers and poets and their food and their differences and similarities — go deeper and go further than I have, but start your journeys. Taste the essence of France by travelling from Clermont Ferrand in the Auvergne and finishing on the Atlantic coast and, perhaps follow our route in Australia: along the east coast and then in a wandering way arrive eventually at Bourke, on the Darling and then wander back again.

And if you do not succumb completely and utterly to the charms, and the differences of each country, I'll... Yes, indeed I will.

Reg Egan

CHAPTER ONE

There is a stream, or creek, as we Australians say, deep in rugged hills and mountains not far from Victoria's Alpine National Park and it is called very simply the Evans Creek. It flows into the King River which joins the Ovens River near Wangaratta and the Ovens flows into the Murray.

My brother and I, aged twelve and ten or thereabouts, walked to that stream many years ago, and I thought then how beautiful it was with its rocks, its overhanging trees and shrubs and its cold and its clarity. It is in a deep and steep gully, covered sparsely but adequately with medium-sized eucalypts, sweet bursaria, wattles and patches of bracken fern, and nearer the stream, a leggy shrub we used to call hazel, and the whole is interspersed with these wonderful rocks. It's as if the rocks have been artistically placed with regard to the density and size of the trees and shrubs, and down by the watercourse, they are flat and smooth, so as to form small ledges and rough terraces. And I know that the scene has not changed even today, for it is still largely inaccessible

How exciting it was for us to set out that day on our journey of exploration! We had been given permission by our father to stay out in the bush overnight and he offered us only one piece of advice about finding our way there and back: "If you think you are lost go to the nearest gully or creek and follow it down. If you do that eventually you will come out at a farm somewhere around Cheshunt or Whitfield."

So we ventured forth with nothing but warm jackets, a billy, a small frying pan, fishing line and hooks and a box of matches each. Oh, and some wonderful ham sandwiches liberally spread with Keen's mustard — enough sandwiches for two meals.

In fact we had fish for dinner that night. And perhaps I do not need to tell you about trout straight from the water, fried and eaten in your fingers as dusk descends over the bush and the stars and a nail-moon emerge overhead. We kept our fire going all night and stayed as close to it as we dared, but we were glad to be up at daylight and fishing for our breakfast.

When we walked out that afternoon we both promised to return. I have reneged on that promise.

My love of streams progressed from that distant camping night on the Evans Creek and after a few years encompassed the trout river known as the Howqua near Mansfield, the King River below Powers Lookout and upstream into the foothills, the Ovens and its billabongs and even the Murrumbidgee and the Murray, and then, with a move to Melbourne, the seductive Yarra.

The Melbourne move was responsible for my getting to know the Thames in London, the Rhine and Mosel in

Germany with their backdrop of vines and castles, the Seine in Paris and its multitude of fine and romantic bridges, the Danube that waltzes through Vienna and charms the gypsies of historic Budapest, the Arno…

In the film *The River* (*Le Fleuve*) made in 1951 by that talented French filmmaker Jean Renoir, son of the painter Auguste Renoir, the narrator, a girl lingers by the river Ganges. She reflects by the river, meditates on the river and its influence on her life and finally she muses that they (she and her friends) might have lived on any river but if they had then "the flavour of the people who live by (that) river would have been different". I concur — the river, the country, the climate…

The first European river that I came to know and to love was that Rhine river, or more correctly, to know in part. We landed in Frankfurt, picked up a car and drove to the Rhine and then along it to Koblenz and then down (or up, really) the Mosel and so into France. The Rhine with its amazing water traffic, its wonderful valley and its vineyards and its castles: what an introduction to Europe. We were there at the beginning of autumn and the weather, although comfortably warm, was also showery and we were impressed and delighted by the activity in the outdoor cafes. After a shower had ceased, the waitresses were on the scene as the last drop fell, mopping the tables, re-adjusting the chairs and making everything inviting for the hoped for customer. You had to stop for a drink or coffee or anything, there was no alternative. And when you sat at your table and looked upwards, there you saw the golden grapes and the changing colours of the leaves.

When we got to the Mosel the scene was even more elegant and the river smaller, but just as lovely. How easy it was

3

to love both the Mosel and Rhine rivers.

The two rivers of France that stand out in my memory are the Rhone (near Condrieu) and the Dordogne (near Sarlat). The Rhone, by Australian standards, is simply immense and I whiled away the whole of one afternoon just sitting on the terrace of our hotel at Condrieu and watching the activities on that river.

What a mass of water: the width, the depth and the flow. Barges of half the countries of Europe thumped away out in the middle with gentle arcs peeling away from their prows and turbulent waters vainly trying to catch the sterns, and yet not far from where I sat there was a wooden fishing boat seeming almost becalmed with a cheerful fisherman casting a flimsy net supported by a mast and some complicated lines and poles. And on the bank almost under the terrace were two grizzled locals in old caps and workingmen's blues with their Gitanes, by the smell of it, and they were patiently waiting for a bite on lines suspended from abnormally long and rather rustic-looking fishing rods.

When we first encountered the Dordogne a storm had just broken over us and the rain was so heavy that it was advisable to stop the car. We were able to do so by the river and we had a view of a limestone village high on the other bank, made all the lovelier by the intermittent curtains of rain.

But, returning to Australia, the river that I most wanted to see was the enigmatic and, perhaps, romantic Darling, the river whose history was so adequately portrayed by the Australian writer C. W. Bean in 1911. I bought his book *The Dreadnought of the Darling* in the 1960s and read it, and re-read it, but it took me until the twenty-first century before I actually got to the Darling. And what did I see? Well, sometimes it is the journey that matters.

CHAPTER TWO

The Dordogne river rises near the centre of France and flows in a general south-westerly direction to join the Garonne some distance to the north of Bordeaux. It is 472 kilometres in length and the streams that mark its origin are the Dore and the Dognon. The Darling rises near Killarney in southern Queensland, Australia and is known there as the Condamine. Several small streams such as the Dumaresque, the Macintyre and the Barwon flow in a general south and south-westerly direction until at the confluence of the Barwon and the Culgoa Rivers that new river becomes the Darling. This river, the Darling then joins the Murray River at Wentworth. The experts tell us that the Darling has a total length of 1867 kilometres — four times as long as the Dordogne.

The Darling, as distinct from some of its tributaries, flows through a relatively arid part of Australia; in fact you could almost claim that today it marks the most westerly part of New

South Wales that should reasonably be farmed and grazed. The Dordogne, on the other hand, flows through one of the richest and most varied parts of France: vines, fruit trees, walnuts, poultry (especially geese and ducks), cattle, sheep and goats (and therefore butter and cheese). The Darling and east of the Darling is somewhat sparsely populated but the Dordogne is a valley of villages, towns, farms, woods, native vegetation. In a word, varied.

Such different rivers, such different people! And the thing that intrigues me at the outset is the question: what is it that makes the inhabitants of one country so different to those of another? Why are the French generally so different from the Australians generally? I know, we all know, that it is in part the language, the mixture of races, history, tradition, and so on, but I maintain that it is more than the sum of those relatively minor things. It is in my view the very country itself, its climate, its soil, its sky its indefinable atmosphere. It is everything about the country; its streams, its oceans and beaches, its *terroir*, to use a French winemaking expression, that produces a population that has characteristics different to and distinct from those, in the case of Australia, of its mother country or countries.

The French have developed the term terroir to a nice point, and it must be said that it has been a commercial success, open to criticism in this modern world though as being rather too unbending. Terroir encompasses more than just the climate and the soil in which the plant or tree grows, or the bird or animal is raised, it encompasses the topography, the geology, the sky, the atmosphere... anything at all which could possibly influence the product, something even in its past, its history, traditional ways and methods. France and Europe are bound closely by tradition and tradition is both good and bad. Australia, on the other hand, may be open to the criticism that we have scant respect for our traditions: we are too eager to be free of everything.

Soil and climate and plant varieties have always fascinated me. Some fifty-five years ago, we decided that we should not only drink wine but that we should grow the grapes and make the wine. I was in the law at the time, and for many reasons, but including the proximity of my practice, we eventually found a four-hectare site facing the Dandenongs in the outer suburbs of Melbourne. We are still there. Now on that small vineyard, we have, for example, three plots of Pinot (interspersed with other varieties) and they all produce differently, ripen at different times and have different characteristics. And yet they are all within two hundred metres of one another a demonstration of *terroir* in miniature.

Varietal characters are another thing that shouldn't surprise me but they do: there you have one apple tree planted next to another — same soil, rain, wind and sun — yet one is distinctly different to the other.

People, plants, *terroir*: a fascinating field for thought and reflection. But perhaps the final word on people and their country comes from an indigenous Australian, Bob Randall, elder of the Yankunytjatjara, the traditional owners of *the* rock, Ayer's Rock. These days that wonderful creation is more correctly and colourfully known as Uluru. A short while ago, Bob was doing a lengthy television interview, which was filmed with the rock in the background, and he had many sensible things to say. That rock! Honestly, I'm unashamedly in love with French Gothic cathedrals, and Uluru is the equal of any of them, and even... But to return to Bob Randall. He said this: "The people don't own the land — the land owns the people." You'd have to applaud such a summation as that.

CHAPTER THREE

The most convenient, and the most spectacular view of the birth of the Dordogne River is from your bedroom balcony looking to your left over toward the forbidding bulk of the Puy de Sancy. (Puy in Celtic is "volcano" or perhaps simply "peak" and Dore is " water").

A long plane trip, a short plane trip, a rental car, and suddenly there it was cascading from what appeared to be a wound in the side of the rocky mountain still partly snow covered at the end of May. You can approach Sancy from the other direction, no doubt, and if you did, equally without a doubt you would come upon small streams which gathered together either short of, or in a cleft in the mountain, but to see it from the Mount Dore side is wonderfully impressive and picturesque. If you walk out of your hotel and up towards the ski lift you will come upon a bridge and under it is the fat and fast stream that the waterfall has begot. This stream plunges straight down to the thriving spa and ski town of Mount Dore and the road runs beside it. On one side of the road are a series of ski lifts and ski nets above the road cutting, presumably to catch unwary skiers before they break their bones, and on the other is this sturdy brown stream and a succesion of chalets, hotels, and the like. You are in the region of the Auvergne but the department of Puy de Dôme; and you are also in the proximity of a young and racy river. Brimful of water and turbulence and excitement, it cannot wait to get there. And despite its impetuosity and its gauche immaturity you admire it and you are intrigued by it. You are beginning to fall under its spell.

The Auvergne is not as well known as places like Burgundy or Alsace or Provence, and it is very different, but so astonishingly beautiful. I must say that my previous impression had been that it was of a land of austerity and mystery. I wonder now how I got that impression. Many years ago we had stayed at what was then the rather passé spa town of Vichy and I had spent a few hours late one afternoon walking in the hills to the west of that town, but why did I have this notion that the Auvergne was remote and sombre? I determined to find out.

I went first to consult our ancient *Fodor*, an old light blue covered and rather tattered volume dated 1971, and I looked at the entry under a section entitled "The undiscovered provinces". It was headed "Exploring Auvergne" and it plunged straight into its spa towns, its healing waters and its health resorts but then it did go on to describe its volcanic mountains, its snow fields and its lakes. It even mentioned the famous literary mother Madame de Sévigné (who apparently frequented Vichy in the seventeenth century) and it went on to extol the architecture of the "beautiful twelfth century church of St. Nectaire". It wasn't a lengthy entry on this wonderful region, but there was nothing derogatory in it.

The aging *Encyclopaedia Britannica* was not adversely critical either–it gave a brief history of the Celtic confederation of
the Averni under the fierce and famous chieftain Vercingetorix,
and it mentioned Julius Caesar and the Bourbons.

I turned to the battered and travelled green *Michelin* and
also drew a blank. Why then this impression? Maybe it was
the Songs of the Auvergne, the lovely but haunting songs
sung and recorded by some of the best mezzo-sopranos.
These songs have a sadness about them which perhaps was
rooted in former days, the days when the farmers and villagers of the Auvergne were poor and remote; but then going
back only a century there was material poverty in many parts
of the world.

The songs of the Auvergne entitled *les chant paysan* were
collected by an unusual Frenchman, Joseph Canteloube
(1879 – 1957). Canteloube was born in the relatively nearby
hunting, fishing region of the Ardeche (where incidentally
Louis Latour has some lovely vineyards). Canteloube was a
man of unusual talents and after graduating in Paris spent
much of his early life in the Auvergne. He was captivated by
the place and its history. He maintained that 'peasant songs
often rise to the level of purest art'. It comes as no surprise
to learn that he entitled one of his operas "Vercingetorix".
You have only to glance at the huge and fantastic equestrian
statue of that warrior near the Place de Jaude in Clermont-
Ferrand to realise what an inspiration he must have been to
the composer. Canteloube, the man with the artistic soul,
became a sympathiser with the once famous but rather aged
Petain during Petain's collaboration with the Germans in the
1939 –1945 war. Canteloube survived the war and Petain,
and died peacefully in the Île de France in 1957.

Vercingetorix was a Celt, or if you prefer a Gaul, for

that is what these tribes were called by the invading armies lead by Julius Caesar in the middle of the first century BC. You may, or you may not, admire the famous crosser of the Rubicon, but what he did at least do was leave written records of his travels and deeds, his "commentaries". And, to an extent, we rely on those records to trace the movements and history of the Celts who, for some centuries, occupied a swathe right across central France before the Romans came to disturb them.

I'm impressed by the Celts and their enterprise and their artistry, especially in all forms of metallurgy, and by their predilection for moving ever westward in a broad band: not too far to the south and not too far to the north. So many Australians could conceivably trace their ancestry right back to France, the Auvergne and the headwaters of the Dordogne itself. They might have to go via Wales, Scotland, Ireland and parts of England, particularly Cornwall, but the line would be there.

Julius Caesar was stopped by the Celtic people at the famous battle of Gergovie, on the plateau just south of Clermont Ferrand, but the war was not over. Caesar re-grouped and at the subsequent battle at Alesia (near Dijon) the redoubtable Vercingetorix was finally defeated. It is thought that there were some six million Gauls in France at the time of the Roman occupation. It is estimated that perhaps one million of those were killed in the wars with Rome or subsequently executed (apart from those who had their right hands cut off for daring to oppose the invaders).

Alesia does not exist on most maps of France for it is the old Roman name for the town. The French name is actually Alise-Sainte-Reine, and yet when you read about that second and decisive battle, it is always referred to as the battle of

Alesia, without any reference to the modern name. Napoleon the Third, the second Napoleon Emperor of France, located the exact spot in 1865 or thereabouts. Before he got the boot over the Franco-Prussian war and other things, he had excavations done on and around Mount Auxois, and as the experts had prophesied there they found the remains of a Gallic *oppidum* (Celtic hill fort) and, of course, a Roman town hard by-as Julius Caesar would have written, I have no doubt, in those famous chronicles of his.

Napoleon commissioned a copper statue of Vercingetorix to mark the historic spot, and it stands no less than seven metres in height and is visible, as you might imagine, from very considerable distances. Napoleon, with perhaps a whiff of his imminent downfall had the scuptor Bartholdi, who also created the Statue of Liberty, give the statue a face in his own likeness. Ah, these great men.

Should you be in the Cote-d'Or, this very, very beautiful part of France, I strongly urge you to go to the village and then drive just a few kilometres to the exquisite and historical neighboring village of Flavigny-sur-Ozerain. According to Ulrike Laule, author of the wonderful hardback called simply *Burgundy*, it is "one of the most picturesque small cities of Burgundy whose historical centre has been almost completely preserved". Its situation in the soft countryside and its wonderful stone and even the production of anis pastilles in the monastic buildings, will enthral you. But back to Caesar and the Celtic warrior.

It is hard to imagine the Roman soldiers mixing too readily with the Celtic women and even harder to think that they stayed on after the occupation or that they colonised the Auvergne and the Dordogne Valley in any significant way. You could say, therefore, that this then remote area of France remained largely Celtic, except, of course, that there were subsequent invasions by the Alemanni (Germanic people), the Franks, the Vikings and no doubt one or two others; and not forgetting the Greeks, Italians, Arabs and others who came as traders in the south and stayed on. A mixed bag; and yet as you wander through the Auvergne and down the Dordogne you often look twice at the villagers, the shopkeepers and the hoteliers and you think, "They are not the olive skinned, brown eyed dark haired French. They are Australians."

And what happened to the brave Vercingetorix, the Celtic warrior who united some of the native tribes and who even had his likeness minted on some gold coins? Sadly he did not die in battle but was captured by Caesar, kept imprisoned and then taken to Rome where in 46 BC he was paraded through the streets as a war trophy and then executed, some say strangled, at Caesar's behest. The only consolation is that Julius Caesar himself was executed a year or two later by Brutus and his mates.

The Celts have left their mark on the Auvergne and the Dordogne and indeed, on France itself, especially in relation to the preservation of trees, streams and the countryside. There is evidence to suggest that the Celts were earth worshippers and that groves, wells, streams, rocks and the like were revered by them. As you travel from the Auvergne south-west down the Dordogne to Bordeaux you marvel at the rich mosaic of the forests of beech, oak, linden and fir trees. There is hardly a hill in France which has been cleared right up to its top, the grazing and the cultivation are confined to the lower hillsides and the valleys. This tradition has stood the countryside well in terms of erosion, climate, winds and rain. The beech forests in the spring in the Auvergne generally, and the Cantal and the Haut Loire in particular, are just as beautiful as the startlingly burnished copper beeches of the autumn. In fact, the shimmering gold of the spring beeches is quite amazing, contrasting as it does with the dark green of the pines and the grey blue of the firs, the deep green of the lush spring grass and the shapes of the puys (volcanoes) against a sky which seems always to have white and silver-grey clouds floating past. It is all rather lovely.

There is not that much evidence of the Roman occupation in the Auvergne for the Romans, it seemed, liked the softer countryside in the Berry and around Bourges and indeed made their headquarters in Bourges. But there is some: the simple but exquisite little bridge at Saurier, the temple of Mercury (and perhaps remains of a Celtic temple also) and of course the statue of Vercingetorix in Clermont Ferrand. The Romans came from a warm climate and perhaps that was a factor in their rather brief and transient occupation of the mountains and valleys of the beautiful Auvergne, an area with a climate utterly unlike that of the Imperial city.

The Auvergne can boast of the birth and/or occupation of many famous people. The first French pope, for example, Pope Sylvester 11, (also known as Pope Gerbert) was born in Aurillac (the capital of the Cantal department) in AD 945 and was educated at the St. Géraud Abbey. He became the pope in 999 at the relatively young age of fifty-four, young anyhow in the terms of 20th and 21st century popes, and he died only four years later in 1003. It is written of him that he "had a reputation for exceptional learning". His statue stands in the Place Gerbert.

Blaise Pascal the mathematician, physicist and philosopher was born in Clermont Ferrand in 1623 (Louis X111) and regrettably died a year before his fortieth birthday. Although he was a mathematician and scientist *extraordinaire*, at the early age of thirty-one he turned to philosophy and theology — a sort of Faustian about-turn. Pascal was a man who reflected deeply and has left us his *Pensées* or thoughts; and just diverging a little, I remember being in a market in St. Julien when I realised for the first time that the French called pansies "thoughts" or *pensées*. So I bought a few pots in full bloom and gave them to our hosts of that evening. But back to Pascal the thinker. Here are a couple of his thoughts:

"Not to care for philosophy is to be a true philosopher", and "If you want people to think well of you, do not speak well of yourself."

Pascal was once beloved by the "systems" men of the gambling fraternity but perhaps is more familiar today for the honour of having the S1 units of pressure named after him. It is said that the famous twentieth century Existentialists drew on some of his thoughts on religion.

A contemporary of Pascal's who lived for a time at Naddes and Espinarre in chateaux in the north of the Auvergne owned by her husband the Comte, was Madame de la Fayette, born Marie-Madelaine Pioche de la Verne. It is claimed that her novel *La Princesse de Clèves* published in 1678 when she was aged forty-four, was "the first true French novel".

Although she was born in Paris in 1634, after her marriage to the Comte she divided her time between his estates in the Auvergne and Bourbonnais before settling permanently in Paris in 1659.

And then there was the birth in 1885 in St. Julien Chapteuil (on the east of the Massif Centrale) of Jules Romain. Romain was drawn to Paris (of course) and did brilliantly in philosophy. Subsequently he turned to writing and in his books expounds his theory of "unanism" loosely translated as "the collective spirit"; for example, the spirit of a city.

My encyclopaedia sums up the word unanism as "the transcendent power of collective emotion...as a whole rather than the individuals composing it". Rather like *terroir*, in some ways. I wonder if we should try and revive unanism. The cult of the individual: the me, me, what about me? has its merits, but perhaps a stimulating dose of unanism say every ten years or so.

Jules Romain also wrote *Les Copains,* which was set partly in the circular town hall of Ambert. As a result, an excellent local restaurant or auberge is known by that name. I always think of Ambert on the Dore River (another Dore), as being on the wrong side of the Massif Centrale, too close to the infernally busy St. Etienne. And besides, the waters of that Dore River flow to the north into the Allier, and then into the Loire. But that river redeems itself by flowing eventually through the oak forests known as the Allier and also the oak forests of the Tronçais (near St. Bonnet Tronçais, *bien sûr*) and those forests are very dear to the hearts of all winemakers, be they French or Australian, for there isn't a winemaker in either country who wouldn't fall to his knees for a whiff of a skilfully toasted *barrique* (225 litre wine barrel) from this blessed region. And perhaps I should say in passing that it is the subtlety of the toast that matters — toast that blends with and complements fruit, not oak that dominates it.

Auvergnats are those people whose hearts will never leave their somehow remote and wild countryside, even though they have streamed and continue to stream into Paris in their thousands. If I were a young man who lived within sight of the Puy-de-Dome, I too would go to Paris, but I would come back, or I would resolve to come back. I would not forget the Auvergne.

There are many reminders of the Auvergne in Paris: in its restaurants and its restaurateurs, its wine from St. Pourçain, its show business, its music, its literature and its politicians. Wasn't Georges Pompidou born in Montboudie and weren't the d'Estaings, both Charles-Hector and Giscard also sons of the Auvergne? Charles-Hector (18th century) and Giscard (20th century) were very successful in France but it must be said that Charles-Hector stumbled a few times as commander of the first French Fleet at the time of the American War of Independence and unluckily was guillotined during the Terror, as a reward for his efficiency as Commander of the National Guard during the Revolution. Giscard can and, no doubt, has claimed that he was a distant relative of the great Charlemagne.

And there was, or rather is, Jacques Chirac, one of the most enigmatic of them all, and long lasting. Chirac was born in Paris but spent some of his early life in nearby Corréze where his family had useful connections. Chirac and then Nicolas Sarkozy, quite a contrast for the conservative French. Sarkozy certainly was *not* born in the Auvergne. It is said that Auvergnants like to describe France as "The Auvergne with a bit of land around it".

And finally we must give the Bourbons a mention. The Chateau of the Bourbon Dukes stands on the top of the hill in the town of Montluçon and the remains of the old feudal castle still exists on the rocky promontory of Bourbon l'Archambault, both in the north of the Allier Department. This general area was once known as the province of Bourbonnais. Henry 1V ("Paris is worth a Mass") was the first Bourbon (son of Antoine de Bourbon, Duke of Vendôme and King of Navarre) and Charles X, who was deposed in 1830, was rightly, or wrongly, the last, or in any event, the last to reign. The old Louis-Phillipe imposed himself on the French for a while but then he made the mistake of preferring the Fleur-de-Lis to the Tricolor, and that was certainly that.

Auvergne, land of mists and snow, of mountain peaks and inverted cones, of icy rivers, waterfalls and gentle lakes, of grass and cereals of the deepest green, of shining clouds and skies of clear blue, of wonderfully long-horned red cattle and short but powerful horses, of sheep and goats and cheese and wine, of the headwaters, indeed the origin, of the Dordogne River, we love you. But we must move on, we must become more specific. You are still around us, but we must go back to Puy de Sancy and then journey south-west down the river to Bourg and Bordeaux. In short, we should become a friend of the river and maintain that friendship throughout its life: its turbulent youth in the Auvergne, its middle age in the Perigord and its old age from the Entre deux Mers to its death in the Atlantic.

CHAPTER FOUR

Picking up the rental car at Clermont Ferrand had not been without a little trauma and amusement, mainly with regard to our rejection of a somewhat battered Citroën, but finally we were on our way. We had determined on a direct route down to Puy de Sancy where we had booked a room, and that direct route was thus: on to the Autoroute the A75, exit 6 on to the D 978, follow the D 996 and straight on to Le Mont Dore (the town) and on to Puy de Sancy. We estimated that we would arrive at our hotel in the early afternoon. We hadn't allowed for the loveliness of the country and the fascination of the villages along the way.

Even as you drive along the autoroute you are struck by the views on both sides of the road: hills close by, volcanic mountains in the distance and everywhere the gold and the green of the trees; the hills, the peaks, the dramatic valleys…It was hard not to stop and to take a D road to the East towards the forest of Livradois or to plunge in amongst the very *volcans* of the Auvergne on the West.

We kept to our plan, however and took our exit along the D 978. At 11.45 we arrived at the quiet village of Champeix. There were two reasons for us to be concerned. Firstly it was a Monday (not a good day for shopping in the French countryside), and secondly it was only a quarter of an hour until the whole village would close for lunch. The *boulangerie* was open and we got our *demi-baguette* and made enquires about the *épicerie*. It was closed, of course, but there was the Ecomarché at the top of the hill on the way out of the village, the less than attractive supermarchés that the French have allowed in thousands of towns and villages.

Never mind, it would have all we would need and indeed it did: walnut oil (essential for picnics in France), vegetables, fruit, water, cheese, delicious *pâté de compagne* (country terrine) and paper napkins et cetera. The punnet of hybrid wood strawberries (*frais de bois*) that I bought in my excitement, however, were well past their use-by date.

Champeix is just a pleasant village but the dwellings above the shops in the main street are all four floors in height. Why such accommodation in a place like this? Was it once home to more people than there appeared to be in 2008? It also had a small building which is somewhat rare in France. A toilet. Never mind that it was for men only. It is well known that women go but rarely. Toilets in France, or rather the lack of them, that is a lengthy subject. It is curious though that they are so little provided.

We found a spot to pull into for lunch and I walked through a meadow of grass, herbs and wildflowers to yet another fast flowing mountain stream. Everywhere there are streams or rivers, small and large and eventually they flow into the mighty Dordogne. If we had but a small proportion of these waters in Australia! There seemed to be more birds here than in other parts of France. I wondered if birds were making a comeback over here.

What a simple but what a satisfying lunch. Once…once a few trips ago we used to go into a restaurant for lunch. It was *de rigour*. How did we do it? And, more importantly, why did we? We hadn't quite finished the baguette, so we crumbed it and threw it in the bushes for those French birds. The diesel fired, and we pulled back on to the road.

After you pass the turn off to the village of Verriers there is a small road on your left and a short way along there is a dolmen-something to gaze at and wonder about. It is a long way short of Stonehenge, of course, but what is it about these simple stones arranged by Celts some two thousand or more years ago. (Past Saint-Nectaire there is a menhir, and another dolmen but on the side road.)

Saint-Nectaire has been highly praised in some of the reference books (as has the cheese of that area) and it was with some excitement that we drove into the town and parked the car. What has happened to this famous little spa town? Our parking bay was next to the town's public gardens, but alas they were overgrown and neglected. We walked up the hill towards a building which announced itself as the Casino. Was it closed for the season or forever? There were grand early nineteenth century houses beautifully set in the valley on one side of the main street and precariously and expensively moulded into the rocks and cliff on the other side. All were empty and many were *à vendre*-for sale.

We turned around and walked back down to the rather sad but once grand and opulent village. There was a hotel which appeared to have no customers at all, houses, no…

mansions, but again most were for sale and the agents' boards were tired, rusty and flapping in the breeze. There were two little bistros or cafés still doing reasonable luncheon business at this rather late hour. The specialities on the blackboards were tripe at one and pigs trotters at the other. I didn't regret our picnic lunch.

We drove up past the Casino and took the road to the haut Saint-Nectaire. Ah, this was better, simpler. Real houses, gardens and shops, and there on the hill dominating the faithful and saluting God was the famous Romanesque church built over the grave of the local saint, Saint-Nectaire. I say it is Romanesque but in the style of the region with more than a hint of "Moorish" or perhaps with memories of what the Crusaders may have seen on their somewhat murderous travels to the Middle East.

The Auvergne, and specifically Clermont Ferrand, had a big hand in the First Crusade of the eleventh century. It was at the capital in 1095 that the former monk of Cluny, the Frenchman Pope Urban 11 made what was said to be some of the "most moving orations recorded in history". He spoke to the crowd in the open, for not even the largest building could accommodate the multitude which came to heed his words. It is said that even the pope was surprised by the response. It was like the war cry of the American Indians or the Maoris of New Zealand. He had set in motion a force of bigotry, politics and plunder that lasted for more than a hundred years.

Don't think of Tournus and its Romanesque cathedral, for example, when you think of the Auvergne and its old churches. There are similarities in construction but you might easily come to the conclusion that Notre Dame du Port at Clermont Ferrand, the Basilica at Orcival, the Saint-

Nectaire church and a few others had been designed by the one architect and had the same builder. Of course they are all built of the dark volcanic rock of the area, and the face of the rock is in all cases relatively smooth, almost as if it had been sawn. In addition each church has a decorative mosaic which is beautifully done, but somehow to me, looks cold and fussy. Orcival is my favourite, partly because of its situation. It is softened by the valley, the trees and the nearby buildings. Saint-Nectaire dominates.

I always have a great affection for abbeys which, by necessity, I suppose are built in valleys near a source of water, but there is friendliness and humility in most abbeys, and their cloisters are very special. I like their background of the forest, the river and the seclusion. Vézelay is classified as an abbey cathedral, Conques has its delightful, exquisite abbey church, and Mont St. Michael is said to be an abbey complex, but one of my first abbeys to fit the description I've just given was Flaran, in the Gers, on the road from Auch to Condom and by the Baize River. It has been extensively restored over the last twenty or so years, but is still friendly and humble. You could spend your life there — perhaps.

You leave Saint-Nectaire and journey on towards Murol with its decaying but spendidly impressive fort or chateau away on the hill to your right and then you go through some of the loveliest grazing land populated by red Salers cattle and stubby, sturdy horses. The houses are few and far between but away off on the sides of the hills and in the valleys you can see these little stone farm buildings. They have great charm, nestling into the hillsides. They are of the same dark grey and black stone, and often have roofs of phondite, or split stone, yet nonetheless they blend into the countryside just as easily as the limestone houses in the lower Dordogne.

We took the Route du Fromage, which was probably designed to service the farms, villages and towns of the area, but which proves to be a scenic road along the ridges. The views of puys, mountains, valleys, drifts of snow and forests continue, and every now and again a mountain horse gazes at you or a herd of red milking cows raises numerous enquiring heads. Good country.

You come across Chambon-sur-Lac almost in surprise. It is quite beautiful, framed by mountains with their peaks still partly covered by slow drifting cloud. We stopped for coffee at a family run place which had dealt with its luncheon guests and was now satisfying its own hunger. The coffee was good.

By the time we got to Le Mont Dore, the afternoon was closing in and we took the cul-de-sac to Puy de Sancy. The mountain peak is spectacular but because you are already half way up the group of mountains it belies its height. It was very cold, painfully cold almost, but we managed to explore the hut near the terminus of the chair lift and to speak to a small mob of goats standing nearby. The hut housed a memorial (or perhaps a tomb) to two men of the Resistance who were killed in September 1944 in this remote and beautiful spot. What were they doing here? Why would the Germans have pursued them half way up this mountain?

How tragic it was that the *maquis* and its members of the Resistance the *maquisards* moved to combat the German occupying force as soon as they did. They were besotted, no doubt, with the euphoria of D-day, 6 June 1944, and overestimated their strength and grossly underestimated the wounded but still powerful German forces.

The town of Tulle is on the Corrèze river, a tributary of the Dordogne, and is just to the west of the Auvergne. The

Resistance determined to seize Tulle and to defend it as one of the first French outposts of the "unoccupied" south. It was surrounded by hills, dear to the *maquis*, and had a small armaments industry. On 8 June the Resistance duly overpowered the German garrison and killed some fifty Germans in the process; they took a further sixty prisoners and executed ten of those on the basis that they were members of the Gestapo and had been responsible for atrocities. They then flew the French flag over the town and basked in their glorious actions.

Unfortunately for the residents of Tulle, a heavily armoured troupe of the notorious SS Division, Das Reich, was nearby, on its way to the Normandy front. It was instructed to deal with the situation. The *maquisards* saw that they were heavily outgunned and withdrew to the hills. The SS Division re-established control over the town and the following day the Germans arbitrarily selected ninety-nine local men and hanged them from balconies in the centre of the town.

Reprisals and monuments to innocent civilians, men, women and children are all over France, especially in the south. The first one that we saw was years ago at Frayssinet-le-Gélat (between Fumel and Gourdon) where fifteen women and men selected at random were shot. You stand in front of the monument outside the church of this lovely village and you gaze at the unusual church with its massive tower and a small tower and pepperpot clinging to it, and you curse all weapons and all wars, and you feel sad for the victims and even for the perpetrators. How could they and how can we? And yet even today it happens, and not only in the "third world" countries: killings, rape, and (and democracies should bow their heads) torture, and worse almost, tacit complicity by other democracies in that torture.

CHAPTER FIVE

My early morning walk is of great importance and on the way to our hotel I had
noted that there was a forest of beeches half way
down the mountain towards the town. Before
breakfast then I put on every jumper, jacket and
scarf I could lay my hands on and set out.

Once in the forest it seemed warmer and I
followed what appeared to be a roughly formed
fire track. Copper beeches! You cannot overstate
their beauty whether in their lime green of spring
or their bronze of autumn. I went deeply into the
forest and around the side of the hill, and finally I
was warm enough to rest with my foot on an old
log. It was so quiet. Not even a bird call.

I had known a boy once and I thought of that
boy as I rested. The first thing he recalls, is lying
in bed and looking at the branches of a laurel tree
which came right up to the window. As that boy
watched the tree he saw the leaves form a picture
of a dog: there was its face, its muzzle, its ears and
its eyes. It was a perfect dog and jumping from

the bed he ran outside to look at it more closely. It had disappeared. He searched and searched but it had gone. He went back to the bedroom and climbed into bed. There it was! He darted outside. There was no dog. His disappointment was acute. Why could not he see and touch that dog which was so clearly visible from the bedroom?

That boy — that boy of long ago. Me, of course, but no longer me. He is a child whose occasional thoughts and actions I can describe but as I look back, it is as if he is a character in a book. I turned and went slowly back through that beautiful forest and up the steep road to our hotel.

Our destination on that day was St. Martin-Valmeroux, or more correctly a *hostellerie* out from that town and in the valley of the Maronne.

We had by-passed the famous mountain peak of Puy-de-Dôme — the haunt of the Celts and the site of the temple of Mercury built by the Romans in the first century BC — and so we had to take the word of the guide books that on a clear day you could look back to Clermont-Ferrand in the East, that Beaujolais was visible and even the summit of Mont Blanc. We would console ourselves with the view from Puy Mary to the south in the Cantal. Anyhow Puy Mary at 1787 metres is higher than Puy-de-Dôme.

When you leave Puy-de-Sancy you descend rapidly to Le Mont Dore (not the mountain, the town) and what a charming bustling spa and ski town it is. How curious that it has prospered while the relatively nearby Saint-Nectaire has declined. We stopped to buy our lunch at a lovely *boulangerie* (half, or a *demi-baguette*). It may be hard to believe but we then had the choice of three fruit shops. One of those shops also sold wine and liqueurs naturally, and so we were able to discuss the merits and shortfalls of one of the local aperitifs,

Gentiane. We did *not* buy a bottle.

We by-passed La Bourbole and took the little yellow D645 which goes uphill and through a dark and lovely oak forest. You meet no one on the road — there is no traffic — but the surface of the road is smooth and adequate. I doubt that I've ever seen a pothole in the French country roads. When you see a profile of the bitumen it appears to be about 125mm in thickness (alright, five inches).

We went through La Tour d'Auvergne and Bagnols and then on to the red road, the D922, and then, how it happened I don't know, but suddenly we were on the road to Trizac and chasing a church and a château. Trizac was sleeping peacefully in the spring sun and the town was quite amazing in its sombre hues of dark grey volcanic stones and roofs of *lauzes*-heavy, shale-type stones. The stone in the walls of the church was, in fact, a rich brown rather than the usual dark grey of the volcanic rock. You have to wonder how they quarried all the stone that there is in the buildings of France. The château that we had sought was closed for lunch, re-opening at 2.00 p.m. We journeyed on and found a very scenic spot for our picnic including (of course) a heavy stone table and stone bench seats.

Puy Mary (I don't know why it doesn't have a "de", nor why it is Mary) is in the heart of the Monts du Cantal, and therefore in a corner of the Parc National Regional Des Volcans. You may not be able to see the Beaujolais or Mont Blanc from here but you won't regret that. The green valleys with their intermittent forests and peaks, cones and rounded summits more than compensate for the spectacular views from the Puy-de-Dôme. The Vallée de Falgoux is not the most direct route back to the D922 but it is charming and a relatively easy drive.

We arrived at St. Martin-Valmeroux in time for a late cof-

fee at a pleasant little café not far from the main road. What
does this village consist of? More dark stone houses, with a
hint of chocolate, a picturesque church and quiet streets. We
found the road to the Valley of the Maronne without much
trouble and soon were comfortably settled in a room with a
view up the length of the valley. A view of stone (of course)
houses with every now and again an isolated hut called a *buron*. These huts were used in the past for cheese making, and
although they no longer serve that purpose, they are well
maintained and add to the character of this lush valley with
its distinctive cattle and its reserves of forest. Oh, but it was a
valley of charm with its trout river, its pedestrian bridges for
the use of anglers, its well maintained track along the river
and its curious fences.

Everyone at the Hostellerie was talking about the village
of Salers and how we must visit it the next morning. And so
we made the short journey

Salers houses are all gables and towers and pepperpots and
lauzes and seem to be in the same condition they were when
they were built seven or eight hundred years ago. The amazing thing about this little town on the hill is that it exists of
its own accord. It is touristy, yes, but it has its own life and
commerce. The visitors make it busier, no doubt, but Salers
would continue on its way even without the tourists. It's easy
to love Salers and I bought the best punnet of hybrid *Fraise de
Bois* — every strawberry was perfect and the perfume outdid
Chanel or Dior, or any of them.

Freda White, in her classic *The Three Rivers of France*
(1953) says of Salers: "Up the valley of the Maronne from
(Valmeroux) lies Salers, perhaps the prettiest little town of
the Auvergne. It was for long a judicial centre, and the towered houses around its tiny square belonged to lawyers, the

'nobility of the robe'." Ah, these lawyers, how often have we knelt and thanked the Good Lord for the profession of the law and its dedicated members.

CHAPTER SIX

Last night after our entrée and main course, we were allowed, or cunningly manoeuvred, to linger over the remaining third of the wine bottle. A cheese trolley was then wheeled alongside the table with knives, forks and plates, and naturally a basket of fresh and warm, sliced baguette.

"Five cheeses, cheeses of the Auvergne, local…" She picked up her knife and fork and leant towards our table looking from one diner to the other.

"This," she said, "is the *Cantal* — very popular throughout France now and very ancient. I think it was mentioned by Pliny the Elder in the first century BC." I nodded, and she skilfully cut a slice and put it on my plate.

Cantal is from the milk of the beautiful Salers cows. It is pressed twice — once when the curd is broken up and salted and the second time when it is pressed into its final mold. You can buy it young, *jeune* when it is at least thirty days old, medium or *entre dou,* when it is between two and six months in age, and *vieux,* when it is more than six months old. As in so many instances *vieux* is…best. *Cantal* cheese comes from what in the Auvergne is known as the *Pay Vert.*

Saint Nectaire comes from the high country around this little town, the communes of the Puy-de-Dôme (of the famous views), and from specified areas in the Cantal. It has been around since before Louis X1V. It is creamy, firm but springy in the mouth, and has perhaps a suggestion of mould, and it has a certain fame. Yes, we would have a slice, or *tranche.*

Bleu d'Auvergne is, of course, a blue cheese, again from cow's milk and is very similar to *Fourme d'Ambert.* Its area of production is extensive and takes in part of the Lozere and even the Lot. And it is delicious. Another slice? *Oui, merci.*

The final cheese that I was tempted to take was from a farmer or *fermier* from the distant town of Saint-Jean-de-Chapteuil, the home of that Jules Romain fellow. And in addition that cheese was from goat's milk, a change from the cow's milk cheeses, splendid though they are. The cheese is dry, soft and full of flavour.

What a way to finish the last of the bottle, and what an excuse.

There is an excellent little book *French Cheeses* written by (yes, it's true) Kazuko Masui and Tomoko Yamuda and they attempt the well nigh impossible and advise you on what wine goes with which cheese. The practical answer often is that you are simply tempted to have cheese to enable you to finish the wine that remains after the conclusion of the main course. Their advice, though, is good. They admit that there "are no hard and fast rules", and suggest trial and experimentation.

Cheese has been made for the last five thousand years at least. Certainly there appears to be evidence of cheesemaking equipment in Europe and Egypt for that period. And Homer (9th or 8th century B.C.) in the *Odyssey* gives an excellent description of cheesemaking from goat's and ewe's milk and storage of the product in baskets in caves. Was it by any chance a blue cheese? Virgil in 52 BC also writes about cheese.

Our Japanese authors reflect on the origin of the "Holy Trinity" of wine, cheese and bread, and suggest that the fifteenth century monk and writer Rabelais may have coined the phrase. I find that his Holy Trinity is much easier to understand than the ecclesiastical one. Cheese, bread and wine — beautiful. I must ask my heart man if the Trinity raises or lowers cholesterol. In this respect I note with pleasure that the very delicious Italian cheeses, Parmesan, *Parmigiano Reggiano* and *Grana* are made from "partially skimmed" milk. Away with thee, cholesterol.

CHAPTER SEVEN

It was hard to leave the Vallee de la Maronne, but we were consoled by the thought of the D roads ahead, the forests and the villages set so unobtrusively (except for *super and hypermarches*) in the rolling countryside.

So it was off. On to the D922, across the river and up the hill, foot hard down on the superb little diesel.

Morning tea was in a forest where wild flowers bloomed abundantly in the grass. There were gentians, of course, wild orchids which remind me of hyacinths, nigella (which I love dearly, but because of my mother, not, I hasten to assure you, because of the English cook), foxglove, buttercups, forget-me-nots, violets, geraniums — very small and quite delicate, scarlet poppies, marguerites, naturally, and…and all sorts that I didn't recognise.

The trees that provided an almost solid background were oak, birch and linden. I can't recall on previous trips seeing so many linden trees nor do I recall their dense foliage or their size. The first of these trees that I ever remember recognizing was in the south-eastern corner of the Flagstaff Gardens in Melbourne. And the first birches I remember seeing were in a delightful coloured glossy brochure advertising the glories of a Renault Dauphine. Unfortunately I was only an articled clerk at the time and people of that income could aspire to Dauphines but they could not actually buy them. Tolstoy describes a birch forest in *War and Peace* and his description is quite wonderful. The birch trees of Melbourne are all dying but there is a splendid Australian "birch" which we hope to meet on the Darling. It is known as the leopardwood tree.

We guiltily ate our *pain chocolat* in the weak spring sun, had a mandatory slurp of bottled water and then resumed our journey. The taste of that pastry and chocolate (pinched from the breakfast basket) remained with me for many kilometres. It is true — stolen fruit and pastry, like stolen kisses, are best.

The outskirts at Argentat presented themselves at 11.45 — the bewitching hour. I stopped outside a *boulangerie* not far from the Dordogne. We took our *demi-baguette* with us towards the bridge, but then I turned and made my way back to the *boulangerie* for I couldn't free myself of the aroma of *quiche lorraine*. I bought two small ones. All this patisserie in one day, but the appetite for pastry is infinite. At least I believe that it is.

Argentat when approached from this direction is dramatic. The river was high, almost in flood and it lapped some wonderful medieval houses overhanging its banks. There were turrets and balconies and verandahs and in the background on your left there was a massive church tower and on your right two elegant church spires. On the opposite bank and upstream along a small beach were cafés, bars and restaurants. Argentat is famous for its old quarter and for its Tours de Merle a short distance out of the town and in the valley of the Maronne. It also attains some fame in my memory for the tall and lean and extravagantly moustachioed waiter who was delighted to show us to a riverside table under an umbrella and to bring us two coffees, *seulement*, despite the fact that it was still lunchtime and he was busy. I left him a tip of two euros, the least I could do, and he smiled and bowed and said "*arrivederci*" as if we had given him a fortune. Bloody flattering Italiani!

The Lords of Merle built the original castle in the eleventh century on a spur overlooking a bend in the river. Sons and descendants of the original Merle built their own towers. The castle and most of the towers are now in ruins but those very ruins evoke the Middle Ages and the so-called Hundred Years War. It was easy to find a pleasant spot for our late lunch and a look at the map for a leisurely journey downstream on the little roads that sneak along the left bank of the Dordogne.

Walnuts and the Dordogne — it's like saying bread and cheese or meat and potatoes: they are the perfect companions. The walnut, I'm informed, is a "native to south-eastern Europe, Central Asia, America and China." It was introduced to France by the Romans, it seems, and how comfortable it has made itself in France, especially in the Valley of the Dordogne. You'd swear it was native to the area, it is so well adapted there. Of course, it is the soft-shelled variety, which I imagine had its origin in Persia, now part of Iran.

Whenever you come across a relatively small plot of land with rich soil you will see walnut trees, and the trees always look young. The French renew the trees about every thirty years or so, for with age their production drops off. And, in any event, the demand for good sound walnut timber is constant, so why not have the best both ways.

There's a wonderful family-run walnut mill at Ste. Nathalène in the Enéa Valley some eight or ten kilometres east of Sarlat. Father and son manage the mill and mother is in the shop and it is certainly worth a visit. The whole of the mill, including the massive and powerful press, is run by a huge water-wheel. Its power is amazing. The nuts are shelled (by various families as far as I could gather) and the kernels are finely crushed and heated to about 50°C. The pulp is then pressed, and slowly, ever so slowly, the oil seeps out. But what oil it is, and how delicious to soak the bread of a fresh *baguette* in it.

My enthusiasm for walnut oil, and its relative scarcity in Australia, combined to cause me to endeavour to press our own oil from our very own tree. So, after dinner one night, I took a bag of our freshly picked nuts and I shelled them and I then put them through the vitamiser. Then I put them in a pot with a small quantity of water and I heated them as mentioned and then I put them in a press, a small press that we use for sampling grapes before vintage. I pressed and pressed. No oil. I threw the whole of my weight and strength into the job — a bent handle on the machine but no oil. I was determined to get some oil so I grabbed a torch and proceeded to the shed and the vice on the workbench. I put the little press in the vice and I applied the screw harder and harder. The press was in danger of collapsing when suddenly I perceived a few drops of oil drip on to the saucer. Eventually I obtained half a teaspoon. At eleven o'clock at night I drank that oil, every bit of it and then I began the job of cleaning up the mess before turning into bed. The oil was so delectable.

It was late in the afternoon when we pulled into the plane tree shaded square in Beaulieu (*Beaulieu-sûr-Dordogne*) and the sun was warm. Out the front of our virginia-covered, three storied, old stone hotel, was a footpath, and so there were small tables and chairs on one side and banquettes, yes banquettes and tables on the other. We sank into one of the banquettes and ordered two gin and tonics. I know, yes how I know, what a risky order that can be in France. They arrived, with a bowl of nuts, and…and the glasses were tall, chilled, filled with ice and a slightly blue mixture. They were delicious, two of the best that you could get in any part of the world. We made them last for half an hour and then there was time for a walk along a secluded track which went through a small forest and up a steep hill. I never did find the monument sign-posted along the way, but the view of the winding Dordogne and the sunset was wonderful.

The feature of Beaulieu is, without doubt, its beautiful twelfth century church built by the Cluniac monks — St. Peter's church, or *Eglise St-Pierre.* It is quite remarkable. There was a jackdaw perched on the steeple. It jumped off as we approached and then flew slowly round and round, only to be joined a few minutes later by a half dozen of its mates. Jackdaws, steeples and bells and old churches, they take me back to our first visit to France all those years ago: an afternoon cup of coffee on the terrace of the little café at Tremolat, the dulcet tones of two English cyclists at the adjoining table and then the clear calls of the jackdaws hovering around the spire of the village church.

The Beaulieu church is said to be in Limousin Romanesque style and on the east end has the usual "tacked-on" round towers of that era. To me, they are clumsy, but apparently there was a cloister joined to the northern side

and that might have made the difference. The south doorway was carved in 1125 and is one of the most famous in the
whole area, with its depiction of a forgiving Christ, a second
coming flamboyant Christ surrounded by apostles and angels with trumpets. For once, thank God, there is no grave
warning, or perhaps an ominous threat, to any backsliders or
sinners. Inside there was a kind and indulgent angel, which I
photographed. I like those jackdaws and I liked the angel.

Beaulieu is the start of the Dordogne proper if you are
going down river. You can now go north, south or east and
you'll be amongst stone villages, churches, gardens, forests,
hills…anything that the eye desires. We went south and
parked in the village beneath Castelnau-Bretenoux overlooking the Céré River. This château can be seen from afar
built as it is on a spur above the two rivers. I say a spur and
yet it is a fertile and cultivable spur — a sort of a small plateau. The château is one of the most appealing you will ever
see: an almost unique mixture of fortifications, and ramparts
on the outside, with an elegant house on the inside. It is
surrounded by extensive lawns and forests and even some
tilled land.

The French writer Pierre Loti said of Castelnau, "(It's)…
the thing you cannot help looking at all the time wherever
you are…a cock's comb of blood-red stone rising from a
tangle of trees…poised like a crown on a pedestal dressed
with a beautiful greenery of chestnut and oak trees."

Now, you may wonder what this naval man and writer of
sea tales and sensuous adventures was doing so far inland. You
may indeed, and as to that I cannot help you, nor can he, as
he died at Rochefort, a maritime town on the west coast of
France, in 1923. Rochefort even has a street named after him
— Rue Pierre Loti as I need hardly write.

CHAPTER EIGHT

St. Céré adjoins the Bave River and has a population of some three and a half thousand only, and yet it seemed very busy when we were there. Our destination was, naturally, the old part going back to the fourteen hundreds and the re-built seventeenth century church of St. Spérie. We walked along the *Rue de la Republic* festooned from end to end with shrubs and trees and stopped in front of yet another plaque to the Resistance. These *maquisards* died in May 1944 (before the Allied landing) and their executioners were once again the Das Reich Division. The town has its old Tudor style quarter around the *Place du Mercardial* but like Salers, it has a life of its own beyond the tourists.

Nearby Château Montal is most assuredly worth a visit, although the château itself had closed just as we got there. The grounds are simple and the château is, somehow, perfectly situated. The story is that in 1523 the owner of the land had a mansion built for her eldest son

Robert, who was in Italy fighting a rather pointless war for François Premier. Robert was killed and the mother in her distress had a motto chiselled underneath the window which had acted as her lookout: "Hope is No More (*plus d'espoir*)." Luckily she had a second son Dordé, but he was a "church dignitary", a priest presumably. Anyhow, he came out, as it were, and had nine children and I assume that one or some of them were boys. The château went through rather turbulent times in the intervening years but was completely restored by a rich Frenchman late in the nineteenth century who then gave it to the State in 1913. Its situation, its park and the building itself are all lovely. I particularly liked a rustic latticed gate beautifully constructed in a diamond pattern.

A village which is off the main road on the little D118 and very much worth the short detour is Loubressac. It's on a hill or perhaps a small mountain, but you could easily pass it by. Well, please don't. Allow Loubressac to draw you off the main road.

There's a small parking area under the trees (chestnut from memory) by the World Wars monument. Having read the announcement and glanced down the list of names, in case I should see an Egan, I went, quite naturally to the little but old cemetery. There's a wonderful view from its gates which takes in part of the valley of the Bave and the Castelnau fortress. To my mind, the peace and quiet of a well-kept cemetery is similar to the peace and quiet of an old, but empty, church.

I left the cemetery with reluctance, and walked on. Outside the church, I stopped and tried to decipher the beautifully lettered acrylic sign. My French had deserted me and the church was closed. The thing about Loubressac is firstly its authenticity and secondly its compactness. The roads are narrow, laneways almost, and every house and tower, every turret and roof is genuine, even if some have been restored. The gardens are alive, the flowers are blooming and the place is occupied. In the space of a half hour you have had a feast. We journeyed on.

Suddenly you are in Carennac and underneath the massive walls of the château. There are places to park and a low stone wall to sit on and watch the river. When you feel like it you walk thirty or forty metres, turn left up the hill and there in a cul-de-sac, or a narrow courtyard is the church of St. Pierre, Romanesque, of course, and with another one of those side doors. Above and around the door are joyful carvings of Christ and his followers but the frieze is mainly of animals. It is a church of great charm and peace. Do not neglect to see the cloisters while you are there.

Perhaps the most famous man of Carennac was François de Salignac de la Mothe-Fênelon — a long name for a man who appeared to be a lover of simple things. His family owned the elegant fifteenth century château some distance down the Dordogne towards Carsac. François Fénelon was born in the château in 1651 and is described in my encyclopaedia as "archbishop, mystical theologian and a man of letters."

Here is a little quote from Francois: "Nothing is more despicable than a professional talker who uses his words as a quack uses his remedies." Now, you almost know the man.

He finished his studies in Paris and was involved for a time in a college where he instructed women who were converting from Protestantism to Catholicism. In 1685 Louis X1V revoked the Edit of Nantes that had granted a measure of religious freedom to Protestants, and persecution of them was heightened. François had the courage to speak out against that persecution.

His next appointment, despite his outspokenness on religious matters, was as tutor to the future Louis XV. During his tutorship, or rather because of it, he began *Les Aventures de Télémaque* (the adventures of Telemachus in search of his father Ulysses), which he completed in 1699.

François continued his searches for spiritual truths and ran foul of the powerful cleric Bossuet, his one-time friend. It was clear that François Fénélon could not be silenced and so he was exiled to his diocese at Cambrai, in northern France on the Escaut River.

There's a lovely and partly ruined tower in the valley below the bridge in the equally lovely village of Carennac and some writers maintain that this was the tower in which Fénélon wrote. The lady at the information office in Carennac said that this was not so. She pointed instead to a tower near the wall of the château. "That was the tower," she said most emphatically. If you walk back down to your car by the river or even to the bridge over the valley you can see the top of this square tower. I think she was right. Before you get into your car, have a careful look at the wall of the château where you will see a striking bust of François. Carennac is a village of great beauty.

You can linger in Carennac.

But going back to Fénélon's fame as a writer — I must say I've not read the *Adventures of Telemachus* and it is a while since I've read *The Odyssey*. Oddly enough one of the most vivid recollections I have of Homer's story is how the enchantress Circe turned some of Ulysses' (Odysseus') companions into swine. I wish that the same lady would revisit the Western world and turn the occasional CEO and company director into swine, she would be most welcome.

But perhaps, come to think of it, there is really nothing further to do.

On the flight over to Paris I kept a resolve that I had made and I read Homer's other book, *The Iliad*. What a task! I don't often use an exclamation mark, but it is deservedly appropriate after that short sentence. The argument between Achilles and Agamemnon gives promise of something worthwhile but thereafter it descends into a description of the manner in which man butchers his fellow man. And all the while Achilles sulked. It was easy to grow tired of Achilles, and Agamemnon too, for that matter.

Our bed and our meal for the evening were near Lacave on the Ouysse River and we wandered in that direction along the southern side of the Dordogne. It was time for coffee which I like to drink at 3.45 (or 15.45) precisely and eventually we saw a pleasant little café. There were only two tables taken and a dog lay under one. We sat down and the aroma of a good roast wafted out to us. The café had shown its proprietorship by enclosing a generous section of the foot path with potted box hedges all immaculately watered and clipped.

I was sipping my coffee and reflecting of things French including their formal gardens when a middle aged woman walked past lead by a trotting, head-up, poodle. The poodle had been artistically clipped and clipped, and clipped — it was all gutters, ridges and plateaux. Arrogant creatures those poodles. The French have a mania for topiary — they'll clip anything: country hedges, trees up to twenty or thirty metres in height (as at Fontainbleau), parterres around vegetable gardens, formal gardens, dogs… There is no end to their tidiness and their formality.

The first formal garden that amazed and utterly de-

lighted me was Vaux-le-Vicomte. We went there by coach
many years ago in the late autumn. I had seen glossy pictures
of the view of the embroidered parterres from the steps of
the château with the Farnese Hercules in the distance and
frankly it left me cold. There were about ten of us only, on
this huge coach and the guide was able to give us his full attention and display his knowledge; "we are going past the
stables, poor Fouquet, the great Le Nôtre, one should always see a French garden from a height, e.g. the first floor
(not the ground floor)" et cetera, et cetera. He rabbited on.
We climbed the steps and stood on the terrace and then
we turned and looked across the tapestry of box, lawn and
gravel. Magnificent.

You need a whole day to see Vaux-le-Vicomte — to
stroll amongst its clipped yew trees, to marvel at the close-
trimmed hedges with the overhanging copper beeches and
chestnuts. It is masterly. And the *pauvre* Fouquet who presented such splendour to his lord the magnificent Louis
X1V, what did he get for his efforts? He got the suppressed
jealousy of a pampered but powerful monarch and he also
got exile, which Louis in his kindness and generosity "com-
muted to life imprisonment."

And what about the master gardener André Le Nôtre?
André got the construction of Versailles, everlasting fame and
a surprisingly long life for those times.

There's a formal French garden in the Dordogne valley not far from Souillac and Sarlat (in fact almost midway
between them and slightly to the north) and it is most certainly worth a visit. I don't say it rivals Vaux-le-Vicomte or
Versailles but Eyrignac is quite beautiful and impeccably
kept. The château has a charm that Vaux cannot match and
the hostesses who conduct you on the tour are just as charm-

ing. There are roses, lawns, hornbeams, yews, boxes — it's all there. See Vaux, you should, but see Eyrignac in the Valley of the Dordogne too, and have lunch by your car in the shade of the oak trees in and around the car park.

CHAPTER NINE

Our room at Le Pont de l'Ouysse was on the first floor, up the narrow and picturesque stairs; and its great virtue was its view of Château Belcastel. This château is not particularly historic and certain additions and alterations have been made to increase its comfort, but it is a pleasure to look at. It stands at the confluence of the Ouysse and the mighty Dordogne and, naturally, it is on a cliff, and therefore, has a great view. This is a quiet and restful part of the Valley and is only a short and pleasant trip from Souillac. We saw quite a bit of Souillac, our starting point on many journeys,

Within walking distance of Le Pont de l'Ouysee is the La Treyne château which is built overhanging the Dordogne. Part of it is four-teenth century and the rest was rebuilt in the seventeenth after being burnt down by the Catholics in the wars of religion. You could be pardoned if you sometimes thought that religion is rather a mixed blessing. The château is now a very smart hotel and restaurant. We parked and ignoring the bustling kitchen staff, all beautifully uniformed, went up into the gardens. Whether the gardens are a state responsibility or are under the care of the hotel I know not, but they could have been quite interesting. The grass is neatly mown and the hedges (ah, those hedges) have been clipped but the roses and the flowers are mediocre. They are, I suppose, the hard work and the expense of any garden. We were somewhat disappointed and we, therefore, journeyed on.

The church in Souillac is another Auvergne-style building and again has a side entrance. Commercial buildings are attached to and form an extension of the church as they sometimes do in France, but the church is none the worse for that. This church, just to even things up, in terms of religion, was pillaged by the English and thereafter, the Protestants. The abbey formerly attached to the church was destroyed but the church survived.

There's another church, or rather the ruins of a church, in Souillac and it is up on the hill towards the Route Nationale. It was called St. Martin and somehow the ruins look more interesting than the Abbey church down on the flat.

When you come in to Souillac from Lacave it is important to stop in the centre of the town, find a parking space and walk down to your left — that is where the good shops, cafés and old houses are. Just above this interesting section (and near the ruins of St. Martin) is a small garden with some statues of famous Souillacrians, including one Amiral Jean Baptiste Verinac Saint Maur who was born in 1794. It was he who brought back from Luxor, the site of the Ancient Egyptian city of Thebes, the obelisk which stands in the Place de la Concorde in Paris. It is said that the obelisk was given to him by the Pasha Mehenet-Ali. The little square where the bust is erected is called the Jean Jaques Chapou square, and who he was, I'm sorry but I am unable to tell you.

Martel is off on the D803 and when we arrived there it was raining, and when we left after our picnic lunch it was still raining. And perhaps, Martel needs rain often because it is an important centre for those precious things with the elusive perfume — truffles. Martel is said to be named after Charles Martel, a brutal leader who defeated the invading Saracens in the eighth century. His favourite weapon, his killing weapon, was a hammer and Martel has celebrated this little predilection of his by having three hammers on its crest. Charming. There's also some nonsense about Richard Lionheart and his brother Henry Short Coat, but honestly it's not all that interesting.

The church of St. Maur is worth the walk but more be-cause of the very old and very lovely houses (*hôtels*) and arch-ways that you see along the route. Oddly enough the church is down one end and is on the rather flatter part of the town. Where we had parked (in the rain) just off the Boulevard des Cordeliers, the garden had been built on and over the site of the twelfth century ramparts which, perhaps I am wrong, still seem to exist in part. There are lovely trees along the side of the boulevard and there is a toilet!

When we arrived at Turenne the rain had stopped; well, to be truthful it was intermittent. There is a quite lovely for-tified gate which gives access to this small but old town, or village rather, and you are requested to explore it on foot. We did so; and yet it soon became evident that a few more cars would not have done any harm. I think I saw only four or five on the whole of our walk. *Michelin* says that the Tour de César "seems to date from the eleventh century". It looks as though it could be one thousand years old. The church is not at the top, again. What went wrong with some of those

Catholic bishops?

Turenne, quite seriously, was a country within a country in the fifteen century or thereabouts: it ruled over vast tracts of the local countryside and it is said enjoyed the allegiance of some twelve thousand villages. There is a very attractive artisan woodworking shop opposite the fortified gateway.

On the way back to Lacave, sort of on the way back, is the most unusual village of Collonges la Rouge. It is quite astonishing for here, in the heart of the pale and sometimes slightly pink, stone of the Dordogne is a village built in nothing but red stone. And it is quite red. You will be lucky to get a park anywhere near the village and even when you do you will have to pay. Don't be deterred if you see an illuminated post blocking your entrance to the gravelled area. You simply put your Euros in the machine and the post disappears into the ground.

This is a tourist village — make no mistake about that. It could not exist if it were not for the gawking herds, and yet for the most part it is delightful. How can I write this. But it is. Apart from the lovely towers and pepperpots and gates and such like, there are gardens, and greenery, and yes, hedges. You'll like Collonges la Rouge. It's fairly big and merits a long and leisurely inspection. Its population in 1976 was 375. It has now climbed to 413.

CHAPTER TEN

You wonder whether the English have changed. I remember, but it could be that my memory is not good, I *seem* to remember then, that the English on their travels were cool towards fellow guests, especially Australians. And yet the following morning at breakfast another Englishman said, "Good morning," and stopped by our table for a chat.

As he subsequently told me he had turned eighty. He had on a pair of red trousers, which he wore with style. How one sometimes envies the English (but not for their red trousers): France and the continent are only a short journey away whether by tunnel, ferry or plane. You can go to France for the weekend.

They had been to his house in the Gers for a couple of days, the bloke in the red pants said, and were now on their way to their son's house near Fontainbleau, did I know of any interesting towns on the way?

"You've been to Bourges and seen the wonderful cathedral with its incomparable stained glass?"

He hadn't, so I waxed very lyrical about Bourges, and then we got on to the writer George Sand and the very special writer Alain-Fournier — one to the south of Bourges and the other to the north. He sat down, as he was waiting for "the wife to come down", and we started talking about George Sand or Lucie Dudevant (nee Dupin) to use her correct name. I told him about the small village of Nohant (near la Châtre) and how some years ago we had booked into the one and only hotel in the village. It couldn't have been staged, but as I carried the luggage from the car to the hotel the sounds of a piano playing one of Chopin's Etudes clearly floated down to us, and later we met the girl, the daughter of the owners, who of course played the piano.

That night at dinner a rather garrulous Englishman (actually a Pom, to be fair) insisted on joining us for coffee. He despised the French and took a great delight in spraying them with smoke and unburnt petrol — so he said. His trick was to hold up an impatient French driver for as long as possible and when the Frenchman got close to him preparing to pass, the Pom would switch off the engine of his Jaguar and then after a moment switch it on again. The result? He covered the windscreen of the Frog's car with oil and petrol — at least he maintained that he did. And having related this cleverness on his part he collapsed on the table with laughter.

George Sand's château is not grand but it is pleasing. Inside, the rooms are reputed to be much as they were when she died in 1876 at the age of 72. Her dining table is set as for a formal dinner and place cards include Chopin, Flaubert and Musset. It's been done before, no doubt, but here it looks genuine, somehow.

She lead an active but a troubled life, and had her share of sadness. Undoubtedly she was a person of courage. There's a poignancy about the little family cemetery and her inauspicious place in it.

The man in the red trousers decided to go there and so we began to talk of that other writer who lived to the north of Bourges — Alain-Fournier. He, in my view had a singular talent and the pity is that he was killed at such a young age in the First World War.

Alain-Fournier wrote touchingly and incisively of the penultimate school days of two teenage boys — one who was prepared to follow and the other who was determined to lead. Both boys had imagination, sensitivity and romance, in fact, they were going through the dreamtime of many an adolescent, whether male or female.

Alain-Fournier's story is set in and around his school and village of La Chapelle-d'Angillon in the Department of the Cher, and as I have said, it is just to the north of Bourges. He wrote extensively for one so young but is known for his novel *Le Grand Meaulnes* which was published in English as *The Lost Domain*. He was born in 1886 and was killed in September 1914 in the first battle of the Marne. He showed great insight and understanding of human nature, especially in the first half of the book.

Our man determined to see Sand's château and Alain-Fournier's village and then return to Bourges where they would stay overnight. I envied him. His wife came down and I said goodbye. When we got back to our room I took out the map of France. We were only a few kilometres from Rocamadour and it had easy access to the A20 which ran almost in a straight line to Vierzon just to the north-west of Bourges. Alain-Fournier's village was only thirty-four kilometres from Vierzon. I began to add up the kilometres and divide by 140 — a reasonable speed on the autoroute. But, then I thought of our limited time and I pictured the Dordogne and so…I unfolded the local map. Today was to be Gourdon and Fenelon and villages on the way there and back — good stuff, exciting stuff.

So Gourdon it was. This is not a big town but it is unusual. If you park in the main street there's an interesting church on your left called Eglise des Cordelliers. It was built by the Franciscans in the fourteenth or fifteenth century, but in the nineteenth century the authorities embellished it with a massive and curious tower. The building is now used for concerts.

I suggest you leave your car where you parked it and that you simply "spiral" your way (on foot, of course) up the rather steep hill to the other church, *Eglise St. Pierre.* On your way up you will see some quite old houses, (even as far back as the thirteenth century), and some interesting shops. Gourdon, for some reason, seems to be a centre for music. We happened to be there on a Sunday which was *La Fête des Mères,* or Mother's Day. The special service had finished in St. Peter's church and fortunately the congregation was just leaving, but someone still played the organ and the smoke of the incense hung over the empty pews. It took me back quite a few years.

Michelin does not remark on the stained glass except to say that there is a "large rose window", but I thought the glass was worth a paragraph. I liked it very much. But then it is fair to say that my passion for stained glass is extreme. I would go so far as to state that there is no painting in the world which can match the beauty of the stained glass in Bourges cathedral, or Notre Dame in Paris or Chartres —

especially the rose windows of the last two.

When you leave the church of St Peter at Gourdon, take the stairs around the side for a great view over the old roofs of the town, the church itself and the surrounding countryside. The walk up to the viewing table had been neglected when we were there and it puzzled me, as the rest of the town is proudly kept. But it doesn't spoil a quite wonderful view.

The Bouriane is said to be worth a visit taking half a day at least and judging by the little that we saw I would agree. It is all rivers and hills and chestnuts and walnuts — not a bad enticement. That is the beauty of a picnic lunch: you always have a view with your baguette. And speaking of baguettes I've come to the conclusion that it's the balance between the dough and the crust that is so precise and wonderful. But then there are so many great breads: Turkish, Italian, Jewish, Indian. English? I cannot think of any delicious English breads and yet they should have some for their splendid cheeses.

And there's pastry — *patisserie*. How could one exist without pastry? So often in France the *boulangerie* and the *patisserie* are separate shops, they are that specialised. I soaked up the last of the walnut oil and looked at my watch. We would have to leave the view and go back to Gourdon and then out on the D 12 to Château Fénelon. It would be an easy and a restful journey.

We had been to the château on a previous occasion but didn't have the time to see over it. Fénelon is more than just the childhood home of François Fénelon, it is a beautifully proportioned fifteenth century château set on a hill rather than a cliff or rocks. There is a softness about it which is partly the building and partly the trees which surround it, especially perhaps on the far side.

When you walk through the grounds of Fénelon and realise that it had to cope with something like a hundred or more horses and their carers, and troops and artillery and the like, you begin to realise why a château of this kind had to be so large. Fénelon is a sleepy and a tame place today but there would have been hectic times when war threatened or actually happened. Now it is views and lawns and roses and tranquillity and beauty. When you inspect the private rooms you realise just how small they were: the kitchen, Fénelon's room — even the reception area and the dining room — none of them were large. I love the history and the stillness of the place.

CHAPTER ELEVEN

Today is to be bastide day but prior to the bastides there is this walk — a before breakfast walk.

The Hostellerie is virtually on the banks of the Ouysse River and I wanted to walk to Château Belcastel which is on a cliff about a kilometre from our hotel. You can go straight up the hill at the back of the hotel but my God it is steep; excellent for the heart no doubt, but hard on the muscles. There is an alternate route, the D road that comes in from Souillac, where the gradient is perfect, the surface is excellent and there are views from every bend, and in addition there are limestone cliffs, and oak forests and sky and clouds, but the distance is about four kilometres.

It took me a while to make a decision standing there by the fast running Ouysse. I had climbed that knee-trembler of a hill last year so...the beautifully graded road with the views from every bend was the sensible choice and I would take the short cut back down the hill on my return journey.

I got to the château eventually and was greeted vociferously by the dog — a frighteningly savage dog which challenged me with its aggressive pose and deep-throated growls. The next thing I noticed, however, was that its tail was wagging and its eyes were smiling. So, we became companions, and as I walked to the gates of the château and peered through, it too poked its head between the wrought iron uprights as if seeing the château and grounds for the first time. A pleasant place — a place worth the walk.

I turned and began my return journey and it trotted along with me. I admonished it and told it in my best French to *retournee* to *le château*. It pretended not to understand no matter how I rephrased or repeated my reprimands. Alright, it could walk with me for part of the return journey while I searched for the appropriate French terms.

We got to the first corner but still it cantered at my side. There was a small field of wheat, excellent wheat in almost full ear, and a stone wall to sit on and so I sat and it lay. How pleasant to relax here on a chilly morning with the sun every now and again puncturing a golden shaft through the clouds. How pleasant to be in France in the spring in the Valley of the Dordogne with a French *chien* by your side. And the quiet — no cars, no loud music, not even church bells. And there was no hurry.

That boy I mentioned earlier who was not me, but a boy I knew; when he was seven or eight, or thereabouts, he too sat one winter's afternoon but not on a stone wall, he sat on the fallen, curly dried bark of a large, old white gum, and he sat there for quite a while. It was after school and he was on his way up to the "Far Hill" to help his father with the digging and bagging of the family's potato crop. His job was to pick up the large potatoes and put them in one bag and then to pick up the "chats", the small potatoes, and put them in a drum to be boiled up and fed to the pigs. This job did not appeal to him.

On his way from the house to the potatoes he began to think yet again about "the problem" which had been bothering him for quite some time. And the problem was this — "How could the world exist before he came into existence?" Surely nothing existed before he was there to see it and listen to it. The world, this bush, this dear old gum tree on a turn in the sledge track, those peppermint gums, that bracken, those gentle clumsy wallabies that he saw on days of mist and light rain, they must have all come into existence when he did. It was inconceivable that they could exist when he did not; but then his mother, and indeed his father too, they had somehow existed when he had not. But if you couldn't see them, how could it be?

He took a twig and broke it into small pieces. He pulled down a tall piece of bracken that had grown through the rough mulch of bark and he felt the soft furriness of the new crook-like shoot. He sat for some time — he may even have dozed.

Then suddenly he got up and made his way along the winding sledge track to the top of the hill. The soil up here was deep and of a rich chocolate colour, and just near a smoking, burning stump he saw a row of yellow-white potatoes neatly laid out and his father putting his foot on a long-handled fork which he then left in the ground. There were full bags of potatoes standing in two more rows and near the edge of the paddock the grey horse Dodger stood by the sledge with a nosebag slung loosely over his neck.

"Where in the name of God have you been?" his father said, as he approached. The boy felt a pang of fear dart through and around his stomach, but he said nothing, he just stood there looking at his father. His mother would understand if he told her why he had been delayed, but not his father. The boy remained mute.

"Where the hell have you been?" his father reiterated, pulling his watch out of his pocket and looking at it. The boy hung his head.

"Better get on with it then," the father said, and as the boy scurried over towards the bucket the father put his watch back in his pocket, looked to the west at the setting sun and sighed and shook his head, he shrugged his shoulders, resumed his digging and, with a quick deft action, turned out all the potatoes from under the next bush.

I got up and the dog did too. Desperately I said, *"Allez, vite…allez à la…non, le château."* My dog looked alarmed and slunk away. My French had come to my rescue. I continued on my downhill short cut.

★ ★ ★ ★

Bastides or bastide towns were a new type of town built mainly in the thirteenth and fourteen century, at the end of the Middle Ages. Although we tend to associate them with France they were also built in England, especially in Wales.

The term bastide was derived from the Latin *bastida* which gave rise in French to the word bâtir : to build. Edward 1 was king of England from 1272-1307 and also of the duchy of Gascony and he was the builder par excellence of *bastides*, but the French also built them.

And you might ask in an aside how it was that kings of England could also be kings in parts of France at a time when the only method of getting from one country to the other was by way of a rather small and rather unreliable sailing boat, and, once there, the only method of continuing your progress was by horse. What an impossible arrangement, but there it was. And, furthermore, you fought battles in France to hang on to your overseas domains and you somehow (part of the time) gained the allegiance of your French subjects.

Freda White has a small and very informative chapter on *bastides* and points out that the redoubtable Edward 1 built most of these defensive villages south of the Dordogne but in a play for more land or more security for his Gascon holdings, he ventured into the Dordogne proper. He was, I think, a little like modern warmongers who talk "defensive" weaponry, when it is plainly offensive. We are in the era of euphemisms, thanks to Hitler and his propaganda and then to his imitators of the late twentieth and early twenty-first century. Modern euphemisms are just as deadly as some of Göebbells' propaganda, but they are more discreetly couched.

Domme had figured prominently in our pre-trip research so Domme the bastide was next on the list. It was not built by the English incidentally but by the brave Frenchman Phillip the Bold. Domme is a natural fortress town with a cliff giving protection on one side and the usual bastide planning and defensive layout and buildings on the other three.

You enter Domme through the solid stone gate at the foot of the village and you walk up through old houses and shops to the church at the top, and you continue on to the cliff. It's hard to be enthusiastic about the boring tourism of the shops on the way up the hill, and when you get to the view from under the shade of the trees (chestnut trees, I believe) you may reflect that it is good but hardly more, but when you take the road to your left and come back down the hill the scene changes. You then walk through some old and very lovely houses (lawyers, I suppose!). How Domme suffers though in not having a sustaining commercial life of its own. You know, on reflection, I would almost suggest that you turn left through the entrance gate and that you do a circuit that avoids the main street — the Grand Rue with all its tourist shops. The church, did I mention the church? Never mind.

Domme has a heart-wrenching memorial to the victims of the 1939-1945 war where it lists in one column those who were killed in combat and beside it a further list of the people who were deported from "unoccupied" France. Wars — how is it that we still accept wars as if they are a matter of course and therefore unavoidable?

The author Eugène Le-Roy wrote two of his master-pieces (*The Enemy of Death* and *Frau Mill*) whilst living in Domme and, as a consequence, not only has a plaque on the house he then occupied, but has had a street renamed in his honour. The French like to do this renaming thing. What about the previous name and the reason for it? What about all the Rue de Charles de Gaulle — will they be renamed in the twenty-second century?

Eugène-le-Roy was a very interesting bloke but it has not been easy to find out much about him. It is fairly certain, however, that he was born in 1836 and that his parents were domestics or servants at the glorious Château Hautefort. He, no doubt, had the sort of childhood you would have expected, and he struggled somewhat in his youth. He enlisted in the French army and served in Algiers and elsewhere, and he rose rapidly through the ranks. Unfortunately, or perhaps fortunately, he and the army parted company after some five years, although he was patriot enough to re-enlist and to fight in the Franco-Prussian War.

His great passion and life-long work was writing and he spent the whole of that life in and around the Dordogne, particularly in his native town of Jumilhac or Jumilhac-le-Grand. But he also lived in Domme and wrote in Domme as we have mentioned. Jumilhac is really just out of the Dordogne proper and is on the D78 in the general direction of Chalus.

And Chalus, well, we all know about Chalus and how it happened that Richard Lionheart was killed there in 1199 by an arrow or quarrel (bolt) from a new long distance cross-bow. Richard, at that time, was king of England, but in his bellicose fashion found an excuse to lay siege to Chalus in La Belle France, and perhaps he met his just deserts when that arrow struck him. The poor defender of the town who fired the shot was flayed to death when the besiegers finally entered Chalus, though Richard, before he died, was supposed to have forgiven him. Jumilhac is worth a visit just to sit and gaze up at its Castle on and in its romantic setting.

Eugène wrote this (my rough translation from the French): "Selfishness makes me indignant, I am exasperated by malice, injustice disgusts me and misery makes my heart bleed." He died in 1907 but some time before his death he quietly refused to accept the Legion of Honour.

CHAPTER TWELVE

Rocamadour and its history and its remarkable buildings squashed against and clinging to the cliff — we saw you from above and photographed you through a telephoto lens but let's be honest, we squibbed it. We did not drive in or walk through the famous town.

What we did do, however, was to park our car in the spacious area of L'Hospitalet and gaze out over the valley and the Forest of the Monkeys. Rocamadour is fantastic, there can be no doubt of that, but even from our park above we could see the buses and the hordes. We beg your pardon for our cowardice.

When you drive from Lacave to L'Hospitalet, above Rocamadour, you take, or I should say you can take, the little D247, a pipsqueak of a road, narrow and almost without any traffic. It is a lovely road that goes past a goat farm, milking sheds, a little *fromagerie* and of course, a tasting room and a sales counter. I had an hour or so in the afternoon before dinner and the usual pre-dinner Campari-soda, and so resolved to go back to this charming spot that we had passed in the morning.

From our hotel Le Pont de l'Ouysse right next to the Ouysse River, we looked up at the picturesque Château Belcastel, but when you actually drive through Lacave and on to the D247 you climb suddenly a cliff that is higher than the one on which Belcastel is built and, lo and behold, you are looking down on Belcastel and on the confluence of the Ouysse and the Dordogne. It is such a rapid and dramatic change of scenery. God, or the French, have left plenty of spots where you can pull off the road and park. I did so, and walked back to look at that wonderful view — rivers, villages of stone and slate and tiles, outcrops of rock of the same colour as the houses and châteaux and churches, cliffs of rock but partially clothed in oak trees in their deepest spring green with the sun slipping lower in the west, clouds, but some blue sky…stone, slate, tiles, trees, water, sky and a gentle breeze, and above all — silence.

The soil here is impregnated with natural limestone gravel and supports moderately high grasses of several kinds and wild flowers of many, many different species: orchids, buttercups, geranium, red poppies, white flowers in clumps and singly. All lovely. I wandered on while the breeze whispered to me of ages past, of history and of peace and of the famous and the ordinary people of France over many centuries.

There were clumps of juniper bushes but their fruit was still green, as I soon found, there were other bushes about head height and there were little groves of stunted oaks. There was a farm further ahead on my right and it had one of those ridiculously flimsy post and wire fences that you see all over France — flimsy but successful it seems. It is hard to believe that they keep in the farm animals but apparently they do.

I turned slowly and looked around the full 360°. What I thought, if God had used different colours, the way that painters sometimes do. Couldn't he have reversed things and made the trees blue and the sky green? Couldn't the sea have been red? Oh, there were all sorts of possibilities, but as I resumed my walk through the grass and the small and scrubby oaks I had to admit that it had all been rather well done. It was difficult to improve on his work, even if you were a painter.

The late afternoon was perfect and I resolved to drive on. A short way down the road was a paddock of grass that had been cut and baled. The round bales glowed yellow and orange and reminded me of Vincent Van Gogh's painting of haymaking in Provence. I stopped the car and went over to lean on the fence and gaze. Definitely Van Gogh-ish. The evening light was just filtering in and the stubble and the bales stood out the more strongly.

The fromagerie was on towards L'Hospitalet and I went there and parked some distance from the buildings. I had seen their herd of goats in the morning and even from where I had parked, you could hear their baa as they were being milked. I reflected that I should go in and taste their product — the area is famous for its goats' cheese — but if I did I could only buy enough for lunch tomorrow; any more and it would not keep. So I reluctantly decided not to trouble them.

Across the road, on this rather dry plateau or *causse* some-one had established a small vineyard which they had first surrounded with low stone walls and had then subdivided in the same way. Perhaps it had once been two very small vine-yards belonging to different people. It was old — one hundred years perhaps. The vines weren't neglected — they had been weeded and tilled — but they showed their age in their knobbly black trunks and many had died and there were gaps in the rows. Nonetheless, the spring growth gave them green and erect bushes which contrasted with the white-grey stone fences and the buff stones in the soil. There were two angular and sparse almond trees along the dividing fence and in the distance, but quite distinct, was a small hut or *buron* with a charcoal coloured roof of flat stones surmounted by a tiny spire in the gold stone.

Romanesque churches, châteaux, hôtels (elegant houses), monasteries, cloisters — we had seen them in their dozens — and we had seen them in all their glory, but was there anything to touch what I had seen that afternoon bordering the narrow D247? I doubt it. Such simplicity. But isn't that the crux of it all, simplicity? And it is a theme that runs through many aspects of our lives. Even in food and cooking there is nothing to beat simplicity — a piece of good fish beautifully cooked and unadorned except perhaps for a squeeze of lemon, a drizzle of olive oil, and naturally, a few boiled kipfler potatoes beside it on a plain plate.

I drove slowly back to le Pont de l'Ouysee with the sun just disappearing behind me and in front of me, on the other side of the river the cliffs holding precariously to the last of the light.

CHAPTER THIRTEEN

"Greed is good" — that is a maxim which has been propounded in recent years. It is put on the basis that the more people who devote their lives to a frenetic pursuit of money and goods, the more employment there is for the masses. Greed is good. It is not the eleventh Commandment but you will hear it trumpeted from time to time and you will see many heads nod in agreement, for it is a daring and a catchy little maxim and no one expects you to analyse it or to linger over it for too long.

We had been in France nearly two weeks and on each and every day in a different town or village I had gone into the boulangerie and in my best French I had said, "*Une (or un),*" I can never remember the genders in France, "*Une baguette, s'il vous plait.*" Half a breadstick, that is all I ever purchased, and I held out a handful of coins on my palm. They, the "*femmes*", presumably the wives or partners of the bakers, picked out the money, smiled, and said, *"Merci, monsieur. Bonne journée."* I made all of those trifling purchases. Half a breadstick! They could have said, "Half a breadstick, fair go mate," or its equivalent in French but they never did.

I must say I am astonished constantly both in Australia and France at the lack of greed on the part of the ordinary person, bearing in mind the adulation of riches, no matter how attained. It is sufficient in contemporary society to be rich — that is fame. Very few people ask whether the money and the assets were well-gotten or ill-gotten.

★ ★ ★ ★

Today we journey to that remarkable château — Hautefort, then to Thiviers and finally to Brantôme — we are striking out in a north-westerly direction, and the morning is overcast and rain is threatening.

The rivers that we see along the roads, and there are many of them, and those that we pass over, are gorged with brown water — they are full to the brim, but not yet in flood. We are to stay at Brantôme tonight and it is all water it seems. The guidebooks talk about it as being the Venice of Perigord. We shall see.

But the first major stop on the journey is at Château Hautefort. Not the old Hautefort, I hasten to add, but the magnificent new one of the seventeenth century, and partially re-built after a bad fire in the twentieth century.

The history of the old one is interesting. It was built by the Las Tours family of Limousin and came into the ownership of the Born family in the twelfth century. There were then two brothers: Bertrand and Constantine. Bertrand had something of a reputation as a writer of songs and poetry, in fact he was what was then known as a troubadour, but he also like to dabble in politics. Constantine also dabbled, but on the side of his liege Henry 11 and therefore, in opposition to Bertrand's fancy, Henry's son.

Bertrand backed his luck and decided to support Henry Short Coat, "the young King" whilst the Young King's father was still alive!

The Young King and Bertrand roamed the surrounding countryside plundering and pillaging and even got as far as Rocamadour where they desecrated the oratory and on the basis that you may as well be hung for a sheep as a lamb went on to steal Roland's sword. The Young King was severely wounded during this little escapade and in his death agony repented and died at Martel "on a bed of ashes". Bertrand wisely galloped back to Château Hautfort and shut himself in. The King arrived in a fury, with Constantine by his side and they and the army laid siege to the château. Bertrand may have been a lout but he was not without brains and he surrendered immediately. The King condemned him to death but Bertrand the troubadour still had a card to play. He begged leave to sing a plaint (no doubt laying special emphasis on the qualities of Henry the son and the pathos of his last hours) and on its completion the king with tears in his eyes, forgave him.

Bertrand continued in his errant ways and his brother Constantine in his exasperation turned Bertrand out of the old château and destroyed it. Bertrand then saw the light (or had no alternative) and he retired to a monastery.

Bertrand was not popular with the very traditional and family loving Alighieri Dante (1265–1321) who wrote him into *The Divine Comedy*. Dante had an excellent companion to lead him throughout the eternal world-the old Virgil of Georgics fame, and he describes their meeting with Bertrand in the deepest and darkest depths of Hell (my paragraphing):

> And since you seek news of me,
> Know that I am Bertrand de Born,
> He who gave ill counsel to the young king.
> I made father and son rebels, the one against the other.

My religious knowledge is a bit rusty and, of course, we do not know how Bertrand conducted himself as a monk, but you would have thought that he could have made it to Purgatory. Didn't Dante, even in his dream, continue through Hell, up through Purgatory and up again to Paradise? We realise that Dante also had Beatrice to look after him, the "divine Beatrice" who was also the wise Beatrice and died when Dante was only twenty-five years old. Dante the romantic, Dante the Italian — one need say no more.

But to return to the modern Château Hautefort.

We saw Hautefort first in the distance, then we saw it from the side of the hill as it towered over us (in the rain) and then we saw it from the car park. On each occasion it was different but never was it less than magnificent. Oh, it is grand, and its gardens, both outside and inside the château grounds, are fitting for such an impressive building. It even has a small museum devoted to our mate Eugene le Roy. It is hard to believe that a huge fire engulfed the main part of the château just forty years ago. It has been restored carefully and completely.

When you have tired of grandeur stroll down through the village that nestles against the walls of the château. It is an old village and it is lovely, including the gardens around the cottages and houses and there is a nice terrace part way down the hill for you to rest and sip a good cup of coffee.

We wandered in a general north-eastern direction towards Thiviers where we arrived just in time for another cup of coffee. Lunch had been in a forest not far from St. Suplice.

Thiviers gets scant mention in "the books", although the old green *Michelin* acknowledges that it is "famous throughout the region for its markets and fairs — foie gras, poultry and truffles". Even Freda White dismisses it as "a good place from which to see [other places]." Well, let me spring to the defence of the town. It is busy, but not too busy, it has some interesting buildings and it has a charming town square where there is an excellent comfortable modern bar which serves superb coffee.

We parked our car under the trees surrounding the square and darted to the bar. Beautiful coffee and brought to our table with a bewitching smile; and there was a clean loo. The day was still cool and so we sat inside and looked over the heads of the smokers who sat outside. France is getting there on the issue of non-smokers and puffers. On one side of the square were three shops almost side by side and they, in effect, are the glory of modern France: a boulangerie, an artisan boulangerie and a patisserie. *Vive la France.*

Château Puyguilhem is lovely but in the style of the Loire rather than the Dordogne. And it was getting late. We jumped on the D3 and headed for Brantôme.

When we got to our hotel at Brantôme the rain had

stopped and as they insisted on taking our bags and parking our car (in a huge cave across the road), we had nothing to do but to stroll off to look at the *clocher* or bell-tower on its famous rock. The church and the abbey and old buildings are sandwiched between wooded hills and the near flooded Dronne which divides into two branches and to an extent dominates the town. There are bridges aplenty, weirs, an "elbow" bridge and a working waterwheel. If it's the one we saw don't get too excited.

There are charming old houses with walls and gardens, especially roses, the town seems to be…introspective and unhurried. It is a good town to linger in, and believe it or not, it has a slightly risqué man of literature who also retired to a monastery. Yes, another one.

Let me relate his story. Pierre de Bourdeille was born further down the Dronne at the family château in 1540 and died in 1614. His misfortune was to be the third son of the Baron, and therefore "a cadet" according to Freda. (Doesn't Mouton Rothschild have a Cadet wine?). It is alleged that he spent some of his childhood at the court of Marguerite de Anguolême, Queen of Navarre (1492-1549). Marguerite was the sister, and a very devoted sister, of François 1 and was something of a racy writer herself. She left us, amongst other works, the *Heptameron* which it is said was loosely based on Boccaccio's *Decameron*. I should mention that she wrote some excellent poetry as well and also some "Godly" meditations.

Anyhow that is where Pierre spent part of his adolescence and even though he was only nine when the good Marguerite died, some of the love of literature and allied subjects, may have been imbibed by the impressionable youth. After completing his education in Paris and Poitiers Pierre was given the abbey of Brantôme, not because he had any particular religious leaning, but simply as a source of income. (And from where did the abbey get its income, one wonders.)

He lead an adventurous life both as a soldier and a ladies' man and amongst other things acted as escort to Mary Queen of Scots on her journey to Scotland (as the widow of Francis 11 of France, who died in 1560). And that was quite a job for a young man of twenty-one.

Pierre was said to be "adventurous by nature" and dabbled in battles in Italy, Spain and Portugal. Finally, not getting advancement in France, in exasperation, he decided to offer his talents to Philip of Spain, but fate intervened and he was badly injured in a fall from his horse. He then turned to writing which included stories of duels and brawls of army men and the love affairs of ladies which were termed "Les Femmes Galantes".

So there you have it, Pierre Brantôme from Bourdeilles.

And where should we go now? Naturally we should follow the Dronne downstream to Pierre's birthplace of Bourdeilles, and so we did.

Bourdeilles, viewed from the bridge on the edge of the town, displays all of its history and its beauty. You have to reach for your camera. In some ways Bourdeilles is more of a river town than Brantôme, but Brantôme has claimed that catchy title and has prospered whereas Bourdeilles seems to have stood still.

The sixteenth century château on the river was planned and begun by Jacquette de Montbron, the wife of André de Bourdeille (Pierre's sister-in-law). Catherine de Medici (1519 –1589) the wife of Henry 11 of France gave advance notice of a visit to Bourdeilles and Jacquette commenced the building of the château in anticipation of the illustrious visit, and made sure that it would reflect glory on her husband's family and herself. Unfortunately the visit did not eventuate and so Jacquette stopped work on the sixteenth century château, and it was never resumed. The château and adjoining buildings are nonetheless worth a visit. There is something soft, mysterious and romantic about them.

The morning was getting on, indeed it was getting towards baguette time. I went down the hill past the historical buildings to the main street passing *un alimentation* shop on the way. I couldn't see a boulangerie and came back to the shop which advertised that it was a *depot du pain*, a place where you could buy bread that had been delivered there. We needed fruit as well and so I selected, in the back of the little shop, a few bananas and tomatoes. There were plastic bags on the floor and like a good Australian shopper I put the fruit in a bag and then went to madame and asked for a demi baguette. She added up my purchases, I gave her the money and she gave me my change. She then emptied the fruit out of the bag, handed the fruit and the bread to me and carefully folding the plastic bag she put it on a little pile of bags on the floor beside her. I approved of what she had done but had to laugh as I juggled my purchases and walked back up the hill to the car. *Pas de* plastic bags.

So much country, so many rivers, creeks and streams, so many villages and patches of forest and we meandered through them on our way to Tremolat situated on the *cingle* (huge loop) in the Dordogne.

After lunch and near enough to coffee time we entered a village called St Alvere which boasted a chemist, a bistro, some other shops and an unusual church built of the loveliest golden-pink stone — quite remarkable stone. We went down the hill to inspect it. There was something about the façade that reminded me of the buildings of ancient Rome:

a simple louvred bell tower high up, a pediment underneath it, a very plain and appealing clock face (and the clock was going), a round window surrounded by what appeared to be a garland of victory, a decorated lintel with some stone cords and a carved head, much weathered, which may have been a lion, and then the arch of a plain doorway.

The church was built privately it seems, in 1783, by a certain Marquis Lostanges and who he was and why he built it I was not able to find out. *"C'est l'eglise,"* followed by a shrug of the shoulders and that was as far as I could get. The church is now owned by the town and is being restored. It is simple and, therefore, in my view lovely. The bistro on closer inspection was not the sort of place for a cup of coffee and so we pressed on for Tremolat.

When we arrived at Tremolat there was a detour at the little church, for it, like hundreds, no thousands of French churches, was being renovated. We were amused to see the name of the local contractor on the side of the van and the name was Andrew Evans, Entreprise Batiment et Restauration. A workman beckoned us on and with some trepidation we drove under the extended arm of the large crane and on to our hotel, Le Vieux Logis.

There are many good things about Le Vieux Logis but all I want to do here is to write about its gardens. I later told the receptionist just how much we loved them and she shrugged her shoulders and said, "Yes, maybe, but the cost of their up-keep is very great." Well, no doubt, but how worthwhile.

The Hotel/Restaurant is on a very slight slope and a stream flows under part of the buildings and through the garden. In the garden there are flowers, of course, but what strikes you immediately, is the extent of the topiary, "the art of clipping shrubs etcetera into ornamental shapes". There is

a species of box which has been planted in a sort of haphaz-
ard but thoughtful way in the garden by the pool, and it has
been hedged into large balls which look as though they are
resting there and are capable of being rolled along the grass.
There are hedges high and low and then in a paddock opposite the reception is a high hedge interspersed with trees
allowed to grow out in a natural and irregular fashion. Along
one side of this paddock is a long row of closely planted
poplars which somehow have contrived to grow to the same
height. They would be twenty or more metres high and
look wonderful and also sound wonderful as they flutter and
whisper in the slightest breeze. They must be remarkable in
the yellows of autumn.

The village of Tremolat is small and pleasant but the meander (or *cingle*) in the Dordogne is very impressive. *Michelin*
describes it thus: "At the foot of a semi-circle of high, bare,
white cliffs coils the river, spanned by bridges of golden
stones…far away on the horizon are the hills of Bergerac,
Issigeac and Montpazier." Well said *Michelin*.

We took the picturesque way out of Tremolat and drove
as slowly as possible through the rocky hills clothed in
dense stands of oak. Our destination was Cadouin along
the D25. The church in Cadouin is an abbey church built
by the Cistercians in the twelfth century and as the books
say it is "severe." Well the order was not given to frolicking
and laughing, religion and religious observance were serious matters. The rules followed by the Cistercians were laid
down by St. Benedict and his successors and those rules
"demanded severe asceticism". The liturgy was simplified
and there were to be no frills or overdone decorations in
the churches. Cadouin, as one of the churches built fairly
early in the history of the order, complies with those re-

quirements. It is worth looking closely at the roofing of the double-tiered belfry at the east end of the church. It is dark grey and consists of chestnut shingles.

The church once had the benefit of the Holy Shroud which had been wrapped around Christ's head when he was crucified, and as you can imagine, it was very good for business. Unfortunately a nineteenth century monk, who should have had better things to do, noticed that the embroidered letters on the shroud constituted a Moslem text. Two experts in 1934 confirmed the monk's observations and that was that, I'm afraid.

I don't care who builds cloisters, be they the most frolicsome or the most severe order, they are always lovely. Admittedly the cloisters here were built at the end of the fifteenth century and even into the sixteenth century and presumably the Cistercians over the intervening period had become a little lax. In any event their construction was financed by the Crown and perhaps that lead to some flamboyance. They are worth a look even if it is by way of a guided tour and even if you are almost blinded by the brilliant lighting. I've never yet seen a cloister that I did not love.

If you continue on along the D25 you will shortly arrive at a turn-off to the Eglise Abbataile de Saint-Avit-Sénieur. Take it, oh most certainly take that turn-off. A little way down the road and on the flat of a hill which overlooks the wooded valley of a tributary of the Couze stands a large church, out of all proportion to the size of the village now or ever, and attached to the church are the monastic buildings which for the most part are delightful ruins. The high front fence still exists but here and there it has also fallen. The church on the hill and the ruins — perfect.

You stroll around the ruins and you can picture the hermit Avitus Senior (also called simply Avit), a former soldier, wandering about and deciding to build his hut there, or thereabouts, within reach of good water from the river anyhow. One supposes that he was mad, or a little mad. Perhaps affected by his war service. The fact is, however, that he gained a reputation and that reputation lasted for more than five hundred years.

In the eleventh century a group of Benedictine monks inspired by something in Avit's life decided to build an abbey and a church. No sooner said than done. Avit's body or rather his bones were buried under the floor of the church. All was peace and harmony until the Huguenots decided to reform the church and the monks, and in 1577 they wrecked the abbey and set fire to it. This method of reforming recalcitrants is still being practised today, and with the same sort of success. There is something about the ruins. They can be looked at whilst your mind pictures scenes more wonderful than ever existed there.

And the church? Just as intriguing. When we walked into the church the lights were on and music seemed to fill the empty space. The music was not loud but it permeated the air from floor to ceiling. After a few moments as we walked towards the altar we saw some men in a side chapel bent over a CD player with two large speakers. They were preparing for a function and their choice of music was perfect — for us and the church.

At the end of the nineteenth century and then again at the end of the twentieth century, extensive structural repairs were carried out in the church. They appear to have been done with a light and understanding hand. Much of the original internal decoration and painting is still there and in good condition. The stained glass windows have been completely replaced with unashamedly modern glass, and it is striking, excellent and harmonious. The glass is high up in this somewhat solid, some may say plain, structure and the glass is clear except for irregular ribbons of colour through it. They have achieved two things with these windows: firstly they have given the church good light and secondly they have created a decoration not in the sense of medieval stained glass, but in the sense of austere simplicity. I found the windows to be rather beautiful.

There is a pulpit part way down the church and the wood carving is excellent. I do not imagine it to be nine hundred years old but it was worth a photograph especially of the angel. I've always liked angels — messengers of God. But will they take messages back, and if there is a reply, will they bring that back to us?

Archangels, angels, seraphim and cherubim. I love you all. And there is also the guardian angel which resembles a PA or these days an EA Does an Executive Assistant have a Personal Assistant? I must admit that my guardian angel has served me well, but with one or two small lapses I have to say. And what about those demons you see depicted on tympanums throughout France, do they have wings and are they as powerful as angels?

I walked down the hill towards the village and became involved with a French basset hound. He may have been French but he turned over for me to rub his tummy in exactly the way ours did many years ago. I would have stayed and spoken to him in my excellent French except that they had begun to ring the angelus. I stood and listened as the music wafted past. Bells-I don't care why they ring or what their tone is for they are wonderful. When the last peal had floated past I began to walk towards the church and then, timed to perfection, the bells of the clock chimed twelve times.

It is worth turning left at the Couze Valley and following the D26 to St. Croix and Montferrand-du-Perigord, and then you should continue south on little and very little roads and suddenly you are at the famous bastide town of Monpazier, built by the English King Edward 1 (also king of Aquitane).

Monpazier has market days, I can assure you of that, because we arrived on one. Fortunately the market was, unbeknown to us, packing up, and suddenly the congestion cleared and we could park, not in the square but in a convenient nearby street. The town has a pleasant outlook over countryside which seems to hedge it in.

The lord of Biron was a partner in the building of the town, which was completed by the end of the thirteenth century. In the sixteenth century and seventeenth century there were troubles with the peasants allegedly led by a weaver by the name of Buffarot who was finally captured and executed somewhat cruelly in the main square. Even so, there is a charm about the main square with its verandahs or covered walkways and its arches.

There is a church, there are window-boxes on first floors and there is the rose Pierre de Ronsard in full and gorgeous bloom over a shop which faces the church. Monpazier is worth a longer visit than was ours. We'll go back to Monpazier one day. (Why did they rob it of its "T"?)

CHAPTER FOURTEEN

Morning walks can be, in fact, are danger-ous, especially when you come to a van-tage point and you have walked far enough to think that you deserve a spell.

I stood on the edge of the river this morning looking at what appeared to be antique machin-ery spread across half the river. It was decrepit and rusty and may have once been for the gen-eration of electricity. It seemed a great pity that it should not be either demolished or restored. Essentially the French are artistic people and yet you come across all sorts of structures that ought never to have been built and decrepit buildings that should be demolished. If I were the French President…

I turned and walked back towards the vil-lage. Tremolat is attractive, but if one can be critical, the village ought to be on a hill rather than a river flat. The walk back was not exciting and instead of paying attention to the scenery I began thinking, and I am the first to admit the danger of thinking.

"That boy" was one of my father's frequent expressions. That boy had erred badly around the time of the Battle of Britain. First there was the "setter" episode.

A setter is a small hand tool rather like a miniature hoe but with a blade similar to a mattock. It's long and narrow, and has a nick on one side. It was used in rabbit trapping: the blade was for scratching and digging the coffin for the steel rabbit trap. Turn it over and there was a head or a hammer for driving into the ground the long steel peg and chain which secured the trap.

His father had erected a new subdividing fence and in his thorough way had strained all the wires in the fence to the tension of an "E" string on a violin. After completing this splendid job he had then gone to attend to the milking of the cows.

The boy was on his way back to the house after setting a round of traps (and was running late for milking as usual) and he happened to pass the newly completed fence. He admired it: the sturdy tree trunk at the end used as a strainer post and its stays and shoes, the new posts in between, beautifully hand bored with a brace and bit, and the small straight droppers in between those; but in particular he was taken with the tautness of the wires. He touched them and felt them vibrate and tremble. He took his setter and struck a wire with its wooden handle. The wire sang. He struck it again. What a beautiful thing his father had made. How thorough and...artistic he was.

The boy wondered. If he took the setter and put that little nick on the side of the blade over the wire and gave it a sudden twist, what would happen? He did this, gently at first, and then he gave it a sharp twist. Wow! The wire snapped with the sharp crack of a bullet fired from the .22 rifle and it went spiralling and coiling up the hill. He was aghast. He had broken the wire and it lay limp and dead beneath the fence line.

That little episode had been early in the week and now at the end of the week, on the Saturday he was sent to do a simple thing. He was to keep the cattle out of the paddock of green and lush oats as his father had not had the time to put up a dividing fence there. It was not a difficult task that he had been set, for there were only fourteen or so cows and there was abundant pasture for them. There was no need for them to stray into the paddock of oats but you know what cows are — mischievous beasts.

He always kept a book of some kind in the pocket of his bluey and he tapped it as he opened the gate and let the cows in to the grazing area. Stupid beasts they were. One of them, old Beauty the Friesian kicked up her heels like some poddy calf and snorting and mooing they all went into the paddock and began eating the luxurious clover and rye grass.

He went over to the headland between the pasture and the beautiful deep green oats. The stools of grain were just high enough to tremble and bend in the breeze of the early spring. The cows had stayed over in the clover near the gate and were eating contentedly. He watched them for ten minutes at least. They would eat in their greedy way for an hour or so and would then lie down to chew their cuds and belch and fart.

It was getting quite warm in the sun and he went to the northern end of the paddock and found a comfortable spot in the tall bracken fern. No one would know where you were. He was completely hidden, but he could still see the cows. He took out his book *The Count of Monte Cristo*. It was a wonderful story and he was almost half way through it. His mother had promised to ask for *The Three Musketeers* when she ordered books again from the Lending Library.

After a while he could no longer see the cows so he got to his feet and took a few steps. There they were. They had moved closer and were in the hollow just before you came up the hill. He went back to his spot but before sitting down he practised a few feints with his sword. Swish, swish, lunge, skip back. "On guard," he shouted. What a writer Dumas was. How splendid if one day he could go to France. "On guard," he shouted across the valley and the little creek below, and he laughed and sat down and re-opened the wonderful book.

Perhaps two hours had passed, he was not sure and getting up suddenly he looked at the sun and then checked the length of his shadow. It was quite short. Yes it would be around midday. He could drive the cows out of the paddock and close the gate. He got up, put the book in his pocket having remembered the page number and set off with his stick.

The cows had gone. How odd. They should be lying down with full bellies under the shade of the shapely blackwood. But they weren't. In fact they were nowhere to be seen. Surely…he was almost paralysed by a dreadful fear. Surely…he began to run towards the paddock of oats just over the hill. As he got to the top of the hill he saw and heard his father approaching from the laneway. "Where is that boy? I'll kill him. Oh, my God. What is wrong with that boy?"

I was perspiring as I walked across the lawn to our lovely two-storey room set out at the end of the garden of Vieux Logis.

★ ★ ★ ★

If you look at some of the nineteenth century magistrate's courts around Melbourne you will be struck by features that also appear in churches. The authority of the state and the authority of the church, and was the authority of the state derived from that of the church?

Rome had its temples before it had its churches and the greatest example of these temples is the Pantheon. It stands in Rome today as solid and indestructible as any building in the world. A pantheon according to the *Encyclopaedia Britannica* is a "building for the worship of all the gods revered in a certain locality…" When you are in the Pantheon and the light is flooding down from the eight metre oculus or eye in the centre of the dome, you may feel that it is indeed a place of worship and that it has a spirituality. As far as I know the pantheon is still the Catholic church of Santa Maria ad Martyres. Cunning people these Micks.

But the building of antiquity which acted as the model for Christian churches was, I imagine, the Roman basilica. Originally the basilica was "a large covered hall for the holding of courts of justice and for banking and other commercial transactions". Perfect for churches.

The heyday of Roman basilicas extended to the fourth or fifth century AD and the Catholic church rather took them over thereafter.

The original churches closely resembled the pagan basilicas. The main hall was known as the nave and sometimes there were one or two aisles separated from the hall by a row of columns. The narthex or entrance porch was at the west end and that is where the sinners and the unbaptised could congregate. I seem to recall in my youth being late for Mass on a number of occasions and so I crowded around the back door (definitely in the narthex) with all those sinners. I remember one day at Wangaratta the blasphemy and boldness of a fellow sinner who stood beside me and who was asked by his mate how he had fared at the races the previous day. My neighbour, wretched sinner that he was, reached across to the holy water font, dipped his fingers in and blessing himself ie. making the sign of the cross, out of the corner of his mouth he replied, "Never backed a bloody winner."

So much money, so much effort has been poured into the churches of the Western world and into France and Italy in particular. Frequently, in fact almost always, the size of the church in any village or town is out of proportion to the population either now or centuries ago when it was built. And we the tourists or travellers, we are drawn to the churches whether or not we have any belief in the creed that they espouse. Why do we seek out these buildings?

Well why? I suppose first and most importantly they are little different from objects in a museum: they attest to a past age and the activities of those people and their designing and building skills. The church was the "opera house" of the community and its communal effort, the most impressive gathering place. In addition it was the monument to a god who was loved but also feared, a god who in many instances had to be placated. But oh, the expense — the impoverishment of the locals who had somehow to pay for those buildings where money had not been spared. And today they have to be kept in repair.

There is an American churchman I hold in high regard, and his name is Ralph Waldo Emerson. It is not a lovely name, I confess, but the man was interesting. He was born in Boston in 1803 and died in 1882. His father was a Unitarian minister (and his grandfather too I believe) but his mother was strongly Anglican — a risky amalgam back in those days.

Ralph's father died when he was only nine but there was money in the family it seems, and he finished his schooling and went on to Harvard. At the age of twenty-six he was ordained as a Unitarian minister and he began his weekly sermons. Ralph's reading was wide and among his favourite philosophers were our friend Fénelon, and the very tolerant, courageous and loyal Michel de Montaigne, who we shall meet as we journey further down the Dordogne.

Ralph's life seems to have been liberally seasoned with deaths — his father, his first wife, two brothers and then later his son. Through it all Emerson retained his balance and his enthusiasm for life, or appeared to do so, judging by his writings. But did he retain his religious faith? Well not in its original form but he did remain an optimist to the last.

And it is a long pre-amble but I thought his mature view on churches and religion might interest you: "I like the silent church before the service begins better than any preaching."

Those words alone would be sufficient to make anyone famous. But how wonderful it is to go into a silent church, especially one that is old. How lovely to stroll through it and absorb its atmosphere and its spirituality, to smell its stone with its impregnated incense, to see a candle fluttering in a side chapel, to relax in its silence — all soothing and thought provoking. It is easy to believe that the stones contain the sorrows and the joys of hundreds of ordinary people and that the patina of the flagstones reflect them up to you. Opera houses, theatres, banks, monuments, houses of parliament — I am sorry but none of them have the soul of a church, or a cathedral, for that matter.

There is a little church in Carsac, which is only a few kilometres to the east of Sarlat. Carsac is not large, nor is it on the Dordogne, not quite, but it definitely has a charm. And the church, which stands by itself, is without doubt quite lovely. The Romanesque belfry is large but in balance, and it is roofed with rough but practical stone. It may have started its life as an abbey church.

Many years ago it was restored, perhaps it has been twice restored, and the restoration has been very sensitively done. The stained glass from the Limoges studio of Chigot, is modern (as it is at St-Avit-Senieur) and is just as successful, and the stations of the cross were done by Zack. Leon Zack was a Russian-born painter of Jewish origin and he wisely left Paris during World War 11 and obtained refuge in Carsac. He went back to Paris after the war but showed his gratitude to the village by creating the Stations of the Cross for the church. They have been called "rather austere," but you may like them, nonetheless.

The texts for each Station were selected from the work of that famous writer and philosopher Paul Claudel (1868 – 1955).

Claudel was born in a village called Villeneuve-sur-Fère-en-Tardenois in Champagne and some distance to the west of Reims, and his life seemed to sparkle like the mousse of a great champagne. He was either an atheist, or a Protestant, or perhaps he was simply disinterested in religion until he went into Notre Dame cathedral on Christmas Eve when he had just turned eighteen, and was thereupon converted to Roman Catholicism. I am prepared to wager that he stopped in the centre of the transept and looked at the rose window on his left and muttered, "Blessed be God (and man)" for indeed you would have to praise something or someone. And then he would have turned away to his right and seen another window of staggering beauty. Ah, the rose windows of Notre Dame, Chartres and the windows of the ambulatory in Bourges, they are divine. How one can understand his ecstasy and his resolve to spend the rest of his life thanking someone.

Claudel pursued a career as a diplomat but at the same time he took up writing and soon became famous for his Symbolism. Claudel the dreamer, the romantic with his impossible notions of the hearts and souls of the fair sex. Ecstasy in religion, ecstasy in love, ecstasy in thought, Dante, poets, poetry… How they all go together.

When Claudel was in his late thirties, he met a Polish woman on a shipboard trip to China and he fell in love. She was married, he was not, but it was adultery and all the sweeter for both of them: guilt, joy, renunciation, sin, until its mutual discontinuance after four glorious years.

Subsequently he married (a French woman, thank God), but he already had material enough for the rest of his writing career.

Claudel's words on the eleventh Station loosely translated are: "The hand which the torturer twists is the right hand of the Almighty." Perhaps it is a Station before which some of the leaders of the West should stop, reflect and then read it, again and again.

Carsac is somehow a place for reverie and as I stood there that afternoon only half looking at the church I began to turn over in my mind, yet again, the hate that I cherish for that definition of time BC/AD — before Christ and Anno Domini, which you Latin scholars would know is the time of our Lord.

The birth of Christ and the death of Christ should not be used to mark the end of an era and the beginning of a new era for they were not that, at the time; and now two thousand years later, they give an artificial but believed line of demarcation. It wasn't a world of pagans before Christ's death and a world of Christians after his death — no, not at all. Christ died, an unusual and remarkable man, and after a time and the preaching and hard work of a band of disciples a new philosophy and religion began to take shape. The world was not changed on his death. All his death did was to mark the emergence, the gradual emergence of something half new and half old. It was new in the terms of some ideas and philosophies but old in its reliance on the existing Hebrew scriptures.

There is, of course, BP, before present, a term used by archaeologists, geologists and others to place incidents in the past, although this seems to mean before 1950. It is better than BC and yet there is something about it that does not quite satisfy.

I wonder if it may not be better, more logical to begin with a date that coincided roughly with the "emergence" of the civilisation of Egypt, say 4000 BC. You would then simply add on the years so that 2008 AD would become 6008. This one step would allow students to see the gradual emergence of the Christian religion against the backdrop of atheism, paganism, Buddhism et cetera. You would see the world as it has actually developed with its sprinkling of Christians and its mass of other ways. It is possible, after all, that Christianity would have been nothing but a rather curious Jewish sect had it not been for the fortuitous help of the Roman Emperors Constantine and Theodosius in the early and late fourth century (AD!) It was Constantine, was it not who converted to Christianity and made it a state religion, even though paganism was still tolerated.

The afternoon was drawing in and we would be too late for coffee unless we made a move now.

CHAPTER FIFTEEN

When we left Monpazier in the afternoon we thought there would still be time for Château Biron and then a quick look at Beaumont and Château Bannes on the way back. And so we turned the nose of the frog car to the countryside and found the little scenic D53, and suddenly in the distance against the skyline was one of the most outstanding silhouettes in France, the Château.

There are parking spaces beside the road and under the very walls of the château and there are shady trees. When you get out of the car you tilt your head back, and back and back to look up at the massive, towering building including the sixteenth century chapel built on top of the old parish church. The château complex was owned for centuries by members of the Biron family but one or two fell by the wayside, great though the family was.

One of the most notable and haughty to tumble was Charles de Gontaut, a supporter ostensibly of Henri 1V, but also ambitious; and why wouldn't you be, perched up here like an eagle on a rock (but with plenty of glorious buildings on that rock). It was in 1598 that a dukedom was conferred on Charles and he became Baron Biron, and, if a Baron, why not take the next step and become a, or the, king. The Baron took that step by making overtures to the Duke of Savoy and the Spanish Governor of Milan. Alas, his negotiations came to the notice of the real king and he was accused of treason. Henri though was magnanimous and granted the traitor a pardon. Charles was encouraged by that magnanimity to try yet again for the ultimate prize, but was exposed and was paraded before the king. Henri said he would forgive him, even though it was a second offence, however, he would have to confess his crime. The Baron had delusions of grandeur and refused. On the 31 July 1602 the guillotine dropped on his neck in the court-yard of the famous Bastille in Paris.

There is an air of arrogant pride around Biron (now owned by the Department of the Dordogne), and you don't wonder that the long-suffering peasants tried to destroy it at the time of the Revolution.

There is also a little, and rather neglected, pond between the road and the walls of the château and as we walked back to the car I distinctly heard the quacking of ducks — bari-tone ducks, to be sure. I looked, but could see no ducks, no birds, nothing. I walked all around the pond, no ducks. Eventually I realised that it had to be frogs. French frogs make noises that are remarkably like the sound of ducks chortling and quacking, hence the predilection of the French diners for sautéed frogs' legs.

Coffee was at Beaumont and good coffee it was too and the hour was getting on. Beaumont is classed as a *bastide*, having been built in the name of England and its then king, our old friend Edward 1. One should remember that often these bastide towns were built at some strategic spot and then people were encouraged to come and live in them. They were not "organic" like most of the villages and towns of France.

There are traces of the fortifications left in Beaumont but the best evidence is in the unusual church, Eglise St-Front. I cannot say I fell in love with this restored and altered building, but it has clean lines and plenty of evidence that it was first and foremost a fortified building. The more I looked at it the more I longed for the warmth and history of Carsac.

Bannes is impressive from a distance so we drove closer. Yes, it is most impressive standing up there on the peak with its lovely soft pepper-pot roofs on its round towers. Yes, quite lovely, but the hour of Campari-soda was at hand and we looked for the bridge and the little roads back to Tremolat.

★ ★ ★ ★

The only disappointment when you stay at Tremolat is the walks, unless you take much longer walks than I did. If you have only forty-five minutes, you are too much on the flat; there are no vistas. Apart from that Tremolat is quiet, peaceful and charming.

We had intended to go to Sarlat before now, or rather go back to Sarlat which we have known on and off for over thirty years. The problem was, and is, that Sarlat is now so busy, as are any of the French towns and villages that are heavily publicised. I don't for a moment say that it doesn't deserve its publicity and its popularity, but I keep remembering when we first went there in 1972 and how quiet and unhurried it was. We drove through the town to our hotel, Hotel Madeleine,

Place Petite Rigaudie and without any difficulty parked outside the door of the hotel. In an open-fronted shop a few metres away a man sat on a stool, with a block in front of him,
carefully cracking and shelling walnuts.

But we had to go back again and so we went there early,
very early, in the morning. We walked across the Place when
it was only mildly infected with tourists and past the church
to the Rue Montaigne and then, naturally, we went to the
Maison de la Boétie and we stood and looked at this charming house built by Antoine de la Boétie a criminal magistrate, in 1525, and beautifully maintained for some five hundred years. It has three residential floors above the arcaded
ground floor shops and its gable reminds me ever so slightly
of Dutch domestic architecture.

Étienne, the son of Antoine, moved into his parents' new
house at the age of five and died there in 1563. He was remarkable in that before he died he had been a writer (and a
controversial one at that), a member of the Bordeaux *parlement*,
a judge, and a great friend of the famous Michel Montaigne.
He lived during the reigns of François Premier (died 1547),
Henry 11 (died 1559) and, in effect the reign of Catherine,
the mother of Henry's tribe. It was a time of unrest and religious persecution and yet Étienne at the age of twenty-two
had written his "Discourse on Voluntary Servitude, or the
Anti-Dictator", pretty solid stuff for those days. He said in
effect that "tyrants have power because the people give it
to them". Well, France at the time had the Estates General
but it also had rather absolute kings. Étienne was a game
Frenchman and a worthy friend of Montaigne. Sarlat is a
necessary visit if for no other reason than the chance to walk
the cobblestones on which his feet had walked a few centuries before — and the cobblestones would be the ones he

actually walked on. And of course for its houses of the thirteenth and fourteenth centuries and later, with their walls
of the golden limestone of the region, and their substantial
but harmonious rooves of split limestone slabs; and for its
intact streets, squares and laneways, apart from the Rue de la
Republique or Traverse constructed straight as a gun-barrel
through the centre of the town.

It was in Sarlat, the old town, that I first ordered and got
morilles in the French autumn. Later, much later, I found
out that this lovely fungus is harvested in spring. Well, we all
have to learn.

On the return journey, St. Cyprien on the hill was our
next destination. Yes, I know that we should have gone to
Beynac overlooking the Dordogne but somehow…Beynac
is so impressive and we had driven past and below it quite a
few times, but as I say, somehow I didn't want to go to Beynac.
I wanted the little back roads to St. Cyprien. I wanted to stop
anywhere and look at the walnut trees in bloom and to listen to the geese as they tut-tutted and tried to frighten you
with their aggressive but laughable waddlings. And so it was
St. Cyprien by way of the woods and valleys and pasture and
walnut groves with the elegant Château La Roque in the
distance on our right.

St. Cyprien gets scant mention in *Michelin*. We are told
that its church was built in the twelfth century and that its
"size is impressive". I think they have been too dismissive.
It is true that it is too large for the town, but I like it and in
particular I like the windows on the buildings surrounding
the church. Many of the windows are glassless, having been
bricked or stoned up at some time. The blank eyes seem to
highlight the decorative window surrounds. St Cyprien is
worth a walk along the side of the hill and down to the main

street. There's a rough but adequate car park on the hill as you come into the town.

Le Bugue has a nice little bar and the town is built on the fast-flowing Vézère river. It's good but is more famous for its caves and chasms (*grottes and gouffres)* than anything else.

Limeul is on a hill and there is something about it. Naturally it is old and it is built of limestone and it is small but it definitely has appeal. Many of the houses are, sort of, one and a half storeys as they are built into the side of the hills and when you walk up their driveways you are in the garden of the ground floor, but there is another ground floor below and another garden. .

Don't make the mistake of driving into Limeul by the main street and going through and out of the town. You will have seen nothing. Take the trouble of going down towards the river (the Vézère), and then you will be rewarded. In fact, one should always make a habit of going down to the river.

CHAPTER SIXTEEN

"Time reveals all that filters is gold" — that's the headline of an article in *The Australian* newspaper of 27 August 2008.

The article deals with research done by one Huai Yong Zhu of the Queensland University of Technology into the effect of gold used in churches, especially gold leaf in church windows. He maintains that "particles of gold absorb light" and "could also destroy airborne pollutants... when exposed to the electromagnetic field of sunlight." It seems that gold heated to 120-200° centigrade can change various chemicals in the air and for some reason, the tendency is to change bad for good. For example, carbon monoxide (as expelled by cars) can be changed to carbon dioxide, which as we all know is the gas produced when we ferment wine. And delicious it is at vintage and delicious too as bubbles in your Champagne or even your sparkling wine. However, you can have too much of a good thing and in large quantities it will replace air and air too is very good for us.

The work being done by this bloke is fascinating and perhaps it goes some further way to explaining the feeling of contentment and wellbeing of Gothic churches. It may even explain Claudel's dramatic religious experience as he stood between the rose windows of Notre Dame turning this way and that. And furthermore, it may explain the contentment on the faces of some ladies whose fingers and bosoms are encrusted and covered in gold rings and pendants.

But Bergerac was our destination and then the vineyards of Monbazillac and finally the château of Michel de Montaigne.

I had been through Bergerac a number of times before I realised just how necessary it is, it always is, to walk down by the river. If you drive through Bergerac on your way to somewhere you can easily come away with a poor impression, as I have in the past. So park that car and go for a walk.

There is a street which runs from the commercial area down to the river and I am sorry not to give you its name, but it is unusual for France in that the verandahs over the footpath are not arcaded as they often are, but are supported by slim posts as in many parts of Australia. It is charming.

Bergerac had its convent (despite being a Protestant stronghold in the Wars of Religion) and the convent now houses the Maison du Vin. It is a splendid building and still retains its cloister. A very good place to ruminate on history and to linger over wine.

The church is the Église Notre-Dame but is only in the Gothic style, having been built in the eighteen hundreds.

It is hard to know whether Bergerac is proud of its famous "citizen" Savinien Cyrano de Bergerac, the seventeenth-century Parisian philosopher who was the inspiration for Edmond Rostand's story.

The real Cyrano died young in 1655 at the age of thirty-six and although he did see service and was wounded at the Siege of Arras in 1649 at the age of twenty-one, he gave up the army and took to the study of philosophy and mathematics. He was a writer who dabbled in what we today call science fiction, and romance, and it is for his romance that he is remembered. Roxanne, the heroine in his play "Cyrano de Bergerac" was based on his cousin who lived in a convent with Cyrano's sister Catherine. Cyrano did have a large, but not grossly large, nose, and although he was reputed to be a jealous and ardent lover, it is thought that he loved men, not women. He may have died as a result of a roofing beam falling on him and whether the beam fell as an act of God or of man is in doubt.

Edmond Rostand was born in Marseille in 1868 but lived the whole of his adult life in Paris. He became a poet and a playwright and was delighted to come across the life and the play of long dead, real life Cyrano. Rostand added an artful twist to his play, and had Cyrano woo the lovely Roxeanne on behalf of his tongue-tied friend Christian. Rostand placed rather heavy emphasis on Cyrano's nose. His play and the real Cyrano's life and original play, have given rise to a gold mine of films, further plays and the like, including a recent film in which the handsome Gerard Depardieu plays the title role.

Neither Rostand or Savinien de Cyrano de Bergerac ever lived in, or so far as I can tell, vsitied our town of Bergerac.

Monbazillac is directly south of Bergerac and is famous for its sweet wine — a dessert wine that may be compared with or contrasted against the wines of Sauternes. It is a lovely area, especially in the autumn when the wine grapes shine in their colours of old gold.

The Château of Monbazillac now owned by the Co-op-erative, is large and was built in the sixteenth century. If you approach it from the very pleasant car park, you may find it confronting. There is something about those double rows of barred windows that takes away the charm of its corner round towers. I couldn't bear to photograph it front-on, but pictures of a tower with vineyards in the foreground are quite appeal-ing. I have seen photographs taken from the "back" and they are much better. The surrounds of the château are beautifully done and it is a pleasure to walk through and around them. Please note, however, that nothing will stop the staff from closing down for lunch. It is *de rigeur*. Could some of the workers keep the place open and have their lunch earlier or later? "*Monsieur, ce n'est pas possible!*" A picnic lunch for us in the treed car park was peaceful and pleasant.

★ ★ ★ ★

I cannot tell you just how much I was looking forward to visiting Michel de Montaigne's château. We knew that the old château had been burnt down after the new owners had had a château-warming party, and that you had to make ap-propriate arrangements to see the new edifice, but we were only interested in Montaigne's tower and it still stood as it always had and it was open on payment of a fee. After lunch, therefore, we took the D936, by-passed St. Foy-la-Grande and streamed on through Lamothe-Montravel and turned right. All the way along the D road were plaques and signs adver-tising and publicising the famous man and the château.

At last we were at the château, but it was hidden away

in the trees and we were only in the remote grounds at the ticket office. These grounds could have done with a trim and a cut — never mind. In the office in front of us were two English couples, not young, not at all young, pensioners perhaps, but driving a new Audi, and they were engaged in an intense appeal to Madame over the cost of seeing Montaigne's tower. They did not want to go into it, their spokesman kept repeating this, "only to walk around it, see it from the outside. Not to walk into it and up those stairs. No, just to glance at it," he repeated the phrase, "just to glance at it from the outside." He wanted her to halve the price. She would not. He began again. There was a girl at a table in the corner and she was following this appeal to Madame with intense concentration. I managed to get her attention and to ascertain that she was a Russian student, but she took our money and issued us with the *billets*. As the three of us walked out into the spring sunshine the spokesman had recommenced his presentation.

It's a moderately long walk to the tower and the rather flamboyant new château. The tower rose up before us and the Russian girl pranced ahead and opened the downstairs door with a set of keys that were appropriate to a door of such venerable age. She then left us, telling us to take our time and "see all".

We first of all walked over and looked at the new château and congratulated ourselves that we had not paid good money to see it. The stone in the old tower though is lovely and has been weathered gently for over five hundred years and you somehow had to touch it. The steps were worn and some of that wear was from the shoes of Michel de Montaigne. We reached the top floor and there was his chair — at least I suppose it was his chair because there was nothing to indicate otherwise — and there in a very small room off the studio was a fireplace. You could imagine a roaring fire there in the winter and how he would come out of the main room to warm himself and to think before resuming his writing.

The atmosphere in the room was evocative and the view was soothing even though the garden was now poorly kept and the grounds a little wild. There were no English people strolling around below. Had he lost the appeal or was Madame still considering his submissions? We looked at the ceiling and there were Montaigne's aphorisms on the beams, said to have been painted in "letters of fire". Well, they are still very bright, quite outstanding really. Had they been re-lettered? We lingered on as you would in a church. Still no English looking up at us.

The best view of the tower, I think, is from the old wall. You simply descend that staircase, leave the tower and walk along by the wall (ignoring the mess in the old conservatory) until you come to some trees. The view of the tower from there with the old stone wall in the foreground is quite splendid.

Michel was born at the château, the old château of course, in 1533 and died at the age of sixty. He had a busy life as a legal official of some kind in Perigord, and then as a member of the Parlement of Bordeaux. We have already written of his great friendship with La Boetie of Sarlat, with whom he shared his humanism and his religious tolerance. Michel was devastated it seems, by the untimely death of his great mate in 1563 and married (for the first and only time) just three years later.

His marriage and his new wife failed to console him, and following the death of his father, Michel retired to his "garden shed". He had given up his official duties and his writing occupied the whole of his time. He resumed his public duties in 1580 and continued his efforts to promote religious tolerance. I write this as if it was nothing, but in the climate of persecution and killings that then prevailed in France it was very courageous.

Michel had published his famous Essays in 1580 and re-published them in a revised form in 1588. He died in 1592 at the château.

We walked back and passed the room in which you bought the tickets. The English people were standing outside. It seemed unlikely that the bloke's appeal had succeeded.

★ ★ ★ ★

"Poverty of goods is easily cured; poverty of soul, impossible."

Montaigne wrote that and much more, and here before we leave this exceptional fellow is one more treasure:

"Unless a man feels he has a good enough memory, he should never venture to lie."

Amen!

CHAPTER SEVENTEEN

Castillon-la-Bataille is on the right-bank of the Dordogne and is so named because of the battle of July 1453 which ended the Hundred Years' War between France and England. And you would certainly be entitled to wonder why those two countries should have been at war intermittently over such a long period. How can I sum it up?

You could argue that William the Conqueror was indirectly responsible. Wasn't it he who set the fashion — a French king or a king of part of France, but also a king of England. If he could do this successfully, and he was successful, then why shouldn't an English king rule France or a part of it? William might have said that he went to England as a result of a promise by Edward The Confessor; but then that was so often the argument thereafter: "I understood, I am entitled by right, a distant inheritance but one nonetheless," et cetera.

So, the start of the Hundred Years' War in

1337 or thereabouts was as a result of the French king Philip V1 seizing the English-held Duchy of Guyenne (formerly known as Aquitania) which had been under English control for the latter part of the so-called Middle Ages (circa 700–1500). Guyenne was important to the English and certainly England was important to the Bordelais and their vineyards.

A long preamble to understand the name of Castillon, a town which takes full advantage of history and promotes *Le Plus Grand Spectacle d'Aquitaine* during July and August. The price of a ticket is a mere twenty euros and this entitles you to watch three hundred *acteurs* and fifty *cavaliers*, and the "show (is) translated into English".

We were too early for the show but it did not prevent us from seeing the town and sampling its coffee. Castillon has some elegant buildings including the Hôtel de Ville (Liberte-Egalite-Fraternite) and a reasonable church but with exasperating stained glass. It is no doubt a personal opinion, but I cannot abide the realistic depiction of humans and angels and saints in human form in glass. It does not work. They look so artificial, so wooden. Ah, for the vague figures and the abstracts and colours of good Gothic glass.

Anyhow, you can park in a very civilized fashion in the centre of the town (under the plane trees) and you can walk back to a delightful and busy shopping centre, or you can walk forward and gaze at the tonnes of water rushing under the bridge over the river Dordogne.

We were going on to a special place in the Entre-deux-Mers (not two seas as you may think but two rivers, the Dordogne and, to the south, the Garonne). Wine lovers will, or may, think of the Entre-deux-Mers as a sea of vineyards. Certainly there are vineyards by the hundreds but there are also areas of countryside comprising pasture and forests. And we had an appointment with one in a little place called Ste. Radegonde. All these saints in France, you wonder if they have all been approved by the Pope. One can use the vernacular: there are more saints in France than you can poke a stick at.

I wasn't going to tell you about Ste. Radegonde (also known as St Radegunda), the girl after whom the village is named, but damn it I will — she is an interesting person and a bit unusual.

We know her date and place of death (13 August 587 in her convent at Poitiers in the Loire) and we know that she was a Thuringian princess who was abducted by a king — Chlotar 1 — during one of his campaigns.

Chlotar, although a Frankish king, was born in Compiègne, and spent most of his life in and around that part of eastern France which is his day was roughly the kingdom of Burgundy. Burgundy got its name from the first century immigrants who came from the Baltic coast and originally was known as Burgundarholm. In the following centuries it continued to attract invaders to add to its original mix of Celts and Romans, and became a melange of many peoples until it was absorbed into France in the seventeenth century. This rather mixed bag was Chlotar's domain but he also longed to posess, in every sense of that word, his Radegonde.

Young Radegonde was not smitten by the king, not at all, in fact she was distant and she was also pious and cold. Nonetheless he married her, but to no avail. She remained pure and chaste, and pious. She did not pity the king, she saved her pity for the poor instead. It is reported that the king "unjustly" killed her brother. That was the end as far as she was concerned and Chlotar definitely got the cold…

shoulder. Her next step was to enter a convent and become a nun. Even so, the lovesick Chlotar still hankered after her, indeed his passion flamed. The bishop of Paris chastised the king and convinced him, eventually, that the devil was firing his lust and so he gave up. Radegonde remained in the convent as the "bride of Christ". She performed the occasional miracle, as saints are obliged to do, and it is recorded that Christ appeared to her a year before her death.

Pujols is a little village, on a hill of course, and in the direction of Ste. Radegonde. The building at the top of the hill at the end of a small cul-de-sac is pleasant, not outstanding and is probably the Hôtel de Ville, if a village of this size can have such a thing. A plaque in the lobby refers to the Celts and the Gauls who would have lived here in the time of our old friend Vercingetorix, but the outstanding feature inside the building is the wonderful wood they have used in the floors and the stairs and the superb way it has been polished. It is outstanding.

We continued up the stairs to look out at the view, but to our surprise there was a view immediately beneath us. It was of a children's circus. I cannot say it was a very sophisticated performance but we watched it for a while as there was no cost involved and really our entertainment was the faces of the thirty or forty local children.

Back to the car and into and amongst the vineyards and their little roads. Near Ste. Radegonde you come to this resurrected (re-built almost entirely, to be truthful) château with one of the most delightful and gentle outlooks you can imagine. We threw our cases into the upstairs room and came down, *"Café?"*

"Oui, bien sûr… Sur la terrace?"

Of course, coffee on the terrace with a pitcher of water

and some *petit fours* and that view: valley, trees, clumps of forests, clouds, blue sky, intermittent sun, and the château surrounded by old-fashioned roses and their perfume, and still three or four hours before dinner. Could you ask for more? It took us half an hour to finish the coffee.

Our room was upstairs and had a glass door that lead on to a small balcony. Not far from the balcony was one of the most perfectly shaped Linden trees I have ever seen. It had on its seasonal complement of lime-green leaves and in addition was in full bloom. Behind it, but some distance away, was the small oak forest on the hill as you approach the château. All rather splendid.

Next morning I went for a long walk, down the hill through the oak forest and out towards the main road. There were vineyards, coming right up to the road and every now and again they were separated by stands of oak. Lovely walking country.

As I went further towards the main road there was a smell, an aroma, that reminded me of home and our vineyard. I came around a bend in the road and saw a man in the distance stoking a smouldering fire of vine roots. A delicious aroma. I turned and made my way back. Despite last night's dinner I was longing for breakfast.

In the bigger places they serve you a buffet breakfast with juices, preserves, bacon and eggs on order et cetera, and of course, a continental breakfast. But in these smaller places they compromise: stewed fruit and yoghurt and perhaps some of that stuff called muesli, but their forté is baguettes (fresh usually but sometimes re-heated or grilled), croissants, *pain chocolat* and perhaps *escargots*, and did I mention it before — coffee. I may be odd but I never get tired of pastry, and bread also, but pastry, and in particular those croissants. The butter in them must be *so* good for the arteries. Breakfast on the terrace again on a perfect morning. It was hard to leave Ste. Radegonde, I sympathised with the old Chlotar. How could she have been so cold to such a daring and romantic king?

CHAPTER EIGHTEEN

I had packed. The cases could be got down in five minutes. I glanced at my watch. "Back before 10," and I was off to revisit the interesting group of houses about a kilometre or so from the hotel. It was not a village, for there would have been a bar and a church if it was, but there had been something unusual about the properties and their gardens and I was delighted to have the time for this last quick glimpse.

Vines, old on my right, and vines new just planted on my left, come right up to the road. No fences. How is it that the French are still planting grape vines, and in the relatively little known Entre-Deux-Mers? It was a puzzle. Until you get to this little enclave of buildings the scenery is rather plain and I found my mind wandering back quite a few years. How old was that boy, that me? Ten or eleven perhaps, about eleven autumns on this earth.

My mother was very religious, very devout. It could be said that she had the gift of faith; the sort of blind, almost thoughtless, faith that was eulogized, and perhaps still is, by certain prelates. If you asked those worthies too many questions about what might have seemed illogical aspects of her religion you were told, somewhat brusquely, that you simply accepted the wise teachings of the church on that point, and — and this was the clincher — that the church spoke with God's authority. If you nonetheless persisted then plainly, you were challenging God himself, and that would not do.

My father, until after my mother died, was not nearly so accommodating. Indeed, he sometimes exploded when my mother talked about the church and its priests. I wanted the comfort and warmth of my mother's belief but my father's logical and probing objections troubled me. Secretly I came to share his dislike of the autocratic parish priest of our childhood.

My parents were country people who ran a family of five children and a mixed farm situated in well nigh virgin bush. Just about the worst farm in the world is one where you grow peas, potatoes, carrots, parsnips, oats, wheat and where you milk cows, keep pigs and chooks and work from daylight to dark seven days a week, and that is what we did. In terms of city occupations we made no money, and yet we all loved that place — most of the time. But it was hard and there was very, very little in the way of income.

And there was, as I say, the priest, who lived in Mansfield in his spacious solid brick presbytery and had his comforts including a dutiful housekeeper, of course. He also had an almost new green Chevrolet "fast back" sedan in which he used to travel out to say Mass at the scattered bush churches, including Tolmie. Mass was not frequent, much to my father's satisfaction and, equally satisfying, there was usually a

sick cow or sheep which needed attention on the appropriate Sunday. Sometimes, though, he was obliged to attend.
Obliged, in the sense I suppose that he could not keep up
the plausible excuses.

Somehow the Egan family was always early for Mass, or
the priest was, perhaps, late, but you would see him swing the
gleaming Chevrolet down the hill, through the paddock of
kangaroo grass and skid to a halt just at the side of the weatherboard church. My mother would nudge me, but I would
hesitate, she would nudge me again and I would glance up at
her. The priest would remain seated in his car staring straight
ahead and looking displeased.

"Reg," she would hiss, "where are your manners? Quick,
go immediately or I will."

I would go over and sulkily open the car door. The priest
would get out and, without looking at me or acknowledging
me in any way, would walk to the church, which mercifully
was usually open. Head down I would slink back to our little
family group. My mother would heave a sigh, smile at me
in the lovely way that she had and run the back of her hand
lightly across her lips. My father's face would be red and his
cheeks puffed out and about to burst and he would tug his
hat further down over his face.

And during the service, there was the "collection" of
course and that was a source of embarrassment and humilia-
tion for my father. The collection plate was of wood and was
handed around with great solemnity by one of the original
parishioners. If you put two shillings (twenty cents) in the
plate it made a solid "thunk". Less than that…well, your coin
made more of a tinkling sound. I regret to write that my father's coins were always on the tinny side despite his attempts
to concoct that heavy, satisfying sound.

One Sunday, the priest, exasperated by the smallness of the collection tally, gave over part of his sermon to remonstrating with the parishioners.

"Look," he said, "I drive twenty miles over a dreadful road, it takes me half a day by the time I hear confessions and say Mass, and what do I get for all my dedication and effort on your part? Eh, what do I get? I don't get enough to buy a packet of cigarettes! You've got to give more. Don't think you're giving it to me. You are giving to God."

On the way home in the old buggy we heard time and time again about Father's diatribe and the fact that our father could hardly afford a few ounces of tobacco a year for roll-your-owns. Certainly he would never dream of buying a packet of tailor-mades.

But Father and his antics and his new Chevrolet has not spoilt my love of churches and abbeys and cathedrals, especially those of France and I will still seek them out for their stone, and their architecture and their peace and quiet, and for their earthy smells. What would we do, what would the French do, if their buildings were to disappear? What can replace them?

Churches, cold, worn flagstones, quiet places of contemplation whether from the outside or the inside: you are so loveable. In praising churches one sometimes has to distinguish between the buildings themselves and the services in them, but I must admit there is a satisfying harmony between an old church and music, especially organ music and choirs, and I have the warmest memories of the Catholic evening service which we used to call "Benediction": incense, Gregorian chants, Latin…

Services in churches should be in Latin, or some language not comprehensible to the congregation. Once a service is conducted in the vernacular you become aware of the triteness of the words and in some cases their absolute nonsense — "Lamb of God who takest away the sins of the world", et cetera. A very odd metaphor for modern times, or for any times when you reflect on it.

Opera is in a similar category: I find it horrible if I am able to understand the words in an opera. How wonderful to look at the singers and the scenery and to imagine vaguely what it is all about. How thrilling to watch the actors and their faces and to listen to the (usually) splendid music, but to understand it — how awful.

I could sum up thus: sermons and preaching are an unfortunate barrier between the churchgoer and God and a comprehensible libretto is an unnecessary distraction when you are watching and listening to an opera.

Such were my thoughts as I continued on my stolen walk to an insignificant but charming group of stone houses, sheds and barns, the last walk regrettably in that quiet secluded part of La Belle France.

★ ★ ★ ★

We ought not to have been late in leaving the Entre-Deux-Mers as we had an afternoon appointment at St. Emilion, but it was hard to leave. Incidentally I committed a mortal sin, one might say, another mortal sin. I wheeled our two cases across the gravel to our parked car, some eight or nine metres. I did glance at the wheel tracks as I went back in to settle the account, *la note*, and I did have a slight pang of conscience, but those cases were not light. When I returned to the car after making payment the offending marks had been smoothed and raked.

On, we must go on.

You can get to St. Emilion by picking up the red D670 as soon as possible, and you will have to get on it to re-cross the Dordogne, for St. Emilion is on the right bank, but let me suggest to you a wandering way and recommend the little roads. You will come to the village of St. Emilion at the bottom of the hill and if you have a moment you will perceive the famous Château Ausone on your left just before you enter.

Alexis Lichine wrote a book entitled *Encyclopaedia of Wines and Spirits*, and in it he states — "Ausone is believed by some to stand on the site of the villa of the fourth century Roman poet Ausonius — and if what Ausonius wrote is true, the wine was a favourite of Julius Caesar". Now, honestly what sort of a wimpish statement is that? "Believed by some", and, "and if what Ausonius wrote is true," "Better," say the theologians, "to sin the whole sin, to be sure that God observes."

So I'll say it. Chateau Ausone there on that lovely south sloping hill is built over the ancient remains of the villa of the poet Ausonius and the wine from here was the favourite wine of Julius Caesar, the murderer of the Gauls. Now, isn't that better?

Decimus Ausonius was a Gaul and he was born in 310 (AD) in Bordeaux and died there in 395. He was a good wine drinker and he, therefore, enjoyed a long life. He was also a poet and a rhetorician (if that can be an occupation) and he taught at some of the best places in Bordeaux and travelled widely. Ultimately he retired to his villa and wrote mainly, it seems, for his own entertainment, but his poems, that trusty encyclopaedia says, had "flashes of an almost Wordsworthian response to nature". He was a patriot of Gaul and of Bordeaux and it seems that he enjoyed himself, and part of that enjoyment would have been the wines of St. Emilion.

Château Ausone and Château Cheval Blanc are accorded the first two mentions in the list of the *Premiers Grand Crus* of St. Emilion and if you have a large amount in the bank or a credit card with a generous limit you may drink them.

We journeyed on through the village and out to our apartment amongst the vineyards just to the north of St. Emilion. It is very soothing to be amongst the vines.

Our appointment was for four pm and we had the privilege of being taken through the cellars and tasting wine from the barrel with their chief winemaker. This was instructive and thought provoking, and the discussion ranged fairly widely, including wine regions and winemaking practices in Australia. At the conclusion of our tour the winemaker pushed a bung into a barrel and said, almost wistfully, "You are lucky in Australia: you can experiment — you can try anything. Here in France all we do is serve the past." That statement was something to reflect on as we drove back just in time to make a reservation for a table in St. Emilion.

Emilion, bless him was a traveller, not a door to door man, but a travelling confessor and a monk, who made an honest living and perhaps a good one at that, good enough anyhow to retire to a cave in the side of the hill. The cave was enlarged into a hermitage and then a church: what is known as a monolithic church, a huge block of stone. Emilion gathered other monks around him and they reflected and they prayed but they also continued the good work of the Romans and Ausonius in the vineyards. But back to the church. It has a long history but you may find the structure to be somewhat sombre.

This is a wonderful area for limestone rock which is easily quarried and it wasn't long before a village in stone grew up around the church. Churches, cloisters, houses, hills, a village: it is a frequent enough formula in France. In fact it is the soul of France. I was taken once under a vineyard in Lussac, just north of St. Emilion, to see the extent of the stone quarry there. Its entrance was totally hidden by trees and blackberries and it went for three or four hundred metres completely under the vines; and just near the centre, many years ago a small area of the vineyard had collapsed back into the quarry. You took a good torch and every now and again you had to dodge roots that hung down from the vineyard somewhere above. What would France be without its stone? It determines the character of the whole of the country from Paris to the tiniest village clinging to some hillside.

There is something special about this village and yet it's not really so different to other villages of the period. Nonetheless, we find ourselves going back again and again. A word of warning. Try to go there during the week, not at *le week-end*, when it is so busy and parking is very difficult.

Apart from Emilion who became a saint and Ausonius who was an epicure, a patriot and a poet, the village can also claim a man of courage from the era of the French Revolution. His name? Guadet, and his first name? Marguerite-Élise. Yes, the French do this, they not infrequently incorporate the mother's name into the name of a son. Jean-Marie, for example. Marguerite Élise was no sissy, despite the name. He was born in St. Emilion in 1758, and was therefore only thirty-one at the time of the "let them eat brioche" revolution.

Although he was young, it is said that he was a "leading lawyer in Bordeaux" in 1789. In 1790 he became administrator of the Gironde *departement* and in 1791 he became president of its criminal tribunal. A very dangerous appointment had he but realised it. Guadet was a democrat and was all for restricting the power of the king, Louis XV1. At the trial of the king, Guadet was one of those who raised his hand to apply the death sentence, but he also supported a stay of execution pending an appeal. He was beginning to tread a dangerous path, even if there was logic and fairness in his favour. He made enemies in the radical Jacobin Club and with the warning signs flashing he decided to leave Bordeaux for St. Emilion. Unfortunately some of his "mates" knew of the village of his birth and he was captured there and guillotined on a lovely summer's day in June 1794.

So there you have it, three very different but three very interesting men from this wonderful, picturesque place of stone and tiles and wine: a poet and a patriot, a travelling confessor and saint, and a brilliant lawyer who lost his head — as lawyers seldom do.

Somehow I was thinking of Guadet when I went on my walk the next morning. I could have turned left at the main road and gone in the direction of Pomerol but almost instinctively I turned right, and followed the gardens of roses until I came to the village of St. Emilion. I had stayed here for a week of winemaking a few years ago, and I thought I would walk as far as the little hotel where I had been so very well cared for. I was going past a better-than-average house with a high wrought iron fence when I heard a familiar bark and a German Shepherd came across the garden to speak to me. He was growling softly deep in his throat but his eyes belied his pretended aggression. We had a chat.

Oh the eyes of animals: the soft, deep understanding eyes. A wave of homesickness swept over me. We had been away too long. This garden, this dog, the roses and the vines, they all said to me that it was time to return and care for the plants and animals at home. I longed to run my hand over his head and along his neck but I doubted that my French conversation had put us on such an intimate basis. I didn't get to the hotel, I simply turned and walked back and as I walked I thought of the eyes of other animals and all they absorbed and expressed.

Cat lovers, please do not be offended but it seems to me that the eyes of the felines are impenetrable: they almost reflect back at you even when their owners are twisting and turning and making themselves agreeable. There is a reserve. I don't see that reserve in the eyes of dogs or cows or sheep or even goats. No, they let you see into their souls. They give themselves completely. Horses are similar but more refined and sophisticated. You are always aware of a high intelligence and thoughtfulness when you look at and talk to a horse.

Animals and birds: creatures of evolution, not creatures created individually by a magical, brilliant mind such as God must possess. No, no, they have mated and mutated and evolved, that is what has happened; it stands to reason, and yet, and yet…

There were fresh baguettes, and croissants and jam (and butter) and coffee for breakfast and I thought I had earned mine.

★ ★ ★ ★

You can drive into and through Libourne, of course you can, but it is getting busy these days. There is plenty of traffic. Libourne is probably named after Roger de Leybourn, the English seneschal (steward "of a medieval great house", according to old faithful) who founded it in 1270 as, of all things, a *bastide*.

Roger de Leyburn (or de Leybourne) was also the Lord

Warden of the Cinque Ports for two sessions (as was our late Robert Menzies, Knight and Prime Minister) and a close friend of Prince Edward, later King Edward 1.

We have already talked about *bastides* but most have remained as villages or small towns at the best, they have not developed in the way that Libourne has. Its old tower gate is fourteenth century and is perfect in its proportions and its simplicity.

Libourne is very much a water town embracing as it does the confluence of the Isle and Dordogne rivers, and being the shipping port for much of the wine from the surrounding vineyards which include Pomerol, Lalande, Fronsac and Canon.

If you can park somewhere, take the time to see the fifteenth century town hall and to stroll in and around the Place Abel-Surchamp where you will see some of the original *bastide* buildings.

Not far from Libourne is the elegant city of Bordeaux. Bordeaux is on the Garonne, not the Dordogne, but it is a city of appealing architecture and history and you may as well see it while you are in the area. The first place I would go to in this city is the Esplanade des Quinconces, where you will have space, a place to stroll and you'll also have plenty of man-made beauty to stare at. There is the Tour St-Michel, the Cathedral of St. André, Le Triangle d'Or, and the public garden — the *Jardin public.*

Ausonius called Bordeaux the "centre of Gaul" and praised its educational institutions. It was said to be "English" from 1154 (Eleanor of Aquitaine) until 1453 when the little fracas at Castillon-la-Bataille saw it return to the French. Edward the Black Prince and his court resided at Bordeaux. Edward was a renowned and efficient killer who wore black armour. He was never a king, dying a year before his long-lived father. And how he had waited, as others before and since have done.

The city of Bordeaux was important in the development of the French Revolution and gave birth to the Girondists. Bordeaux was of major importance in the 1939-1945 war and it became the seat of the French government for a short time. The Free French forces made certain that they were responsible, or primarily responsible, for liberating the town in August 1944.

Bordeaux has an air about it. I think it wears its past with pride and elegance and it is certainly worth deserting the Dordogne for a couple of days and getting involved with the more pedestrian Garonne which has made a long journey from the far-away Pyrenees.

Incidentally, here is a quote to ponder on from the Roman Marcus Antoninus 121–180, (I know he has nothing to do with Ausonius but Antoninus was a great thinker and talker): "Remember that to change your mind and follow him who sets you right is to be less free than you were before."

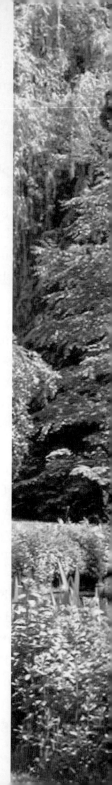

CHAPTER NINETEEN

The Dordogne and the Garonne rivers merge just to the north-west of the wine village of Bourg and they then become the Gironde which exits to the Atlantic ocean at Pointe de Grave. The Gironde is a mighty waterway, a mixture of salt and fresh water, but the turbulent brown waters of the mountains, hills and plains of south-west France are a force to be reckoned with and they carry the fight to the sea right out into the ocean.

Bourg is not famous in the way of St. Emilion; in fact, you could be excused for saying that Bourg has seen better days, and is in need of some re-suscitation. And yet I find that it has great appeal and individuality. In addition it is surrounded by modest vineyards with modest but interesting and in some cases quite historical châteaux. And there is a lovely small church where you would never expect to find such a church. And there is a view over the water, brown though it may be, and there are boats and yachts and things nautical in the foreground…and the ferry, and on a clear day you might even see Château Margaux — you might. Am I protesting too much?

Bourg's main street goes off at an angle and if you follow it you will come to a square and a church nearby. The square is a small plateau perched quite high above the Gironde. But don't take that main street. Instead drive down the side street and park beside the estuary. This little manoeuvre gives you an easy place to leave the car and also a wonderful view of the old buildings and the parapets of Bourg with its overhanging chestnut trees.

Then, you walk up the flights of stairs and you look out, and you wander the square and you ask yourself how it is that most of the shops are in the main street and that the square is half empty. There is even a Turkish house to look at. A retired seaman's house it seems. Quite a few of the fishermen hereabouts were of Turkish origin. Bourg has two restaurants so far as I am aware. But the only places to stay are the bed and breakfasts in some of the vineyard châteaux.

Out of Bourg in the vineyards is the tiny village of Tauriac and it is worth a drive just to look at its relatively unknown but lovely little church, the church which I mentioned earlier. It seems to me to be quite perfect in its weathered stone and its discreet and classical façade. Château Falfas at Bayon matches this modest church in its simple but beautifully proportioned outlines.

We left the church reluctantly and regained the yellow D669 and drove towards Blaye, the centre for the principally white wines of this area. It was becoming late and we were in need of a cup of coffee, or at least I was. There, near a school on our right was a bar and a place to park. We pushed open the door and were met by a startling sight. The woman who greeted us wore a scarlet red blouse and black flared pants, her face was decorated and painted in the glowing colours of the night or very early morning and between the fingers of one hand with its brilliant enamel finger-nails was a cigar, half smoked, but still alight and active. In the corner of the bar there was another woman similarly decorated and attired but she was bent over a large table and was ironing. There was a washing basket half empty and a pile of neatly folded articles beside her. She was cigarless.

"*Bonjour*," I managed to say, and was answered in the usual courteous fashion. "*Deux cafés, noisettes, s'il vous plait.*"

"*Certainment, monsieur.*" She moved behind the bar and operated the machine in a professional fashion and handed the coffees to us. The sheila in the corner continued in her duties and the coffee sheila smiled and talked to us about the weather and other things until we finished our coffee and departed. A most unusual bar, the first of that kind we had encountered despite our many tours of France over a number of years. I still puzzle over that little bar, and in particular I puzzle over the two girls. Never, no never…well, it doesn't matter.

But on to Blaye. There is no doubt that Blaye can be busy, even downright commercial, but if you get into the back streets there is something to see and of course there is the Citadel across the road. It covers a huge area and there is a tourist train which they say runs from time to time and, of course, there are pralines "the famous sweets…invented here by the chef to the Maréchal de Plessis-Praslin." There, you have the name of the nobleman but we cannot identify the inventor, and I have tried.

I know it is "drawing the long bow" but if you have the time, drive north from Blaye along the little D road which starts as the D255, and continue on despite the seaside attractions until you arrive at a quite small village perched on the edge of the sea — Talmont. Let me tell you about this thirteenth century bastide, this jewel overhanging the rolling blue and green Atlantic.

Talmont is not large and some people including *France This Way* proclaim "that it is reminiscent of small villages in Greece". Well, I don't say that I would subscribe to that statement but it is very lovely and in spring and in early summer, it becomes a village of hollyhocks. There is a simplicity about hollyhocks that suits the plainness of the houses in the village, but which at the same time decorates and highlights the plainness. Hollyhock, as gardeners know, is part of the mallow family and can be an annual, biennial or even a perennial. It is a native of China. It seeds prolifically and comes in a range of soft colours from white through pink to bright red. And why is it so outstanding and so prevalent here? Sorry, but I can't help you.

The hollyhocks, the sea, the white cliffs and the simple houses are captivating but the real reason for our visit was the church of St. Radegonde. Yes, another church dedicated to this disdainful dame and what a church and what a position. There is no doubt about the skill of the catholic hierarchy. Even in the eleventh century they chose a site to advertise their creed and dominate the town or village. There was no hill on which to build the church so it was put on the bare stone cliff overhanging the sea. Brilliant. It is like a lighthouse but one that has been built in the Roman style. There is a splendid picture of St. Radegonde in the book *The Love of France* by those two girls Marie-François Golinsky and Alice Vidal, who regrettably, are no longer girls.

But to return. As I have said, the Dordogne and the

Garonne merge just to the north of Bourg at the Bec d'Ambès and the river, or the estuary becomes the Gironde. Bourg and Blaye are on the east side of the estuary and their vineyards tend to have a westerly aspect, whereas those on the other side — the vineyards of the Médoc — have an easterly aspect.

When you speak of the Médoc you speak first of the great growths as they are called: the châteaux Margaux, Lafite, Latour, Mouton Rothschild and Haut Brion but you may think also of some of the lesser but beautiful châteaux, for there are others, many others. Now, I know that strictly speaking we have left the Dordogne but there is a lovely château that has something different about it, and it happens to be just a short ferry journey from Blaye. So, drive your car through the very pleasant public gardens of Blaye and board the ferry which will land you at the port of Lamarque. And not far from the port is Château Lamarque.

The village just outside the château gates is not large; it does not even have a boulangerie but there is a depot du pain and a few other shops. The gates of the château are actually on the opposite side of the road and the château itself is some two hundred metres away along a lovely gravelled driveway lined on both sides by mature and shady trees. The perimeter wall of the château is quite high and of stone and has false gates and decorated pillars and the like and it is worth a stroll and a close inspection. If you follow the wall to your right (as you face the château) you will come to a most unusual church. It is not part of the château and it stands aside from the village and it has a definite Russian appearance. I was unable to discover its history.

But to return to Château Lamarque: the drive is classic and the stroll is pleasant but the lovely white pebbles roll under your feet, so wear sensible shoes. When the château finally comes into sight you are looking at part of the eleventh and twelfth century section although the "courtyard" château itself is mainly fourteenth century. Henry 1V, the *vert galant* stayed here. Henri was admirable, in the main, and did much for religious tolerance, but his private life and his propensity for younger and younger women (girls) procured by his staff was less to be admired. He was assassinated in Paris in the spring of 1610 at the age of fifty-seven. As you walk towards the château you see first a wing which overlooks the park. There are balconies on this wing and it took very little imagination to see Henri standing there laughing, with his arm around the waist of an attractive young lady.

If you continue on along the driveway you come to the courtyard of the building in its different styles. The château is not grand: it is low, its garden is small and neat. It is altogether an unassuming château where you could imagine you would feel at home. This modest but historic château represented the end of our trip. It remained only to return to the car and drive the relatively short distance to the friendly airport of Bordeaux at Merignac.

Bordeaux airport is not Charles de Gaulle, oh no, it is small and it is easy, and you don't have to worry about other drivers, knowledgeable drivers sitting on your tail while you try to decipher the signs and get on to the correct cloverleaf. Bordeaux is relaxing. I handed the keys to the girl and told her that the car had survived our journey and that it didn't so much as have a mark on it, therefore, she should refund the whole of that extra insurance premium we had paid. "Monsieur," she replied, "A nice try but no refund."

136

CHAPTER TWENTY

We flew from Bordeaux into Charles de Gaulle to await our flight to Tokyo and as there were two or three hours to spare we decided to have a cup of coffee and a croissant at a slightly grotty but pleasant and democratic café/bar that we had discovered the previous year. The walk to the bar seemed very long and the crowd hurrying both ways seemed to be grubbier than we remembered and rather more jostling. Eventually our recalled bar showed itself over the bobbing heads.

Alas, and alack, the bar had changed! The waiters no longer waited on the little tables, you simply ordered at the counter and stood there while they made the coffee, and you then took your tray to the table. Worse, a hundred times worse, the coffee no longer came in that wonderful clay called china, no, it was now served in waxed (or plasticised) cardboard with a plastic lid. Oh woe is me. How can you serve that noble drink in manufactured tumblers with plastic lids? Why is it so difficult today to have decent food, decent drinks and decent china and cutlery? By all means have a cheap place or places but let us also have some civilised places as well, even if it costs a bit more. I know that there are better bars in other parts of the Paris airport, but to have walked a long slog out of our way just to return to this nostalgic bar and to be confronted with cardboard tumblers and indifferent coffee…no, it was too sad.

To console myself I remembered as we sat there, that other part of Charles de Gaulle and our flight from there to Rome only a few years ago. We were leaving France and so I went to their splendid cheese shop and I bought two well-matured goat's milk cabecous and put them carefully in a proper compartment of my overnight travel bag. I won't say that I forgot them but they remained there for two or three days, at least.

We were driving from Rome to Venice and I had had about enough of the smoke and heat and speed of the Italian *autostrade* when quite suddenly the turn-off to Soave appeared. And we were going to Soave. In the twinkling of an Italian eye we were off the roaring madness and proceeding at a slow and civilised speed into the village of Soave, the wine village where we had an appointment. Oh, but this village is lovely, and quiet; and it is surrounded by old stone houses and walls and trees and there are people who are strolling under those trees. It was, and no doubt it still is, bliss.

After our interview and our wine tasting we re-emerged into the autumn sun and drove down by the old walls and parked under a tree. It was time for lunch. What did we have for lunch on a warm day in late September? Well, we had the shade of the tree, old stone walls to look at, two (well-aged) cabecou, an Opinel pocket knife, paper plates, two real wine glasses, four small brown Italian pears and a half bottle of chilled Soave white wine given to us by the winemaker and his wife. I don't have to tell you that the lunch was one of the simplest and the best I have ever had, and its memory consoled me as I sat and gazed at this revamped and now tawdry bar. Progress, economy, "the bottom line", "the big picture", "down the track", "the level playing field", "the window of opportunity" — you and your plastic tumblers, you should all be put into a giant mulcher and spread on the garden to rot.

We went to an airport lounge and as I sat there, in comfort I must add, and waited for the departure of our flight to Tokyo I thought about France and the French and I tried to evaluate them in some objective way.

I know there are people who laugh at my much loved Encyclopaedia Britannica, and they gesture towards a keyboard and a thing called a computer, and I admit the advantages of these modern devices, and I use them and they are used for me by others, but for a very quick reference there is nothing to beat the speed of a book. Nothing. The other thing about an encyclopaedia is this. You get an idea in consulting it of just how often certain nationalities are featured. And I tell you that in the case of the French it is often: whether it is a painter, a sculptor, a scientist, a doctor, a writer, an archaeologist... I say to you they populate the annals of the books more thickly than famous people of any other country. France has always been a thoughtful nation and continues to be so today. What about this: "[France] one of the oldest and historical and culturally most important nations of Europe and indeed the whole of the Western world". Yes, what about that?

On our first trip to Europe we flew to Frankfurt, picked

up a car and drove north and west through Germany: along
the great Rhine, through some mountains, into rolling countryside, through villages and so on. All good, all lovely and
interesting and with plentiful food and excellent wine along
the way. Then we came over the border and in to France.
We had done no more than to cross a bridge, but what a
change. The architecture was quite different, the cars (mostly
Citroën *deux chevaux*) were very distinct, the way the people
dressed was different. Everything was sharply distinguishable,
including the language. I stopped to fill our petrol tank and
as I spoke to the woman in my wretched French I thought,
"I am home."

A week or so after our arrival I had to take our car to a
garage for a minor ailment and as I came back to the *hostellerie* in the taxi I listened in to the girl at the depot as she was
giving directions to her fleet of drivers, and realised just how
lovely the French language is. English has an interesting pedigree and can claim to be a language of the classics, German
is expressive, can be a touch hard, but can also be romantic,
Italian is certainly romantic but can perhaps be criticised on
the basis of being too mellifluous but French, I reasoned,
as we drove back to the mill on the river near Angoulême,
French is perfection. I don't wonder that the French endeavour to protect its purity and yet words like le *"parking"* and
le *"camping"* and le *"week-end"* have managed to creep in and
make themselves at home.

And speaking of speaking and language, have you ever
watched the faces of the French when they are talking? The
face is working vigorously and in particular the lips are extremely active, pouting, relaxing, narrowing and the whole
time moving with forcefulness and decision. It is fair to say
that the French articulate, and yet oddly, it seems to me, they

are unwilling (or unable) to aspirate. This inability or disin-
clination to pronounce the letter "h" is on the other hand
one of the charms of listening to a French person speaking
in English: "I 'ate you, you are 'orrible."

Perhaps you have heard that the French are distant and
arrogant, and we have found evidence for this proposition
once or twice in Paris. But in the Provinces, never. You sneak
into a lovely picnic spot under the shade of a tree by a stream
and you have a tad of doubt that you may be just encroach-
ing on private property, but you reflect, you are safe for no
one would ever come along this little track. A cyclist appears
and you glance up at him, "*Bon appetite,*" he calls with a smile
as he rides on.

You get an introduction to the head of a famous house
in Champagne, a man who also distinguished himself at the
end of the last world war and when you call at his office and
are kept waiting for a while a glass of Champagne is served
to fill in the time; you are taken on the mandatory tour, then
you and your children lunch at the firm's château; you are
booked into a good hotel and when you present yourself at
the *bureau* next morning to pay the account you are told,
"There is nothing to pay". And when you go back to France
again and yet again the hospitality is not only repeated but
expanded. There are whole weekends at a hotel-restaurant in
the country, dinners, champagne breakfasts, pheasant shoot-
ing (if you like that sport) and so on. Just try to recipro-
cate that hospitality, and you will not be allowed. The same
generosity is meted out in the Rhone Valley, in Alsace, in
Burgundy…

You might suppose that we were important people at
that time: perhaps rich and famous, and therefore deserving
of all the attention. We were not. I was a solicitor with my

own practice and a vigneron who had made wine for three or four years on a small vineyard in the Melbourne area. We were hardly important customers, nor was there any likelihood that we would ever be of significant commercial value to our hosts. Nonetheless we were feted. Ah yes, the French will not be outdone in kindness, generosity and hospitality.

"The French are, paradoxically, strongly conscious of belonging to a single race and a single nation, but they hardly constitute a unified racial group by any scientific gauge." Yes, objectively my Encyclopaedia is correct but have you ever heard the proud utterance *"La France"* and watched the uplifted tilt of the chin, *"Ah oui, la France."* So why is it, why this pride in homogeneous France when Montmartre is crowded with those colourful, elegant, but somewhat newly arrived black French people and the rest of France is a mixture of Celts, (or Gauls), Greeks, Italians, Germans, Normans and even English and the occasional Australian?

First it is, perhaps, their pride in their language and their endeavours to keep it as pure as is possible despite the encroachments of the electronic media. They are serious about their grammar (and their bloody genders), their syntax and their pronunciation. You do not trifle with the French language. And if you speak it with the murderous inaptness that I do they shudder, they apologise, but they adhere to their duty to their language and they switch to and stay with English.

Another quality that sets them apart from the English in particular, and many other Europeans, is that the Parisian loves his Paris but he also loves and is interested in the countryside, the rivers and the seas; and the country people are closely bound to their villages, their towns, their farms, orchards and vineyards and they respect their capital Paris, and even love it a little.

In former times I might have said that they were also united by the Roman Catholic religion which is in a sense the state religion, but today the Sunday worshippers do not crowd the beautiful churches as they once did. In fact, the recruitment of priests is not exactly thriving.

When I arrived back in Australia and allocated a Saturday morning to thinking, reading and writing, I picked up Volume One of the beloved Britannica to test my earlier statement that French people featured thickly in its pages. Opening it at random, I started to read about the composer Berlioz (1803 –1869) who at the age of twenty-seven wrote his magnificent Symphonie Fantastique. Now I know that this part of my book is about the valley of the Dordogne and that Berlioz was a native of a rather plain village called La Côte-Saint André which is somewhat over the hill and on the side of a mountain quite a distance from the Dordogne, but, but, and I digress, and ought not to do so, but it is such wonderful music. Heavenly music. Hector Berlioz was the son of a well-to-do atheist father, a country doctor, and of a very devout Catholic mother. He had been sent to Paris to study medicine but had become involved with the artistic world and various musicians, and on a home visit he announced to his mother that he was abandoning medicine and devoting himself seriously to music and its study. His mother knelt at her son's feet, embraced his legs and begged him to give up the world of the arts and all that that sinful world involved. He told her that he could not; she wept, he refused; she begged and cried, he continued to refuse. She had his allowance terminated. Berlioz went back to Paris and meditated sourly on her religious faith, on her "stupid doctrines — relics of medieval times".

But mother was right, as mothers sometimes are, and Berlioz got involved with an English actress Harriet Smithson who he eventually married, then he became enamoured of a singer Marie Recio and had one or two other affairs. So you see, as I have said mother was right, in a way but oh, what a loss it would have been to music. Mother was wrong.

I apologise for the diversion, but that Symphonie Fantastique, how aptly it is named.

And, yes, I admit it. There follows another digression, and again I apologise, but if you are at La Côte St. André you may as well jump in the car and travel up to Belley in the Department of the Ain. Belley is famous for its wine from the regions of Bugey (once part of Burgundy) and its cheese called *Tome de Belley,* and extremely famous as the birthplace of the great lawyer (another one!) and gourmet Brillat-Savarin.

Brillat-Savarin lived at the time of the French Revolution and he was not a lover of the Jacobins. Indirectly he made his views known: a very dangerous thing to do when the Jacobins had both the power and the guillotine, as the man from St. Emilion found to his cost. In 1792 at the tender age of thirty-seven, Brillat-Savarin fled to Switzerland, but even there it became uncomfortable so he managed somehow to get to the coast and to board a ship for America. In the land of the free they had little use for a French jurist and gourmet, and to support himself Brillat-Savarin taught French and played the violin. There was no end to his talents.

In 1796 it was safe for him to return to Paris where he was kindly remembered by friends in the new regime and made a judge of the Paris Supreme Court. He was a good judge, it seems, but like so many in the law he had an intense interest in another subject — cookery. He went into print on that subject and his publisher launched on behalf of "an anonymous author" his great classic *Physiology of Taste*.

The book was ahead of its time, and is still read today, two hundred years after its publication. Some of Brillat-Savarin's essays into the science of food are now shown to be rather wide of the mark, but he investigated, and he tried, and he theorised. Eventually his colleagues on the bench discovered the identity of the author and were not amused. He was being too trivial and had compromised the solemnity of the law. Brillat-Savarin soldiered on and it is said that he eventually became more famous as a cook than a jurist.

Now, Brillat-Savarin died in 1826 and just fifty years after his death a French baby was born in Geneva. His name was Marcel Rouff. Born in 1877 and dead in Paris in 1936. Marcel conceived a novel which perhaps had as its inspiration and background some aspects of the life of Savarin. He called it *The Passionate Epicure*, and it followed on the success of *La France Gastromonique* written in collaboration with his friend Curnonsky.

A word or two about Curnonsky, whose real name was Sailland. The man was a dedicated and brilliant gastronome. Look at his words on cooking: "Above all keep it simple." Curnonsky died in 1956 at the age of eighty-four whilst on a strict diet. It is thought that he was standing by an open window gazing out at Paris but thinking of dinner when he fainted and fell head first into the street. But let us return to Rouff.

The hero of *The Passionate Epicure* is Dodin-Bouffant, an epicure par excellence, and also a magistrate who lives in a village in the countryside around Belley. We hear very little of Dodin's legal career but we learn much about his love of food and wine and his surgeon-like dissection of their components. Dodin wants the appreciation of food and wine elevated to the same artistic level as music, literature, painting and the arts in general. "Art", he maintains, "is the understanding of beauty through the senses, through all the senses, and in order to understand the dream of a Vinci, [Leonardo presumably] or the inner life of a Bach, one must...be capable of adoring the scented and fugitive soul of a passionate wine." Or winemaker, one might add.

The book was translated into English in 1961 and the wonderful illustrations are by the Englishman Charles Mozley. I love, in particular, a sketch of the French village and all its characters, and I fail to understand why the book is so little known.

But we have strayed a long way from the valley of the Dordogne, and even some distance from a general commentary of France and its history and habits and customs. We must return, we must hark back to the artists and the entertainers and the intellectuals and famous people of France. We should take up that encyclopaedia. I invite you to turn the pages of the Encyclopaedia from Berlioz onwards. You will find Bernadette of Lourdes, Saint, born Lourdes, George Bernanos, born Paris and author of *The Diary of a Country Priest* (odd book though it is), Bernard, comte d'Armagnac, Claude Bernard, born St. Julien, physiologist, Emile Bernard, born Paris, painter and friend of Van Gogh, Tristan Bernard, born Besançon playwright, novelist, journalist *and* lawyer.... And you will have turned only two pages since the entry on the magnificent Berlioz. Q.E.D.

France and your stone, your villages and your people, your magnificent châteaux, cathedrals and churches, your intellectuals, composers, dancers and your writers, your lovely forests, your food and your wine and perhaps most endearing of all, your peasant-style gardens beside modest houses, your superbly kept vegetable and flower gardens combined, we must leave you and return to one of the most unusual islands on this globe. An island that was largely isolated from most of the other countries until almost the end of the eighteenth century, or to put it in French terms, until the time of the French Revolution.

PART 11

PART II

CHAPTER ONE

Australia, often called the largest island on earth, has been inhabited by man for between twenty and fifty thousand years. And how that "man" came here, or came to be here, we do not really know and perhaps we never will. Some say that ancestors of the Australian Aborigines would have come from neighbouring islands, but of course it is equally possible that they peopled those islands.

Boats, the lack of boats, isolation, the lack of rain and consequent lack of abundant fruits and vegetables …the land imposed its pattern, and many Aborigines were nomads by necessity. Yes indeed, the land ruled.

The continent now known as Australia had been chanced upon by European explorers in the 1600s, perhaps even before that, but they did not invade and settle here until the British settlement in Sydney Cove in 1788. New South Wales was the newcomers' base, even though subsequently there were settlements in Tasmania (1804), Queensland

(1825), West Australia (1829), South Australia (1834), and Port Phillip in Victoria (1835). It is fair to say that New South Wales was the principal colony until the 1850s and it is not utterly unfair to allege that the particular characteristics of Australians were largely formed and nurtured in the Western Plains of that state.

Australia's name is said to have devolved from *auster* (Latin) south, hence austral (southern). Its official title in English circles was Terra Australis. Matthew Flinders, the intrepid sailor liked the sound of the simple word "Australia" and in 1804 he made strenuous representations for it to be adopted. Sir Joseph Banks was against this careless, lackadaisical "colonial" approach and insisted that Flinders use the formal title — hence his report "A voyage to Terra Australis".

Robert Brown (could he have a plainer name?) in his book published in 1810 on the continent's botany ignored officialdom and frequently used the adjective "Australian".

Governor Macquarie, good, progressive, independent Scottish-born Lachlan Macquarie, liked the title "Australia," and he not only used it in his dispatches but strongly urged its adoption, especially from 1819 onwards. The Colonial Office reluctantly agreed and recommended accordingly to the Admiralty (which apparently had the say) and in 1824, Terra Australis became Australia.

So in 1824 we are finally and officially dealing with blokes and sheilas called Australians. What and who were those original white Australians? First there were the expatriates — the officers, naval men and officials, who were anxious to go back to England; then a sprinkling of relatively well-to-do "gentlemen" who saw a chance either to enrich themselves and remain here, or enrich themselves and go "home", the ambivalent ones; and there were the ordinary soldiers and sailors. As time went on, more and more "free" settlers arrived, along with immigrants who came out on assisted passages. Other members of the population were the emancipists ("free from slavery") who had had their prison terms expunged or whose terms had been served, and the convicts who were indented to settlers and who called themselves "Government men". A rather curious category was the "remittance men", those who had been obliged to leave their homelands by well-(or ill-) meaning parents or near relations and who could look forward to a steady payment from the Old Country so long as they remained discreetly in Australia; and finally there were the "currency lads" (and lasses) — those who had had the good fortune to be born in this southern land.

Initially the groupings above were divided into their races — English, Welsh, Scottish and Irish — and subsequently, especially during and after the gold rushes of the 1850s, Chinese and Europeans, especially it seems, Germans but with a liberal seasoning of Italians. We also had sprinklings of Dutch, Norwegians, Swiss, Russians, Afghans and some, but not many French. The French have long taken the view that you do not readily leave such a splendid country as theirs, or if you do then it should be on a temporary basis.

One of the first things you observe about this mix of people and races is that it bears no relation to the mix of the general population in Britain at the time. Nothing like it. But then that mix had been forming for centuries and had long since solidified. England could, and can boast of a society where the classes are defined. It is true that money and fame can and do make inroads into the class system but it still remains intact. The nobility and the "upper classes" may have been frightened by that eighteenth century bloody revolution just a beret throw across the channel, but they held their nerve and they kept a stiff upper lip and they survived intact.

Even today in London (and elsewhere) you see evidence of the lines of demarcation and distinction — in the clubs, in the "right" restaurants, in the manner of dress and speech and of course, in the deference paid to the tottering but still rich and powerful "Royals".

Let me digress for a moment, and tell you of a silly and a trifling incident in London in the 1970s. On one of my early morning walks I came upon a "private" park or garden. I should state that my wife, who prepares properly for all trips, had made me aware of the existence of those places, and lo and behold I came across such a phenomenon. Now, I don't mean a private garden attached to a house or a stately home, I mean a small park that is utterly houseless and is plonked right in the midst of London's buildings and squarely in the way of your walking track. It had, this one, a cast iron fence and a cast iron gate, locked with the appropriate key, and a discreet but distinct sign "Private. Entrance only to members", or some such phrase. And the path that I was on went right up to this gate. Now what would any normal Australian do when faced with this provocation? He would put his foot firmly on the top of the gate, he would grasp the gate in his right hand and in one bound he would be on the other side and he would be walking respectfully, demurely and admiringly through this charming reserve. So that's exactly what I did.

Half way through the delightful refuge I met a rightful one and he certainly had a disapproving look on his privileged face. To do him justice, he said, "Good morning". There may have been the faintest suggestion on his part that he would be quite happy to stop and have a longer conversation. An evil impulse floated through my head — I would say "G'day". I resisted the temptation, I would not sin. I replied "Good morning", made room for him and we passed within a few inches of one another. The garden was quite beautiful and well maintained. I did not turn my head or look back. I simply repeated the little exercise that got me into the enclosure and then continued my walk through the historic streets of that old capital. I was back amongst the populace.

But we must return now to early Australian history and continue with my hypothesis about the make up of the general Australian population of the nineteenth century.

Where were the nobility, the upper classes or even the wealthy or rapidly growing wealthy middle class and manufacturers? There was a complete absence of some classes and a predominance of the poor, the under-privileged and the peasants. But, and in my view this is of the utmost importance, the dead weight of the nobility and the like never oppressed the ordinary people of this Southern land. It is true that the convicts had plenty to resent, apart from, in some cases, the trifling or the political offences behind their transportation: they had ill treatment to an extent it is hard to imagine less than two hundred years later, including floggings, and they had no rights — initially. And yet their resentment was remarkably moderate. They quickly learned to adapt and to curb that resentment and once emancipated they got on with their lives. They stood in the sun, they took a deep breath and they marvelled at the expanse of their new country.

"Liberty, equality, fraternity". The French Revolution has enshrined that phrase in France for over two centuries and it might well have been the motto of the new Australia — the Australia which emerged following on the construction of the road over the Blue Mountains by the supervisor William Cox and his loyal band of twenty-eight convicts, who gained their freedom when they gained the wonderful view over the western plains of New South Wales.

"Liberty, equality, fraternity" — a great achievement by those quarrelsome bloodthirsty patriots but oddly enough more apposite to Australia than La Belle France. Yes, the motto is emblazoned over the doorways of every Town Hall or *Marie*, in France but it is an ideal rather than a reality. How is it after you have beheaded the King and Queen, and thousands of others, and adopted the somewhat gruesome "Marseillaise" and the above motto, how is it that there are hundreds of the old regime, the nobility, from one end of France to the other? How is it when you speak to the French and read their newspapers you are addressing Comtes and Comtesses and the like, and reading about them in the press — with their appropriate titles? It is a *mystère, monsieur* and you accept it as you watch them somewhat apologetically shrug their shoulders. *C'est le mystère.*

Yes, it is curious, and I remember how appalled I was many years ago when we were wandering around the cellars of a "great" chateau in the wine growing area known as the Médoc and I was introduced to a workman who was topping the barrels. *"Bonjour Monsieur,"* I said and held out my hand, *"Bonjour"* came the reply, but instead of taking and shaking my hand he grasped me by the forearm. The reason may have been that he did not want to soil my hand, but then what about the sleeve of my jacket? It was a shock for an Australian, this act of what appeared to be subservience.

But I have to admit my admiration for France and its manner of addressing fellow human beings. It is democratic, egalitarian and so simple: *monsieur* and *madam* and *mademoi-*

selle. We have no equivalent in English speaking countries. We have expressions such as mate and cobber, and then at the other extreme, sir and madame. I loathe, and most Australians loathe, the use of sir, even by a waiter. I detest the word "guy" and "you guys", but I'm not happy with the word mate, except in the appropriate circumstances. We have to admit it, the French have the wood on us there. Monsieur — brilliant.

And I fear I may have digressed. We shall return to the conjectures surrounding the Australianess of this continent.

CHAPTER TWO

For the first twenty-five years the growing settlement of New South Wales was hedged in by the Great Dividing Range, which includes the rugged Blue Mountains. The land was developed north and south of Sydney and there was a reasonable percentage of agricultural land including orchards, as well as larger grazing properties.

Quite a few Englishmen coming out to the new colony complained that it was too like Home — they had expected something quite different. And even today you see the English influence along some of that same coast and nearby accessible areas like Bowral and Moss Vale in the Southern Highlands. It was the opening up of the land west of the range by the famous three, Blaxland, Lawson and Wentworth, in 1813 and the completion of that exploration by George Evans and others that freed the new country Terra Australis from the tight grip of Englishness. Australia may have been officially recognised in 1824 but Australia as we know it — assertive, democratic, independent Australia — cut the umbilical cord when those first men sat on their horses, shaded their eyes and looked west across Bathurst and Forbes. There was no holding "Australia" from that time onwards.

There are many things about Australia that amaze me but one in particular keeps cropping up: the speed at which new arrivals became Australians and defied "the mother country". Take that bloke Lang for instance. Not Jack Lang, the "big fella" and the brother-in-law of our Henry Lawson, but Dr John Dunmore Lang, the Scot born in Greenock on the south shore of the Firth of Clyde and not far from Glasgow. Dunmore Lang had all the confidence and assertiveness of many Glaswegians and he arrived in Australia in 1823 at the age of twenty-four in full possession of his formidable powers. He was already a fully-fledged Presbyterian minister and all he needed, it was said, was a pulpit.

His old acquaintance, or more correctly perhaps the acquaintance of his childhood, was Thomas Makdougall Brisbane, the governor of New South Wales, Scottish soldier and "acclaimed astronomer". The young preacher, shortly after arrival here suggested to the Governor the desirability of a new and independent Presbyterian church for Sydney and intimated that a contribution from the local revenues would be appropriate. Governor Brisbane, somewhat understand-ably, demurred.

The Governor himself was a Presbyterian but he pointed out that there was an Anglican church and that it had set a standard in tolerance. Lang expostulated that it was the Scots themselves who had won their civil and religious liberties "by the swords of their forefathers". They ought not and would not be beholden to the Church of England. Lang sailed to England the next year and after an audience with the Earl of Bathurst came back with an order that the authorities advance one-third of the cost of the new church. Lang was away!

Lang had plenty of support from his two well-established brothers and from his mother and, of course, his church, which after all was founded on the principals of Presbyterianism, i.e. government "by elders all of equal rank". He became a representative member of the Legislative Council of New South Wales and applied the same "equal rank" principles to the government of his adopted country. He was instrumental in bringing some four thousand Highlander immigrants to New South Wales — good stout Presbyterians all and hardy independent workers and farmers. He would use them to balance the Irish immigrants with their love of the Papacy. He lampooned the use of English names for our rivers and mountains and agitated for local names. He ran newspapers to spread his gospel and he also agitated for the Republic of Australia. America was a republic and why shouldn't Australia follow suit?

Lang had drive. He travelled back to England and Scotland no less than eight times in his life, eight times halfway around the world in nineteenth-century sailing ships, and despite these journeys and his newspapers and his books (his secular activities) he still had time for his religion. Undoubtedly he contributed an immense amount to his adopted country, and it can rightfully be said that he helped to establish that "Australianess" which we all know and take a pride in. His name is commemorated in the Dunmore Lang College of the Macquarie University, and his face and body is commemorated in the charming park known as Wynyard Square, near the Wynyard Station of course.

There was another Australian, a currency lad, and a con-

REG EGAN

temporary of Lang's: William Wentworth (1790–1872). I say William was a currency man but actually he was born on a ship en route from Sydney to Norfolk Island. But then Norfolk Island was in many respects just an extension of Australia in those times. So we will call him native born. He first came to our notice in 1813, when he joined Blaxland and Lawson in crossing the Blue Mountains.

There is a significant grey area about the background of William's father, D'Arcy Wentworth, and it was not until William had gone to England in 1817 to study law preparatory to his admission to the Bar, that he found out about his father's peccadilloes. His father was obliged to leave England because of some prank or perhaps actuality in connection with an armed hold-up. Regardless of the doubts and uncertainties, what was certain is that his father D'Arcy married a convict woman, Catherine Crowley. The D'Arcy Wentworths did well in Australia; D'Arcy came out on the boat as assistant surgeon, was promoted to Superintendent of Convicts, surgeon of the new Sydney Hospital and assisted in the foundation of the Bank of New South Wales. He was on the best of terms with Governor Macquarie and died in 1827 a respected and wealthy landowner.

Was it any wonder that William, the son, aimed high in his matrimonial plans and from England wrote to his father about a union of this nature with John Macarthur's daughter Elizabeth to whom apparently the family was "connected by such ancient bonds of friendship". William had benefited from his upper class English education and was able to show the effect of this in the concluding remarks in the matrimonial letter to father: "[it] would not fail to secure your approbation, even without reference to that predilection and regard which I know you feel for the object of my affection." How elevating it would have been to have eavesdropped when William put the marriage proposal to Miss Macarthur. Sadly, or perhaps fortuitously, the proposal was not made after William learned in England of his father's youthful indiscretions.

William shrugged off his lofty ambitions in the social hierarchy, wrote excellent poetry of a kind, and on his return to Australia plunged into things local. He supported the political claims of the emancipists, started a newspaper, the *Australian*, with a legal acquaintance Robert Wardell and after the appointment of Governor Darling, William lead the attack on Darling and his autocracy.

Darling called him that "vulgar ill-bred fellow". Darling was able to acquiesce in the flogging of convicts or "brutes" as he sometimes called them, and was famous for his "iron necklace": specially devised shackles which included an iron collar with spikes. He is also remembered for his attempted control of the press and his banning of a colonial theatre, yet he was able to put his nose in the air when it came to the young Wentworth's "breeding". Pure bred dogs are, I am the first to admit, wonderful creatures but crossbreeds and mongrels can be very appealing and, dare one say it, of equal or greater intelligence than the well-bred.

William Wentworth was a rabble-rouser and a democrat in his youth and a supporter of the emancipists (and no doubt Darling might say — "and why not?"), but sadly, as he gained more and more property mainly through his own efforts, and became an even larger landholder, he also became conservative or even reactionary.

It was from the elegance of his residence Vaucluse House that Wentworth put forward his plan for the "bunyip aristocracy". England, ultimately, controlled the common people through the House of Lords and, of course, through the nobility, the aristocracy and, thank heaven, that good, wise woman Queen Victoria. She was Queen of New South Wales (and would be Queen of Australia in due course), and why not simply adopt the (God bless it) reassuring wisdom of the English nobility, translated into Australia and Australians, of course.

Lord Wentworth! Duke of Vaucluse! The daydreaming William must also have had the occasional thought along those lines. But it was not to be. He was attacked by that damned Presbyterian John Dunmore Lang who alleged that he was an "equivocal" patriot, and also by Daniel Deniehy, that colourful, theatrical, artistic young currency boy (born of Irish emancipated parents) who made himself quite famous in his 1853 speech describing Wentworth as the foundation member of Australia's "bunyip aristocracy". The ebullient Deniehy was a lawyer, a member of parliament (1857–1860), a writer, an excellent speaker, a lover of conviviality (perhaps too great a lover) and was dead at the age of thirty-seven after falling from his horse at Bathurst.

William Wentworth had had enough. He felt that the Australian atmosphere was not quite to his standard and at the ripe and wise age of sixty-nine he took himself back to England. He died there ten years later.

Wentworth was an enigma. Yet in some ways you might say he always wanted to be one of the "exclusives", that group typified by the Macarthur family who believed themselves to be a cut above the rest of the community, and simply went through an opportunistic interregnum. Nonetheless, his achievements on behalf of New South Wales were considerable. Vance Palmer, that illustrious writer, points out that his contemporaries were of the opinion "that he was a great man". Palmer also heads his chapter "William Charles Wentworth — The Emancipist". Was Vance being serious or was this some of his sardonic humour? I doubt that the possible Duke of Vaucluse would have been amused. At least William's body came back to Australia, but you might reasonably ask where his spirit finally rests.

Vaucluse House is splendid, it is historic, its setting is superb and yet there is something cold and awkward about it. I am not a fan of the Macarthurs, but I do like the lovely house, Elizabeth Farm.

So, we've written briefly about a Scot who certainly became an Australian, and a man of English/Irish descent who was at best ambivalent in his Australianness, so let us now look at an Irish family who certainly became Australians — those "Kings in Grass Castles", the Duracks.

What a contrast it was for Patsy Durack between his country of birth and his country of death; Patsy Durack came out to Australia with his mother and father at the age of eighteen. He was "blue-eyed with a mass of dark, curly hair... [and] loved to dance and could play by ear any instrument from a tin whistle to the fiddle". The oldest boy in a family of seven children, he would have remembered very well the country of his birth and their little rented farm in the western hills of Ireland almost on the borders of County Galway and County Clare. The Durack families had lived in the area for generations and were very familiar with the river Bow and their little village of Capperbaun. The seaside town of Galway was some distance to the west, the north/south river Shannon flowed to the east, with Limerick near the mouth of the estuary, and Tipperary, too, was relatively close, by today's standards anyhow, so they lived in a rather romantic and colourful part of the old Ireland. But also a blighted part in the 1850s, for there was the Irish potato famine of the mid 1840s and the systematic and determined clearing out of the tenants by the largely foreign landowners. The land holding of Ireland had to be modernised and consolidated or "Ireland would be ruined". Little thought was given to the ruination of the country's indigenous people. And so to the relief of the foreign masters, the Irish peasantry in its millions began its exodus to America and Australia, and elsewhere. Two Durack brothers and their extended families were part of that exodus and came to Australia as assisted migrants, virtually penniless. They entered into an agreement to repay that part of their fare advanced by the New South Wales government.

It must have been a shock to land in this young and vast country and to travel by horse and dray from Sydney to Goulburn where both families settled — one in 1849 and the other some four years later. The family we are primarily concerned with is Michael Durack's family and of course their relations and friends, the Scanlons and Costellos and Dillons and Brogans…and the rest of them.

They all found positions and commenced to acquire property in and around the Goulburn district, so that by the time of Patsy's marriage to Mary Costello in the spring of 1862 they were a clan of some power and influence. Patsy, after the untimely accidental death of his father Michael, was clearly the head of the Durack family and to an extent the leader of the western Irish in that part of New South Wales. Most of the clan had been in Australia for less than ten years but it could be said, and later it was written by Mary Durack in *Kings in Grass Castles* that: "The land was moulding them…to a certain uniformity. Shading the raven hair to brown, the flaxen to honey gold, blending dark eyes and blue to tawny hazel, a smoky grey. Even their voices were losing the distinguishing traits of country, county and class, Australia imposing an intonation and emphasis of her own…"

These Irish people had come from a country steeped in tradition, rich in history, bowed down by a tyrannical foreign power and suddenly they were completely and utterly free in a land whose frontiers seemed infinite. Is it any wonder that their emerging prosperous grazing properties though large, now in the vastness of Australia, seemed cramped and small? Is it any mystery that they succumbed to the freedom and unlimited space of the beckoning outback? They left behind the comfort of Goulburn and the eastern flowing Wollondilly and Shoalhaven Rivers, they crossed the western flowing Murrumbidgee and the Lachlan, they left the Darling and the Warrego in their wake and they settled in the vast outback near the corners of the Northern Territory, South Australia and Queensland in the plains, the valleys and the mountains of Coopers Creek, the Diamantina and the Barcoo. You might have thought that the hungry Irishmen had found their new and final home at last, and yet not even this space, this freedom, this expanse was enough. They had to journey on.

After his Kimberley adventure, Patsy Durack went back to his old home in the west of Ireland where he found that it was much as he had left it some forty years before. He was disillusioned though. Of course, he was. Like so many who cherish romantic and sometimes erroneous memories of their homelands, he grieved to see "so much evidence of apathy and neglect. Surely a stable door could be fixed in two shakes of a cow's tail." Why, he complained, did his people find "solace and inspiration only in the past"?

Perhaps too he thought about the old Irish cry of the early and mid-eighties: "You cannot live in Ireland. To get up you must first get out."

CHAPTER THREE

There is a fascination about Australia because of its origins and its remoteness, even if the remoteness is largely a thing of the past. France may be different, is different, to other countries in Europe but it is and always has been very similar, basically, to its near neighbours. France has never known a truly nomadic population, not even the Celts, for all their steady westward migration and their wanderings… The people of France have clustered in settlements almost from their beginnings and this has developed a regard for material goods and comforts far beyond any need felt by the Australian Aborigines.

Apart from our monsoonal north and the eastern and southern coastal belts of Australia we have only moderate sized rivers. It is often a question of a flood or a trickle in this continent/island — there is the mighty Murray of course, but how does its flow compare with the huge and steady volumes of water in the Dordogne, the Rhone, the Loire and the other streams of a country with abundant water? The cry is, and always will be, that Australia is hot and dry, that its deserts dominate the inland and that our greatest drawback in lack of water. But Australia has its rivers, nonetheless, and a river that has imposed its character on all Australians is the romantic and enigmatic Darling.

And yes, Australia is different to France and Europe and its climate is unusual and its rivers are sporadic and its animals and its vegetation are unusual, and there is a race, an ancient race, which has adapted to all these differences and has made itself at home (indigenous) here.

At the end of the eighteenth century the Aborigines of Australia numbered three hundred thousand or thereabouts in total and were divided into nomadic tribes, each with their own customs and language. They had neither the background nor the need to consolidate into a group or groups larger than the traditional tribe: the tribe sufficed and had done so since time immemorial. So, when the first white men arrived and the Aborigines faced the invading British, they did so singly or in small groups. There was no pitched battle as was the case with Julius Caesar and Vercingetorix. There was no victory and no victor's sanctions such as the lesson of the severed right hand. No, things were different, as perhaps they should have been, after all Caesar's capers were some eighteen hundred years away.

What happened in Australia between the indigenous people and the newcomers was odd in a way. The Aboriginal men, one assumes, carried their spears and throwers, but showed curiosity and friendliness rather than aggression. Governor Arthur Phillip (1788–1792) was the first governor of the first Australian settlement by Europeans and, although there were incidents with the Aborigines, he goes down in history, write the editors of *The Oxford Companion to Australian Literature*, as a "humane, energetic and determined governor, (who) was sustained by a positive vision of the Colony's future". The pity is that he stayed such a relatively short time.

Governor Phillip by all accounts earned his good name, but the authorities in England were by no means entitled to call themselves "humane", nor were the captains of some of the convict ships. Look at this for an indictment of the English authorities towards the end of 1789 — it is from a letter written by Reverend Richard Johnson detailing the condition and casualties on three convict transport ships which arrived at Port Jackson (New South Wales) in June 1790.

"The *Neptune* — 520 convicts, 163 died on board and 269 landed sick, The *Scarborough* — 252 convicts, 68 died on board and 96 landed sick, The *Surprise* — 211 convicts but 42 died on board and 121 landed sick."

Or to put it another way, close to 30% of the convicts died on the voyage out. That's almost one in three. And today we make a fuss about a few sheep in the live export trade to the Middle East! The Reverend goes on to describe his visit to the newly arrived *Surprise*: "went down amongst the convicts when I beheld a sight truly shocking to the feelings of humanity. A great number of them lying, some half and the others quite naked without either bed or bedding, unable to turn or to help themselves…the smell was so offensive that I could scarcely bear it."

The Reverend proposed to inspect the cargo of the *Scarborough* but was dissuaded by the Captain. "The *Neptune* was still more wretched and intolerable, therefore never attempted it." As the ships came near the shore, bodies were still being tossed overboard and were washed up on the beach. The cleric pointed out this rather untidy behaviour to Governor Phillip who gave orders for the bodies to be collected and buried. These convicts were transported for major and exceedingly minor offences and were treated vilely, but then many were Irish or Scottish and most of the rest were from the lower classes. It makes the cutting off of a few thousand hands seem almost kindly.

And if the authorities could turn a blind eye to the transportation of the convicts, and to their frequent floggings, then you wonder that the Aborigines were not treated more harshly. Yes, the trusting, often helpful, friendly, puzzled Aborigines were, for the most part, simply used or swept from the path of the white man.

Mary Gilmore (1865–1962) sums it up in her poem "The Waradgery Tribe".

Harried we were, and spent,
  Broken and falling.
Ere as the cranes we went,
  Crying and calling.
Summer shall see the bird
  Backward returning;
Never shall there be heard
  Those, who went yearning.
Emptied of us the land,
  Ghostly our going,
Fallen, like spears the hand
  Dropped in the throwing.
We are the lost who went
  Like the cranes, crying;
Hunted, lonely, and spent,
  Broken and dying.

The poet and writer Mary Gilmore (nee Cameron) was proudly and almost aggressively Australian, but was also, and I think above all, a lover of humanity, who throughout her life, supported the disadvantaged, the poor and those puzzled people of this earth.

But, let us return to the first Governor of New South Wales, Arthur Phillip of the English Royal Navy and Arthur Phillip the reasonably successful farmer in England. Phillip needed the money, it is said, and came out of partial retirement to take on the momentous task of commanding eleven sailing ships on the journey from England to Australia — or more correctly Botany Bay in New Holland, just south of Sydney. Botany Bay had been discovered in 1780 by Captain Cook, and the botanist Joseph Banks had collected a large number of native plants there and had taken them back to England — hence the name. As it turned out Botany Bay was not a very good location for a settlement and Phillip soon moved the whole crew and soldiers and convicts up to Sydney Cove. The entourage consisted of seven hundred convicts, two hundred and fifty free settlers and soldiers and sailors.

It is hard to imagine the extent of Phillip's task. The overseas journey was itself heroic, let alone the arrival, the disembarkation, the accommodation, food, water, discipline, treatment of the Aborigines…You could say, "I take my hat off to the fellow", and speaking of hats it is worthwhile looking at the hat that Phillip wore (presumably) on his arrival in Australia. It is a ripper. Just have a look at the portrait of Phillip in the National Gallery London in the hat. (And yes, you can view it on the Internet too.)

The flotilla landed on 26 January 1788 and that day, rightly or wrongly is currently our national day — Australia Day.

John Hunter, also of the Royal Navy, succeeded Phillip

in 1795 and ruled the new colony and its convicts and free settlers and all, until he was recalled to England in 1800. Hunter made the mistake of opposing that formidable bloke John Macarthur. It is said that Macarthur, a former member of the New South Wales Corps, who retained a strong allegiance with the soldiers, helped to depose three governors and Hunter was the first of them.

Macarthur's initial move was to grab a large amount of land, his second was to become the spokesman for the Corps and his third (after the recall of Hunter) was to shoot Governor King's representative dead in a duel. Sent to England to answer for the death he avoided a trial and then set about organising the wool industry for Australia (and his family). He returned to Australia and "inspired" the Corp's Rum Rebellion against Governor Bligh; was sent to England where he continued, amongst other things, to promote the Australian wool industry, aided and abetted by his formidable wife Elizabeth, who ran things back in Australia. He returned to Australia eight years later and then managed to extend his land holding to sixty thousand acres. After all that activity, he got himself elected to the New South Wales Legislative Council and served there for two terms. Governor Bourke was the only governor to get the better of this "English" abrasive Australian.

But back to our early governors.

Captain (Royal Navy) Philip King was governor from 1800 to 1806 and was a man of considerable energy and courage. He took on the rum brigade, devoted money and time to public works and expanded agriculture. He allied himself with the "little" men, the convicts and the emancipists. King was the first of the governors to bring his wife out to the new country — a man of courage indeed. There were not too many sheilas in the sunburnt country at that time.

Governor (Captain of course) Bligh is the third last of the early governors to claim our attention and he is surely one of the most enigmatic and without doubt, daring, and perhaps inquisitive, of men. I must say that I had rather a poor opinion of Bligh until I saw his lonely bronze overlooking Circular Quay in Sydney. I was surprised that Sydney should have had him made and cast and so I persuaded myself to reread a précis of the man's life.

Bligh was a Cornishman born in 1754. He took to sailing at a very early age. He accompanied Captain Cook on one of his voyages and subsequently was given command of HMS *Bounty*. The crew mutinied off Tonga and Bligh and eighteen of his mates were kindly put in an open boat by the mutineers who shoved them off, wished them luck and sailed away — in the opposite direction. They had not shot them but it was tantamount to a death sentence. Bligh and his open boat however reached Timor some six or seven weeks later after a voyage of about four thousand miles.

Bligh, not in the least daunted, returned to the business of commanding ships, survived a subsequent minor mutiny and then managed to get (or was thrown) the job of governor of New South Wales in 1805. "Enough," you will think, "the man's had enough," but no, the slightly stooped Bligh was just hitting his straps and readily accepted the job just on the age of fifty. And what the man had packed into those fifty years!

Deputy Governor George Johnston was a major in the famous New South Wales Corps and was matey with our notorious John Macarthur. Bligh had taken on Macarthur who he maintained had violated some port regulations and had thrown him into prison. Macarthur's influence was such that he persuaded Johnston (from prison) to swap Bligh and himself. Johnston, in turn, persuaded the corps to do Macarthur's bidding and they duly entered Government House and arrested Bligh. Macarthur was released. Johnston then took over the administration of the new colony until the arrival of the genial Macquarie as the new governor. In the upshot Johnston was sacked, Bligh was vindicated and Macarthur went on his merry way and further developed his business of sheep grazing and the production and sale of his wool. Clever Macarthur. I did not see a bronze of Macarthur in Sydney though.

Lachlan Macquarie (more about him later) succeeded Bligh as Governor in 1809 and was followed by Major-General Thomas Brisbane (1821–1825). Brisbane's reputation is mixed: he encouraged agriculture (as distinct from grazing), he supported immigration and exploration but he had rather poor financial ability. His great forté apparently was astronomy and he, therefore, did a lot of stargazing. And that brings us back to the anachronistic Ralph Darling, the upright flogging, iron necklace man: "the King's authority has been upheld".

But enough of Governors — let us move on.

CHAPTER FOUR

In Australia today we have many prominent Aborigines: painters, musicians, singers, activists, medicos, lawyers, sportsmen and women. It is a long list. And as a white Australian I have the distinct feeling that, at last, the Aboriginal culture is being recognised and that people are beginning to value it. The non-Aboriginal section of Australia is being attracted to and becoming interested in, and, in some cases, immersed in things that belong to and can only be obtained from the indigenous people. There is less emphasis on trying to absorb the Aborigines into our society, and more on us absorbing their knowledge, culture and arts. It is a refreshing change.

There is a parallel, of course — well, a sort of parallel, and that is with the Italians and their position in Australian society since, say, the Second World War. Many will remember when the Italian migrant was blamed for every crime and in particular any incident concerning the use of a knife:

"That would have been one of those Ities. Yeah, typical of Dagoes." Yes, to my shame, that is an expression we used when speaking of the Italians in a derogatory way. And we blamed them for huddling together in the inner suburbs like Carlton in Melbourne. Naturally, we poured ridicule on their living and eating habits: "They live on the smell of an oily rag, yer know."

But look at the Italians today and look at things Italian. Olive oil is almost drunk by the Anglo-Saxons (and Scottish and Irish) and how "in", how fashionable it is, to have planted your country property with olive trees and to make your own oil. Everyone drinks coffee, as indeed they should, and we are all aspiring baristas. There is a pasta pot in most households and we speak knowingly of carbonara, bolognese, and marinara. There is carpaccio and parmigiana, and tiramisu and gelati, there is espresso and machiato and affogato, and… everything Italian. There are even Italian shoes!

Now, I know that the Italians are historically part of "the West", and that it is a far cry from the Aborigines and their isolation in this southern part of the earth, and I do not want to press the similarities too hard, but there are some. And in particular, I come back to the point that we have not so much converted the Italians to our way of life, rather, they have converted us. They are part of Australia but on their terms, as it were. They have enriched us. In a different way, the Aborigines and their culture and their skills, are enriching and will continue to enrich the "westerners" of Australia. This enrichment began years ago and its pace is quickening.

I was in Sydney recently and I saw and heard an Aboriginal busker playing a didgeridoo. He was painted, he was artificial perhaps, he was commercial, he was just a circus performer playing for whatever he could wheedle out of the passers-

OF RIVERS, BAGUETTES & BILLABONGS

by and the tourists, but…he was good. There was an aura, a mystery, a beauty, an artistry about him, his instrument and his music. I loved it, and was obliged to make a contribution, for he had not cadged it — it had been earned.

Not in the same category, not at all, but years ago many people, including me, saw for the first time a wonderful Aboriginal girl, Yvonne Goolagong was her name. What a sportswoman, but more important, what a person! She was possessed of all the qualities I admire in a sporting champion; skill, determination, courage, manners, moderation, tenacity, humility, intelligence, balance…it was all there. Oh, she was a delight to watch and although she was a champion (French Open, Wimbledon, Federation Cup, et cetera) she took it all in her stride. It is alleged by some that when occasionally her concentration lapsed, she went "walkabout", and again there is a valid comparison with the Italians who sometimes give the impression that excellence at sports is all very well but it might be preferable to be sitting down at a table spread with a dish of antipasto, some ciabatta and a few gleaming wine glasses to go with the bottle of wine there on the table — the Italiano's "walkabout".

It seems to me that there is a crop of Aboriginal culture, which is just coming to maturity, and inevitably there is a pride that goes with it. I do not believe that the Aboriginal person has changed or indeed should change to fit in with or to impress society, but rather that he should have the confidence to show his talent. It will be of great benefit to Australia if the trend that I and others have perceived continues and develops.

★ ★ ★ ★

What, one wonders were the thoughts of the Aborigines when Phillip and his ships and all those people landed at Botany Bay and then Port Jackson?

As we have already noted, the Aborigines were never in a position to give battle, as was the case with the Celts and the invasion of Gaul by the Romans, for example. It would not have been possible to unite the Aboriginal tribes under a leader as the Gauls united under Vercingetorix. In addition you have the impression that the Aborigines were neither belligerent or warlike. They were prepared to talk, to enquire and observe. These new creatures were interesting with their clothes and uniforms, their guns and their horses. For indeed, when first seen, a man on horseback must have seemed a remarkable four-legged composite creature — a veritable centaur more real than the Greeks ever imagined. No doubt the realisation that these coloured creatures had come to rob them of their land and their food came slowly. It took a while for the imported animals to take over the land of the native creatures, but if you helped yourself to one of the invader's beasts, those beasts which had displaced your game, what a fuss they made.

If the figure of some three hundred thousand Aborigines on the mainland of Australia is correct, then you are obliged to wonder why the Aborigines had populated the *whole* of Australia including much of the inland deserts. I know that to an extent they followed the rivers including the Darling, but why, with that rather meagre population, weren't there more living around and near the coast and on the slopes of the Great Dividing Range and elsewhere around reasonably fertile hills, mountains or plains? Why occupy the relatively barren interior?

Then, of course, we come to question the attitude of the

invaders towards the indigenous people. How much easier for them, in a way, it would have been if there had been a traditional war. A few skirmishes, a few more shiploads of soldiers and cannon and the like, and a pitched battle — a slaughter and retribution and the imposition of the victor's will. It did not happen. In fact you virtually had to provoke the Aborigine. He was prepared to share and to negotiate. He was curious about these apparitions, and he was to a degree friendly.

I suppose the British acted on the reports of Captain Cook (or his subordinates, as it turned out) to the effect that the natives had confronted the explorers in small groups and that they were poorly armed and on the whole friendly. There was no need for a Rome versus Gaul battle. The instructions to the early, and indeed I think to all governors, was to treat the local populations well. You could, oddly enough, incarcerate your fellow beings (and the dastardly Irish and the Scots) in ghastly conditions, you could starve them and flog them (to death if need be) but you were to treat the locals better.

To be fair, the governors endeavoured to carry out their humane orders but whether they realised it immediately or much later, they were forced to acknowledge that the settlers, once they had found their feet, came to enrich themselves and to seize large tracts of land. Once they possessed that land they stocked it with sheep or cattle and with horses, and the local people had better get out of the way, and had better not spear any beasts, or they would be taught a lesson. That attitude had prevailed all over the earth: in South America, America, South Africa, anywhere there was a relatively sparse local population which was not well organised.

You might say that having regard to the times, to the

dominance of the "white" and western nations, the then-attitude to slavery (which of course still prevailed in the USA), the treatment of fellow countrymen and neighbouring countries, and the overall attitude of conquering nations to the conquered, that the indigenous people of Australia were not badly treated. But, oh, to be able to look back and to say that we had treated them fairly. To have our consciences clear. Australia would be an even better place today if it were possible to say that. We have apologised, at last, and so far as I am aware that apology has been generously accepted, but how pleasant if we had had less to apologise about.

★ ★ ★ ★

It took the early settlers quite a while to get to the Darling River. Indeed the Darling was only discovered, officially in any event, by the explorer Sturt in 1829, some forty years after Phillip and his ships had landed on the east coast. Sturt had been commissioned by Governor Darling and having succeeded in his commission had been good enough to name the outback river after his patron. The crossing of the Blue Mountains which had locked the invaders into the coastal belt did not occur until 1813 (Blaxland, Lawson and Wentworth) and the fertile slopes and plains to the west of the Great Dividing Range held back the avid pastoralists for a few years but it was not long before they were squatting and pegging out claims along and in the vicinity of the Darling and its tributaries.

And then the cry was westward, westward, forever westwards in New South Wales and in Queensland. The rationale was simple: be the first out there and grab what you could and in large areas. If the season had been good then you simply continued and you gave little thought to the bad seasons: the seasons of no rain at all.

And the outback Aborigines? They could make themselves useful or, once again, they could get out of the way.

It is as well to keep in mind that we are dealing with the nineteenth century, the era of Queen Victoria and Prince Albert, of Rule Britannia and the ever-increasing wealth of the Empire. We were content to buy and sell slaves until 1834 (1864 in USA) and it took until 1850 to stop the transportation of convicts to Australia. So the treatment of the indigenous population whilst it was anything but praiseworthy was about all that might be expected.

So, there is some background. The canvas is no longer bare, but has a primer and some broad brushstrokes. Let us see if we can fill in the details.

CHAPTER FIVE

We approached the Auvergne and the headwaters of the Dordogne by way of Paris and Clermont Ferrand and so it seemed logical that we, as Melburnians should approach the country to the east of the Darling and the headwaters of that stream by way of Lakes Entrance, Narooma, Ulladulla (Mollymook), Moss Vale, Port Stephens, Port Macquarie, Yamba, Stanthorpe and Killarney (allegedly the source of the Darling — the Condamine). And so we set out.

As you get down to Lakes Entrance you encounter patches of native bush: wonderful gums with a judicious mixture of ferns, bracken, acacias and various rushes. How comforting, how absolutely wonderful to be drifting along surrounded by the tall eucalypts. I have decided that one of the beauties of our gums is the way they display their limbs: their structure and their superstructure. In this respect they can perhaps be likened to the Australian girls on our wide sandy beaches. Those wonderful golden beaches of summer with their flattering and moving background of blue and rolling foam. The European trees, on the other hand, although they are quite superb, they have to wait until the winter season until they can show you their design — and their limbs — they have first to be quite naked. Not so with our Australian beauties who are somewhat scantily, but adequately, clothed through all our seasons.

We drifted into Lakes Entrance just in time to throw our bags in the unit and dash across the road to a little café which was there on the water — actually on the water and built on large pontoons. Good coffee.

As I walked back along the Lakes Entrance waterfront, seeking an elusive chemist, I decided, after all these years that there are four very important day to day things. Important? No, I have understated the position: four things that are essential to leading a reasonable life. They are — wine, bread, olive oil and coffee. I could easily add a fifth and if I did it would be croissants. In fact, if I were to become the prime minister of Australia, or, having regard to our constitution, premier of all the States, I would legislate and make it an offence for any café or restaurant which opened for breakfast not to have croissants on their menu. I would go further and I would stipulate in the statute, the law, that some of the croissants should be displayed in a basket in a prominent place in the breakfast room. Australia has so readily accepted the habits and cultures of so many races and countries, so, let us embrace this little necessity from the French (who might have pinched it from the Turks).

Lakes Entrance has a rambling shopping centre, or so it seemed to me, and the next morning I tried, without success, to purchase a bottle of walnut oil. Olive oil is, after all, quite wonderful and it would have to do. Bread was another matter. The town is big enough for two bakeries but no, supermarket bread is all that you can buy. I know that some of those breads are good but how one longs for a baguette, a bread stick, which has been baked that morning and which will stay crisp until lunchtime. Fruit, tomatoes... we drove on.

Just before we got to Orbost I saw a swagman, a man with "a traveller's bundle". The swagman was riding his bike very carefully along the side of the road and I marvelled that he could keep his bundles and bags from getting caught in the spokes, not that the wheels of the bike were rotating that fast. Right on top of the clobber on his back was a billy, a rather blackened billy which swung back and forth. We passed him but I watched him for a while in the mirror. Seeing him took me back a few years.

Whenever we went potato digging on the Little Hill or the Far Hill my father took morning and afternoon tea and of course lunch, and, most importantly the billy, the seasoned and blackened billy. Before you arrived at either hill there were convenient springs, both of which flowed into ponds and then away through the bush or a gully. One spring had a slightly gassy smell and its water had a faint suggestion of sulphur, but the other was absolutely cold, pure and pristine. My brother or I would fill the billy at one of these springs and we would journey on.

Dotted throughout our few acres of potatoes were old tree stumps, in need of being cleared from the path of the stump-jump plough, but grey and stiff and dry and absolutely perfect for a long and slow fire. If we had been there the previous day a fire might still be burning and smouldering along the roots, but if not, it was an easy task to gather some twigs and branches from the nearby bush and light one. The wonderful old billy was placed against the fire and its position adjusted once or twice during the morning so that it would be on the boil for morning tea. No lid. We never used a lid. When the billy boiled you threw in the right amount of tea leaves and you left the billy there for about half a minute while it continued to boil. Then you took a convenient stick and lifted the billy of tea clear of the fire. You struck the side of the billy sharply with your stick and the few floaters sank. The slightly smoked tea was now ready for pouring into the three mugs. And then, after morning tea you put the potatoes in to the ashes to cook for lunch, potatoes that later emerged with a blistered skin, a thin layer of fragrant brown crust and then, as the steaming smoking white flesh was begging for a generous dob of butter and pepper and salt, you simply obliged it.

We had decided not to detour into Orbost on our left, and so we ignored those directions and the signs and concentrated on the way ahead. The bridge over the Snowy River and the Snowy River flats surprised me. Surely these flats are the most extensive of any in Australia. This was the embryonic river I had sat beside near Kosciusko, the river which was no more than a stream but a stream which was artistically landscaped with rocks and trees and shrubs and a swarm of midges hovering over a pool as the afternoon faded to dusk.

★ ★ ★ ★

The road we were travelling along was, of course, the Princes Highway and I thought how aptly it was named. Any prince would count himself lucky to be going through the South East Forest in the vicinity of Mt. Imlay National Park. The bush here is glorious and the road threads its way through it in a graceful and easy manner — relaxing driving. I had admired white gums and blue gums, peppermints and mess-mates, red gums and scribbly gums, mountain ash and iron-bark, but this was the first time I had encountered apple-topped gum and Maiden's blue gum and I have to admit that I was captivated. Every now and again you would see a squat and venerable Maiden's blue gum flanked by a coast grey box with huge rocks set harmoniously in the background. It is the contrast of the colours that camouflage the trunk and the way the light brown bark blends in that fascinates you. This is a very stimulating introduction to the south and east of New South Wales.

As you continue up the "coastal" road some kilometres in from the sea, it does in fact become coastal as you come in to Eden. There is something about Eden and its deep blue waters which are never still, something more than the diction-ary definition. It has an atmosphere. But did it have coffee? Yes, it did, right down near the jetty. When I asked the lady to fill my café latte glass only two-thirds full, she did it! Lovely coffee and a lovely setting.

When you visit at the weekend you are hardly aware that Eden is an important centre for the export of woodchips. In fact some 90,000 tonnes are exported each year, making good use of the wharf which is about two hundred metres long. Eden acts as the general or service port for the coastal towns of Bega, Merimbula, Bombala and Cooma and you will of-ten hear it mentioned as a haven or rescue centre for yachts which might strike trouble in the Sydney to Hobart. Once a whaling centre, Eden is still an important fishing town and a good spot for watching whales at play, now they are no lon-ger hunted by Australian fleets. The Killer Whale Museum is worth a visit and enjoys one of town's best look-outs

Apparently Eden is named after Baron Auckland, secretary to the (ahem!) Colonies and its name was approved in 1843. Eden may be old but Boydtown (Benjamin Boyd) preceded it as an inspection will prove. Some day, some day soon we will have the time, the capacity and the energy to walk through the forest and the coastal area in and around the Ben Boyd National Park. It should be on everyone's list.

We were sorry to leave Eden, the notorious port "exactly half way between Melbourne and Sydney", but we drove on to Bega.

Bega has a number of things. First it has an agreement dated the 13 June 2001 between the Shire and the Aboriginal people of the Bega Valley, and this agreement and recognition of the Aborigines is broad. It is "not confined to archaeological sites". And it includes on occasions the flying of "the Aboriginal flag at the Council's main office". Quite a remarkable agreement and well worth a study.

Bega and Tilba are also the centre of a thriving cheese industry. The district is famous here in Australia and the industry is also a big exporter. So far as I am aware the cheeses are made principally from cows' milk but no doubt there are goats' cheeses and sheep's cheeses too — I cannot see how it could be otherwise.

But what really fascinated me as we drove was the countryside. As you continue north (ever northwards) you are on a sort of plateau with the South Coast Forest and then the Wadbilliga National Park on your left and the Biamanga Park on your right. The plateau is, nonetheless, a series of gullies and streams and I imagine has a reasonable rainfall. This is dairying and fat cattle country. The settlers who cleared the land had the good sense to leave a generous sprinkling of local gum trees — large trees — and how noble they are and how they break up what would otherwise be nothing but hills and valleys of lush green grass. But…but wisely in my view, they also planted myriads of deciduous trees, especially around their homesteads but also in the valleys, where the predominant tree is the Lombardy poplar. Well, all of these trees were in the full glow of their autumn colours: golds, crimsons, red browns, purple, and how they contrasted with but complemented the grandeur of the gums. This is a very picturesque part of the South Coast and indeed of Australia.

We could have turned sharp right and gone up the real coast to Bermagui but we were aiming for Narooma and it was getting late. The sun was hovering just above the distant peaks of the Great Dividing Range and dusk was threatening from the Tasman Sea, or perhaps the South Pacific Ocean. There was smoke ahead and coming around a bend we saw a fairly vigorous fire in the bush there on our right. Two forestry trucks were parked by the side of the road and the men were simply watching the flames as they were pushed by the wind towards the coast. We drove on through Tilba Tilba made famous by Zara Holt (and cheese) and through her a reminder of Harold Holt, our Prime Minister who for some unknown, but to him no doubt adequate reason, apparently swam out to sea. On and on he swam, never to be sighted again. A year or so after his disappearance I picked up a sand-shoe on the beach at Portsea and I was convinced that it was one of his. Sadly, I threw it away after trying unsuccessfully to find some evidence for my conviction.

Narooma has a good restaurant and the couple at the table next to us that night ordered oysters kilpatrick — not an inappropriate choice I suppose when you are in an oyster producing area and can get the beasties sea and rock fresh.

I can recall when I chose that dish: it was before I learned to appreciate the subtlety of both the texture and the taste of those molluscs. Our neighbours had finished their bottle by the time the oysters arrived, and I assure you it was not because service was slow. Another bottle was ordered and arrived at the same time as the oysters. We could smell the deliciousness of that grilled bacon, with its hint of smoke, and I could picture the oysters nestling there in their glossy shells surrounded by the pungent liquid. The lady diner, though, did not seem happy even before the plate was put in front of her. He on the other hand was ravenous apparently, and plunged straight into the feast. As a result it took him some time to realise that she was poking and picking at her dish.

"They're not good," she said.

"But mine…" He had to stop eating and yet he seemed reluctant to do so. "What's wrong with them?"

"Chilli. They've got chilli in them, and… and the Worcester sauce is not Lea & Perrins." She put her fork down with a resounding clank.

"But mine…"

"You just said that. I know what oyster Kilpatrick should taste like." She pushed her plate away and looked sourly around the room. Madame saw the face and came to the table.

"Everything all right?" she said in a positive way. "Happy with your oysters?"

Well, the floodgates had been opened and we were assailed with a litany of complaints and we heard again and again about the alleged chilli and that the Worcester was certainly not Lea and Perrins. What is it about that famous sauce. Is there another?

Madame offered to change the dish, but no, it was too

late for that, the mood had passed, she just wanted them re-moved. He surreptitiously began to eat his.

"I don't know how you can. What *is* wrong with you!"

He was cowed but he put his fork down slowly and I thought reluctantly. There was still the wine. Thank God for the wine.

The main course was picked at but again and again we heard the assertion that the sauce on the oysters was certainly not Lea and Perrins. Did she have shares in the company?

★ ★ ★ ★

Narooma is on the Wagonga estuary and is famous for its oysters (but no mention is made of bacon) and its golf course, which they tell us is suspended above "a raging sea".

Next morning I decided to see the view from our hotel at close range and I set out for the "raging sea" and the man-made exit to that sea for the fishing boats and the pleasure boats. There is a cliff above the point that leads down to the rock exit channel and with my scarves and jacket secured against the wind and the light showers I made for it. To my surprise someone was already there peering over at what turned out to be a wind-swept native garden clinging to the cliff and the rocks. The garden was quite remarkable, better in so many ways than the most brilliant man-designed effort. I recognised the bloke standing there as a fellow diner from last night, not from the next table I hasten to add, and he and I walked back towards the motel together.

He was, of all people, a grazier from the area that we had driven through yesterday, a man who now runs beef cattle and whose grandfather had built the homestead and had planted deciduous trees around it. We talked, naturally, we talked until we arrived at his holiday unit on the side of the hill. He asked me about our terrible bushfires this summer and we stood there for ten minutes whilst the hunger pangs gnawed away at me — there would be croissants for breakfast surely. He had an unusual suggestion concerning bushfires, but had nothing to say about croissants.

He pointed out that we had, to an extent, Europeanised Australia and he maintained we had therefore, to recognize that and to carry Europeanisation to a logical conclusion. If we had modified the countryside and in the process had made it more fire prone then we should go the whole way and endeavour to protect our native vegetation by planting swathes of non-volatile trees through the bush and in particular around all plantations of blue-gums, pine trees etc. "You shouldn't get permission," he said, "to establish plantations unless you first took those precautions." Burning off? No, he answered, in the first place it was "damnably polluting" and in the second place "it eventually changed the bush". He said more and might have said even more, except that our motel was only a short distance away up the steep hill and I could definitely detect the aroma of good coffee. We parted and I reflected on his words of…wisdom, perhaps, until I was in the dining room foyer. My wife was already down to breakfast and was seated at the corner table, undoubtedly the best table in the room, but the one that *the* couple had occupied last night. What if?…And in they walked. The assertive sheila cast a glance in our direction but said nothing. I hoped her breakfast sauces were genuine and from famous manufacturers.

I suppose the coastlines of any country are picturesque but the east coast (and the only coast) of New South Wales is outstanding for its variability and its often rugged beauty. If you had to choose between a house on the coast or a house in the bush (with a view of distant mountains) I wonder which you would choose. It occurred to me on the way up here that the Aborigines probably had not lived in the bush in and around the forest reserves and in the Great Dividing Range. Why would they do so? They may have hunted in the bush but they would have lived by the rivers and on the sea. Three hundred thousand Aborigines? I wonder who made that estimate.

Bateman's Bay has a new and a prosperous appearance. If you owned a house or a unit on the hill overlooking Beach Road and the Bay you would count yourself as lucky, and well-off. The town is situated on the Clyde River and is part of the Far South Coast area. One of the most wonderful sights around the inlets and hills are the stands of spotted gums. We have some planted on our vineyard in Melbourne and although I like them, they are open to the criticism that they have grown into huge and somewhat coarse trees. When you see the forests of them in this area all you can think of is grace and elegance. I liken them to vertical herds of immobile leopards. When we return I will look at our gums in a fresh light. Bateman's Bay is said to be the seaside playground of the Canberrans, and after all if you sped along the King's Highway the relatively short distance from the capital and found this coast, why would you go on to the north or the south?

Well, as we discovered, you might easily turn north from Bateman's Bay, because if you did so you would come to Ulladulla and Mollymook, and they are worth looking at, and indeed staying at. Mollymook is a suburb of Ulladulla and is located on a hilly spit. The surfers congregate on the front beach and the "lookers" on the back beach. There is a spot there where you can stay and it has an "infinity" pool (!), a wonderful view of coastal trees and rocks and blue and boiling sea, and more than all of those, your room is filled with the sound of the waves. Very relaxing. And there is good tucker, a good wine list and excellent espresso at the end of the evening.

Sydney lay ahead and we had not decided what to do about Sydney. Why not prevaricate? Why not put off the decision? And so we did.

If you drive up the Princes to just south of Shellharbour you can take a small road to Bowral and Moss Vale and so on. We did that by way of Nowra (wildlife Park and Fleet Air Arm Museum) and Kiama (blowhole and Saddleback Mountain lookout).

I had half an hour to stroll on the beach at Kiama and during that half-hour I examined and re-examined the curious and fanciful notions that I have always entertained for the Australian writer Charmian Clift, born here in 1923. She, as a journalist, met and married a fellow journalist and writer George Johnston in 1947 and they moved to the Greek island of Hydra in 1954 and brought up their three children there.

Somehow her writing has a haunted character and yet on re-reading her *Peel me a Lotus* it is hard to quote any passage which would demonstrate my point. Why do I find a sadness about her? She and George had found their back to basics island retreat and this enabled them to live their simple, untroubled lives. And yet in July 1969, Charmian committed suicide, weeks before the publication of Johnston's Miles Franklin award-winning novel *"Clean Straw For Nothing."*

I thought I'd drive to her house near the hill as you come in to Kiama from the north, and so I journeyed to the excellent municipal library to discuss this local lass and to have them identify the actual house. They looked rather puzzled when I talked about her, but eventually solved the problem by looking her up on the internet!

Charmian, I would have liked to have met you but I thank you for your company this afternoon with the South Pacific Sea breaking over the sand and whispering its secrets to me.

Then we turned towards the Southern Highlands and Bowral

★ ★ ★ ★

Now you can criticise Bowral and Moss Vale on the basis that they are just too Olde Worlde, but I did not find them so. And the trees! The trees blazed in their autumn finery. They were grouped in and around traditional nineteenth century cottages, houses and mansions and they lined the streets and thickly populated the parks. Perhaps we saw this area at its best but it charmed us. We did not go to the Bradman Museum — it is not mandatory. Nearby Berrima is quite outstanding. It was founded in 1829 on the banks of the Wingecarribee River and its court house, gaol and stone houses are something to drool about. We are going back to Berrima.

There is a little tragicomedy that is worth relating. It happened at the lovely village of Berrima around 1834, almost two hundred years ago, and it involved one Lucretia, her paramour and of course Lucretias's husband.

Lucretia's parents looked at their delightful baby daughter and were immediately inspired to name her after the famous beauty of ancient Rome. It is true that that Lucretia, the original girl died by her own hand, but she lived such a virtuous life. Lucretia, princess Lucretia lived in the Rome of the sixth century BC, and beautiful and graceful creature that she was, was married to Lucius. One Sextus Tarqunous, an Etruscan and therefore a savage, fancied Lucretia and made overtures to her. She waved them, and him away, but Sextus, who also happened to be the son of the self-styled King of Rome, was only inflamed by her modesty and he took her by force. Lucretia was determined that she should not be raped again and so she drove a dagger into her heart.

It was rather after the event, but her sorrowing husband and her father got together an army and drove the Tarquins out of Rome. Thus was the Roman Republic founded.

Our Lucretia, she grew up and became a married woman, Mrs Dunkley. She was greatly admired by a lusty young local named Henry, and she acceded to his approaches voluntarily. The thing developed, as these things do but there was the encumbrance — the husband. The lovers removed the encumbrance by chopping off its head. They were convicted of murder and sentenced to death by hanging. Lucretia Dunkley is unique at Berrima in being the first and the last woman to be hanged at the local gaol. Somehow the Surgeon General got involved in the affair and he ordered that the bodies be buried "standing up", so that "they would never rest in peace." I was unable to find out if the sinners were buried in the one grave, and if they were, whether they faced one another…or what.

The Surgeon General was not finished with Lucretia and Henry though; as an afterthought he had their heads lopped and sent to Sydney for "scientific research". One cannot help wondering if this was the only area of research that should have been explored.

Kangaroo Valley is not widely known but it is quite outstanding in its mixture of European trees, native trees and shrubs and picturesque farms and properties, and of course its superb old bridge. We had a very relaxing picnic lunch on the top of the escarpment, but rather sadly, the bread we ate was not from the lovely ovens that apparently still exist at the back of the Old Bakery Tearooms.

Our destination was Sutton Forest and the former home of a one of the Katers, who built the house in 1926. Kater had some distant claims to royalty and, therefore, made one of the rooms in this large house "baronial", i.e. exaggeratedly high ceiling, a huge and ornate fireplace, stairs along one wall flying up to distant bedrooms, and of course stained glass windows depicting coats of arms. He called the home "The Manor House", and today it still carries that name and is, without doubt, a most comfortable, gracious and elegant country hotel. It is situated in an area that is made for walkers and even the early morning rain could not deter us. Lovely old trees, including giant plane trees and a new fence and gates at a nearby property which are not excelled by those of many a chateau in our beloved France. Sutton Forest was a favourite destination of the early governors of New South Wales and in many ways it was responsible for the "gentrification" of Bowral.

And before we move from Bowral in the Southern Highlands and make a dart for Nelson Bay and Port Stephens to the north of Newcastle, I must comment on the rather curious statement and inference in a website on Bowral: "The Roman Catholic church was banned in the earliest days of the Sydney colony and although Catholic Churches had previously been established in Berrima and Sutton Forest, the first church in Bowral was built in 1891. ...It was customary to build Catholic churches on the highest location within a town, yet this is the lowest in the subdivision. The existence of a number of Masonic and other lodges since the earliest days…attest partly to the fact that Bowral was a 'Protestant' town."

Well, there are a few loosely connected observations. If they were intended to persuade us that the Catholics of Bowral were discriminated against, I can find no evidence for such a proposition. As for Bowral being a protestant town, the Protestants in Australia have always outnumbered the Catholics, but many of them have tended towards agnosticism and secularism rather than active proselytism. English, yes, I would agree that Bowral exhibits "Englishness", but it is none the worse for that.

Incidentally, whilst doing research into the position of the Catholics in Bowral I was told about the old ban that apparently applied to Catholics in Ireland: a prohibition on the ringing of church bells, and for a time from building new churches. It was said that the bell ban was talked about as a law that also applied to Catholics in Australia. It seems that Australians, both Protestant and Catholic very quickly debunked that notion.

★ ★ ★ ★

And dart past Sydney and Newcastle we did, but with lunch, nonetheless on the water overlooking Kur-Ring-Gai Chase on the way. This picnic spot is one of the best you will find anywhere and despite being located just off the busy freeway there was hardly anyone using it. The Hawkesbury and a couple of creeks wander into the bay here and mix their water with those of the Tasman Sea.

Port Stephens and Nelson Bay to the north are well off the freeway, and of course are located on the sea, but the journey to the coast is more than worthwhile. Housing is spreading over the peninsula faster than the swine flu is spreading around Australia, but there is still the water and the coast and islands and reserves and although it is intensely developed it also has pockets of charm — in other words, a few good cafes with "barista" coffee, some civilised restaurants and some beach and sand and salt water. We pretended that we were exhausted from the trip up from Melbourne and stayed at the port on the water's edge for two days. This enabled us to go to both of the lookouts and to Shoal Bay and to see the surf coming in "side on" near the life saving clubhouse. Whenever you watch the surf, even in a bay, you will see the waves conform to the shape of the land so that they fit in with the contour of the coast. But here, they go racing past you like great lines of naked grass hay. You actually do see them from the side. I had never seen this phenomenon before.

And finally, before you leave the beach at Port Stephens let me recommend you to a great walk in the bush on the hill at the back of the boat club. If you go right through the reserve to the far corner you will come upon another residential development complete with one of the most Italianate, Tuscan-like villas you are likely to encounter outside Italia itself. It even has an aged and weary, almost decrepit air about it. Worth the walk.

Some of the bush on the way up this coast has been nothing short of wonderful: spotted gums, blackbutt, ironbark, yellow stringy-bark, tallow-wood, monkey gum, grey gum, stringy-bark, Sydney blue gum…And now on both sides of the road you come across dense young bushes and trees, gums and acacias and banksias and so on, and they are all massed together, and their leaves of green and blue and grey and bronze twist and twinkle as you rush towards them and then away again. They will have to be hedged in some fashion soon, but how lovely they are in their young and natural state.

Port Macquarie is a leisurely drive from Nelson Bay and is some ten or so kilometres from the Pacific Highway and the first thing you notice when you get to the beach is the proliferation of the imported Norfolk Pine. This tree is exotic, of course, and carries with it a reminder of the convict days. It is very geometrical, very formal, and I must say that I am surprised at its popularity on the New South Wales coast. I find it hard to like.

The history of the town is interesting. John Oxley managed to reach the Pacific Ocean in 1818 after his exploration of central and western New South Wales, and he designated it as a future port and noted the Hastings River, emanating from the Werrikimbe National Park, the fine spring, and the abundance of native game.

He named it Port Macquarie, after one of Australia's most competent and democratic governors.

Lachlan Macquarie — honestly, what a man. If Australia has a reputation for egalitarianism, if we can lay some claim to being a society that thumbs its nose at snobbery and class distinctions and the nonsense of "nobility", then that reputation is based in part, at least on his actions, his deeds, and his writings.

Macquarie succeeded Bligh as Governor in 1809 and the British Government broke with tradition in appointing him, an army officer, rather than the usual naval bloke. But Macquarie had much to recommend him apart from his army career: the fact that he was a wiry tough Scot from an island off the coast of Scotland, the son of a mother who was the daughter of a Maclaine chieftain, his extensive experience as a soldier in the American War of Independence, his service in Egypt and India, his re-doubtable second wife, his cousin Elizabeth Campbell (a Campbell!)… Yes, indeed he had a pedigree and a good background.

Lachlan's education seems to have been no more than rudimentary as one might expect for a boy born on a poor, cold, windy and sparsely settled island to the north-west of Glasgow, but look what he did with his career and his life. Appointed Governor of Australia (New South Wales at the time) in 1809, Colonel in 1810, Brigadier in 1811, Major-General in 1813; planner (through the surveyor James Meehan) of the lay-out of Hobart; instigator of some of Sydney's most historic buildings in Macquarie Street and elsewhere, built under the guidance of the renowned colonial architect and emancipist Francis Greenway; founder of the splendid city of Bathurst following on the famous exploration and later development of the Blue Mountains pass by Blaxland, Wentworth and Lawson and Evans and Cox; the democratising of Australia by the insistence that emancipists should be treated as social equals (they even balanced cups of tea on their knees at Government House) and generally he guided the development of the former penal colony on the basis that it was a new country with a promising future.

Macquarie has been called "an enlightened despot…the last British proconsul to run New South Wales as a military autocracy". And the thing that you wonder most about is how he came to acquire those "enlightening" ideas, a man who spent the whole of his life in the British army…in England, America, India, Egypt and elsewhere. And yet the man was so humane — such a democrat.

The free settlers and the upper classes were not ready for Macquarie's democracy and managed to persuade England to send out an investigator, Judge Bigge. His Honour was on the side of the establishment and was critical of Macquarie. The Governor tendered his resignation and returned to his home island but also found time to defend the actions that he had taken whilst in Australia.

In an extract from his "defence" presented to the Colonial Secretary Earl Bathurst in London in 1822, he wrote:

"Finding on my arrival many persons free, who had come out originally as convicts, and sustaining unblemished characters since their emancipation, but treated with rudeness, contumely, and even oppression, as far as circumstances permitted, by those who had come out free, and viewed with illiberal jealousy the honest endeavours of the others to attain and support a respectable station in society, I determined to counteract this envious disposition in one class, by admitting, in my demeanour and occasional marks of favour to both, no distinction where their merits, pretensions and capacities were equal."

The salty winds of the Hebrides blow over his island grave with its lengthy and touching inscription part of which I will quote —

"...the wisdom, liberality and benevolence of all the measures of his administration...the unwearied assiduity with which he sought to promote the welfare of all classes of the community...rendered him truly deserving of the appellation by which he has been distinguished "The Father of Australia"; and, I am told, his grave is maintained by the National Trust of Australia.

But back to Port Macquarie. Governor Darling of iron necklace fame was most impressed by its remoteness and made it a special convict camp. He sent there troublemakers, the so called "specials" or "literate" convicts — those who were critical of him. He also had some bright ideas about convicts with various disabilities. He wittily designated one-armed convicts as stone breakers, those with a wooden leg became delivery men and the blind were given night duties. Ah, that man.

Port Macquarie has the Town Beach and Oxley's Beach but it also has — bless it — excellent coffee. Yes, here in a town of less that fifty thousand people there is a thriving café (Italian of course) which serves out-standing coffee, and very good tucker. Oh, to be sure, it is worth a long linger this town. There are also some good buildings and a classic thir-ties (or forties) picture theatre, and an excellent bronze bust of Edward Barton our first Prime Minister.

As we walked towards this wonderful coffee establish-ment we saw a bloke in an electric wheelchair. He was mo-toring along at a sedate pace and his dog ran along comfort-ably beside him, on a lead. He stopped his machine near the café and dropped the lead. The dog edged up to the chair itself, and sat down. It seemed to smile at him. He patted the dog. It waited. Painfully he got out and somehow managed to grab his crutches from the back of the chair and put them under his arms. He turned slowly and with great determina-tion made his way gingerly towards the café. The dog moved beside him glancing up from time to time and watching his face, its tail swinging to and fro. Without doubt it was smil-ing. I reflected, as we walked to the café, that here surely was proof that there is a God, a Creator. I cannot believe that dogs happened by chance. That they have evolved Darwinian style — yes. But that they just happened by chance — no.

In this godly café you can get café latte in the following sized glasses: "Piccolo Latte" – ¼ volume, "Puné" – ¾ volume, "standard" size, "Mugaccino" – 2 shots BIG, "Massimo" – 4 shots HUGE. Now they ought not to serve the noble drink in the giant size, that should be beneath their dignity, but what an idea to have a cafe latte in the piccolo glass. Inspirational.

When you drive from Port Macquarie to Yamba the road is frequently bordered by young bush, and all I can say once again, is that it is delightful, just delightful. How lucky we are in Australia, how damnably lucky.

We got out of the car at Yamba to be greeted by two butcher birds singing their hearts out. What song. Different, slightly different to the fluting of the Victorian butcher birds, but just as lovely. It was a great welcome to this quiet seaside spot with its secluded Pippi's beach and the benign Pacific rolling its waves gently on to the sand. I decided to pick the brains of the motel man on the distances we still had to travel: tomorrow Killarney, the little town located near the source of the Condamine, (and then a large town to stay in and get a feed), the next night — query, and the next night Bourke on the Darling. What did he think?

He thought, and he expressed his thoughts as politely as he could, that we were mad. Too far, definitely too far. The headwaters of the Condamine were not worth the trip. Why go up into Queensland? Yamba and Bourke were roughly the same latitude. We would be going up through Warwick and then turning around and coming back through it again. Killarney had been an important and growing historic town until it was hit by a cyclone in 1968 and it had never really recovered. The hills were lovely, the waterfalls were outstanding, especially the Queen Mary Falls but after all they were just waterfalls. His wife had come from Goondiwindi and it was more or less on a direct route to Bourke. Go through Tenterfield and the pretty and historic Texas (never mind the name) and then through Moree and Walgett...His friend from Queensland who had been listening to most of this intervened in his support.

But we had seen the waterfall at the head of the Dordogne and in fairness we ought to see from Carr's Lookout above Killarney, the start of Australia's longest, if not its fullest river. And so we did, by way of Stanthorpe and the back road — lovely country — soft country, which in some way, seemed to me, an ignorant vigneron from the south, to be better vineyard country than the famous Stanthorpe ("and the monkeys sing soprano, round Stanthorpe in July"). And yes, the Killarney of today is a long way from the optimistic report by the Killarney & District Historical Society on the village of the 1880s: "one of the most flourishing towns in Southern Queensland".

It was getting late when we were leaving Killarney but I lingered for a while near the Condamine where it is crossed by the Ellen Backhouse Bridge and the local crickets burst suddenly into song. I looked around at the attractive hills and small mountains with the evening shadows across them and I wished that the early white settlers, Irish though they may have been and feeling a touch nostalgic about the "Auld Country", I wished that they had said that the district reminded them of home but they would find out the Aboriginal name and give it that. It is understandable, this nostalgia, but there is a lilt too and a very lovely lilt about names like Boorungle and Marrapine, and Nundoolka, and Windamungle, and so on. A name change (and some vineyards on the back road from Stanthorpe) might change Killarney's fortunes.

We had come to Killarney from Yamba by way of the graceful Clarence Valley, Maclean, Casino, Tenterfield and Stanthorpe, and now with dusk approaching we kept to the main roads and returned to Stanthorpe via Loch Lomond (yes, Loch Lomond is only a short distance from Killarney!), Warwick and Thulimbah. Stanthorpe has a few motels, a bridge under repair and it appears to have been in that state for months or even years, and a very good Italian restaurant which is buffet on Saturday nights, but none the worse for that.

Our destination for the following night was Moree, then Bourke, but first there was breakfast at Tenterfield. You couldn't say that the main street of Tenterfield was crowded with people or cars, but to the credit of a local lady there was a small place to eat breakfast, at tables on the footpath and the food was fresh and the service was excellent. The town gives the impression that you are on the plains and yet it is in, or perhaps adjacent to the Great Dividing Range. It is virtually surrounded by National Parks and nature reserves — Basket Swamp, Bald Rock, Boonoo Boonoo, Demon...

It has seen busier days, especially when it was first reached by the railway line in 1886 and ten trains were needed to transport the official party headed by the Governor, who was a lord. The station building is quite charming and was designed by John Whitton, "the father of the Australian railways", but trains no longer whistle and clang along the line.

Sir Henry Parkes' famous speech, the first impassioned cry for Federation, was made at the Tenterfield School of Arts on 24 October 1889. The attractive red brick building still stands. There is also, of course, the Tenterfield Saddlery on High Street. This old bluestone and granite building was originally bought by Sir Stuart Donaldson of Tenterfield Station. George Woolnough owned the saddlery for some time and he grand-fathered the Australian expatriate the piano-stool-turning Peter Allen. One of Allen's most touching songs was and is "The Tenterfield Saddler"

Another of Tenterfield's adopted sons is a local solicitor called James F. Thomas, who became better known in the Boer War as defence counsel for Breaker Morant and his farrier Handcock. Thomas never achieved the fame of Morant but in some ways perhaps he should have. He was born in 1861 (three years before Banjo Paterson) in Sydney to parents who could afford to and who did send him to The King's School, Parramatta. He graduated in law at Sydney University and commenced practice as a solicitor in Tenterfield in 1887 at the age of twenty-six. He is said to have been in the group of townspeople who persuaded the New South Wales Premier Henry Parkes to give that Federation speech of 1889 and to give it at Tenterfield. James Thomas made Tenterfield his home. He bought some properties in the nearby countryside, and in the town added the local newspaper *The Tenterfield Star* to his portfolio. He wrote poetry and paradoxically, or perhaps innocently and romantically, he involved himself with the local reservist group, the Tenterfield Rifles.

Despite his ties to what was now his home town, he volunteered for service in South Africa in the horrible Boer War. In November 1899, aged thirty-eight he, as a captain, took his horsemen and riflemen, the A Squadron New South Wales Citizen's Bushmen, to South Africa. They acquitted themselves well in the killing fields and the famous Sir Arthur Conan Doyle, (who at this stage in his writing career had also killed off Sherlock Holmes) then a war correspondent, wrote of their Eland's River encounter: "When the ballad-makers of Australia seek a subject, let them turn to Eland's River, for there was no finer fighting in the war." Was Sir Arthur, in passing, having a dig at our

Australian poets?

Thomas came back to Tenterfield but was reluctantly persuaded to return to the War in 1901, only to fall into the task of defending "The Breaker" and his farrier, at the insistence of the British Army. Any lawyer will tell you the difference in advocacy skills between a barrister appearing in court every day and a country solicitor doing the occasional appearance before the local magistrate, especially where the charge is that of homicide. James Thomas was in the latter category and the Brits would have known it. In fact it was precisely what they wanted. They had been seen to do the right thing, as a matter of law, and that was all that concerned them.

James Thomas, however, shocked them with the rigour and skill of his defence and with his blunt criticism of Lord Kitchener and his method of conducting the war. The convictions were, perhaps, a foregone conclusion, but somehow they came to him as a shock. He must have become very close to his clients during the conduct of the case and was devastated by the verdict and the swift execution by firing squad.

Morant, the horseman and poet, would no doubt have discussed his last poem with his legal advisor and perhaps would have handed it to him. It was called "Butchered to Make a Dutchman's Holiday", written on the eve of The Breaker's execution and published in the *Bulletin* on the Red Page on 19th April 1902. It was the sixtieth poem by a dashing horseman and a poet whose verse was said to be "lovely, breezy and entertaining". Anyhow, after the killing Thomas and his colleagues reclaimed the bodies and saw to their burial at a "truncated burial service" — for God would not have liked a full service for those two blokes.

Thomas returned to Australia as a haunted and shattered man who thereafter refused to use his military rank of "Major". The Army was pleased to part company with him and he with it. He started a book on his war experiences and lobbied the New South Wales Premier on behalf of the farrier Handcock's children. His law practice went downhill and gradually he sold his country properties and the *Star* newspaper. He became something of a recluse and an outcaste and sometimes slept in a tent at the local cemetery.

He died at his country property of Boonoo Boonoo on Armistice Day 1946 at the age of eight-five, a bachelor, a poet, a solicitor and a derelict, broken man.

Tenterfield and the outlying Tenterfield Station in particular have other claims to fame. The station was the home of Banjo Paterson's wife Alice Walker, and she was quite a girl. Banjo obviously spent time in the town (and at the station property no doubt) and he is said to have been a customer of that saddlery. No way that you can contradict that claim.

The morning sun was shining more and more strongly on our breakfast table (without its umbrella), and it was time that we were resuming our southern journey on the New England Highway.

Glen Innes is famous, well a little bit famous for a few reasons: it is at the intersection of the New England and Gwydir Highways, it's on the western slopes of the Great Dividing Range, it was a gold rush town (and its buildings benefited accordingly) and it is Celtic. Yes, I have left the best reason till last, the same as you do when eating your favourite dinner: you save your favourite morsel until the final forkful.

It is written that the district's first settlers (in the 1840s) were mostly Scots.

Well, maybe, but the Micks (and presumably many of

211

them were Irish) put up a bloody big church. I am not often impressed by Australian churches, but this lofty brick thing has a bit of style. The façade is simple and good and the bell tower is both unusual and artistic. Something has happened to the girls of Glen Innes though — they are no longer secluding themselves in the convents as they once did. As a consequence the large, and somehow cumbersome, convent has been sold off. With any luck it has been bought by a restaurateur/hotelier, and we too will one day be able to stroll those former chilly corridors. I have never yet been in a convent that wasn't cold. My recollection is that my sisters suffered from chilblains every winter at the Wangaratta Brigidines.

But Glen Innes, the sapphire prospecting and mining town like most of the gold rush and gem fossicking and mining towns, has secular buildings as well as religious, and they are worth a leisurely stroll. There is the post office erected in 1896, and you may wonder as you progress through central New South Wales why it is that so much money was spent by the Postal Department only three or four years before Federation. There is also the Court House which is still in use and lastly there is the magnificent town hall and its clock tower (1896). And you wonder afresh that the citizens and rate payers of the municipality could or should erect such an opulent building, and finally there is the CBC (Bank building) of 1890 and you don't need to wonder about expenditure by that commercial entity.

We had to do a right angle, right hand turn at Glen Innes, and this meant turning our backs on the Great Dividing Range which we had been skirting on our left all the way down from Queensland. We felt sad at leaving these mountains and foothills, even though the plains had been beckoning to us. What country this is — how expansive, how liberating. Just imagine that you had come from some miserable, damp, cold, poverty-stricken room somewhere in England, Ireland or Scotland — cribbed, cramped, shut in — and within a few months you are a horseman on a station property somewhere on the western plains: expanse, freedom, blue skies, sun, space, stars, open…

You might come to this little bit of paradise and have worked for any squatter or grazier, or you might have worked for the Cambridge educated Scotsman and barrister Archie Boyd. Boyd took up quite a few properties in the New England area, one of which is now known as Stonehenge Station. Honestly, Stonehenge Station! Change the bleeding name — please.

We made that right-hand turn onto the Gwydir Highway which commences at Grafton and ends at Walgett. The highway is named after the Western flowing river the Gwydir and it flows into the Barwon just north of Collarenebri. The Gwydir River's name originates in a district in North Wales and includes the rather lovely and historic mansion of Gwydir, now renovated, restored and going strong it seems. These Celts with their influence in France, in Scotland, Ireland and Wales, and in Australia, they were and still are a formidable people.

Inverell's origin and naming is attributed to Alexander Campbell who arrived here in 1835 and who established both Byron and Inverell station. Campbell's father's property in Scotland was named Inverawe: "Inver" meaning "meeting place". Alexander's homestead was at the junction of the McIntyre River and Swanbrook and so, continuing father's tradition, he named the area Inverell, "Inver" for meeting place and "ell" meaning swan. The first building in what is now the town was a store established by Colin and Rosanna Ross.

One of the travel guides says this of Inverell: "What this place lacks in character it does not make up for in any other way." What a churlish, and if I might say so, an inappropriate remark. The town is full of history and well-kept streets and trees and gardens, and some of its buildings are just splendid. Let me list a few: the Court House, all opulence and balance and Victorian decoration topped by an Eastern European tower; the (now) museum with its crop of minaret-style towers along the front; its nineteenth century gold/gem rush hotels (some now converted to other uses) and finally in Byron Street (good poet but that name for an Australian street — pity), in Byron Street the quite wonderful string of two-storey shops known as Hong Yuen's Building. Congratulations to the early settlers who decided that Inverell would be a place to remember with pride.

Not far from Warialda on the Delungra-Bingara road is the Myall Creek. This spot is infamous as the place where in 1838 some revengeful white Australians murdered approximately thirty Aborigines on the basis that they had stolen cattle and that generally they should be taught a lesson. This sort of stupid, spiteful, and sadistic behaviour was not unique in the history of human beings and similar kinds of mindless brutality have occurred since and no doubt will occur again. No mercy had been shown to the blacks, and after the second trial and the conviction of the perpetrators in Sydney at the end of that year, no mercy was shown to the gang of white men. Governor Gipps was absolutely steadfast in the face of considerable opposition to the death penalty. He was a man of courage and integrity, without doubt. But what a sorry event: massacred blacks and brutally hanged whites.

A memorial to the Aboriginal victims was belatedly constructed and unveiled in 2000. A commemorative ceremony is held there on the 10 June each year, and it may be of comfort to our black people to know that it is now included in the Australian National Heritage List.

Plaques to the maquis in France, and plaques to some of Mary Gilmore's people in Australia — they don't bring back the wronged and the dead, but perhaps they are of some consolation to the living.

Almost half way between Inverell and Moree is the small town of Warialda, and it was there in 1880 that a remarkable girl was born to an Irish farmer Michael Kenny and his Australian wife Mary Moore. She was Elizabeth Kenny, later known as Sister Kenny, the polio innovator, even though she never qualified officially as a medical person.

Warialda is, I imagine, very proud of its progeny even though the family moved to Nobby on the nearby Darling Downs when she was eight. Elizabeth became interested in muscles when she was injured in a riding accident at the age of ten, and she never lost this interest and never ceased to reason out its amelioration and cure. She was intelligent and courageous and she was helped to treat remote country cases of poliomyelitis by qualified Queensland doctors and surgeons, despite the general ridicule of many in official positions in the medical profession.

Elizabeth fought for her ideas throughout the whole of her adult life and saw with satisfaction the establishment of her clinics in Australia (Queensland in particular), England and America. She also had the thrill of viewing the film "Sister Kenny" released here in 1946 which "eulogized" her life's work. What a fighter she was, what a girl. She died in 1952 and has been described as "a big woman with (in later life) white hair which she often covered with large hats." She was buried at Nobby in Queensland, a small town between Toowoomba and Warwick.

Back to the Gwydir and westward — westward all the way to Bourke and the Darling River. Moree is the next big town and it did not have a recommendation that was without some reservations. It is easy to see why when you come in from the east and you stop at a motel in that area, and then go for walks from your motel. It has its blemishes, including its door and window screens and its security bars and grills. But go for walks I did, and no harm came of it.

Short walks are excellent, but why not a longer walk across the bridge that spans the Mehi River. The Gwydir River flows parallel to the Mehi at this point but for some reason Moree is on the Mehi. When you cross the bridge you soon enter the main shopping area and you will see slightly "classical" columns at various intervals along the footpaths, with plants around and over them. You might feel like smiling at the…artificiality of these. But I urge you not to. The municipality has made an effort and it continues to make an effort. I say congratulations generally for that effort and heartiest congratulations on the hedged olive trees in the side street. They look marvellous.

Moree is one of the cotton towns and there is plenty of the stuff along the roads and quite a few cotton factories and storage facilities throughout the general area.

But, I hear, the district is also a grower of those delicious pecan nuts which are gaining in popularity every year. The pecan comes from Mexico and its natural habitat is in the "arid areas." So, well done Moreean farmers. Moree will re-emerge, it has some inner spirit.

CHAPTER SIX

W hen you leave Moree you are definitely headed for Bourke, so fill up the petrol tank and top it up as you go.

Collarenebri does not mark a sudden change in the trees and undergrowth, but, nonetheless you become aware that the topography and the plant life are gradually altering. The Barwon River asserts itself on your left, and soon you are in the town of Walgett. The Gwydir Highway ends north of the town and you travel on the Castlereagh for a short distance before you join the Kamilaroi in the township. This highway is trumpeted as running from "the Great Divide to the Great Outback and provides the quint-essential [!] Australian Bush Experience". It was named after the original Aboriginal people who roamed over much of the area.

Walgett may have seen better days, and cer-tainly some of its hotels have, with their doors boarded up and their windows sealed with sheets of corrugated iron. They are deserted apparently, but have not fallen down and have not been pulled down. They are waiting for a big opal strike up at Lightning Ridge, or a richer harvest in grains from the huge expanse of the nearby and surrounding black-soil plains.

There is a high percentage of Aborigines in the town including young people, who are quite happy to exchange greetings with you and to flash you an infectious smile. And there are plenty of signs regulating or banning the sale and/or drinking of alcohol, and they seem to be observed. What do the Aborigines do here in a westerner's environment?

I got back into the car and drove around to a well-kept petrol station and store. The cashier was a white girl in her early twenties and I asked her about the place and intimated that it must have its difficulties: living in Walgett. "Not at all," she replied. "It's a good town. I like it here." And she was not defensive, just corrected me in a matter of fact way.

We drove out of Walgett on that Kamilaroi Highway with the now friendly Barwon River somewhere in the distance, and the road flat and straight — there's not much reason for it to turn as there are few gradients to surmount or hills to skirt. Every now and again though there is a deliberate trough or spillway to allow for the movement of floodwaters. Odd, isn't it in such a normally dry landscape.

The scenery had become so different that we took the next dirt sidetrack we came to, and parked the car and got out for a walk. What granulated, gravelly soil it was and how did those shrubs keep their leaves and their grey-green colour? There was grass, and then saltbush on the small rises and eucalypts of moderate height, scattered but not too sparse. There were all sorts of small bushes, scrub you would call it I suppose, and the whole thing was captivating in its austerity and its strangeness. This had to be Australia and it had to be the beginning of the outback.

As we resumed our drive towards Bourke we were intrigued by the thickness and the height of the grass under the trees and amongst the scrub. On our right in a small clearing we saw three emus strolling along, heads down. Further on there was a semi-trailer parked by the side of the road with what appeared to be a rough type of hut taking up the whole of the tray. Then a little further on and some twenty metres in the scrub we saw a bloke on a four-wheeler and then we saw the sheep. For the next kilometre or so there were hundreds of sheep eating the rank grass and there were also another couple of shepherds on their four-wheelers. No horses. The horses have been superseded.

As you get closer to Bourke you see thousands of acres of grain soil, and when we were there it was either fallow, being readied for planting or in one or two cases they were already sowing. Huge areas and huge machinery.

Eventually the green and gold sign came up on our left: "Welcome to Bourke — Gateway to the real Outback". We had crossed the Bogan River some distance back (and the Barwon just out of Brewarrina) and now we looked forward to our first glimpse of the glorious and historic Darling; the river of Lawson and Bean, of squatters and boats and barges and wool by the thousands of bales.

The entrance to Bourke is unusual and we drove slowly down to our retreat almost on the bank of the Darling itself. The garden was full of roses which were still in the full flush of the autumn season and our room, or suite perhaps, was called "the Bush Poets". How charming! And on the bedroom walls were two photos, one of the rather sad Henry Lawson and the other of the rather joyous romantic, Will

Ogilvie, who was the originator or in any event the pro-moter of the phrase "Back o' Bourke". More of Lawson and Ogilvie later but what about this from a Scot who fell in love with many things in Australia and who in the last few lines of his poem "At the Back o' Bourke" wrote:

It's the bitterest land of sweat and sorrow
But if I were free I'd be off tomorrow
Out at the back o' Bourke.

Will (1869–1963) was born near Kelso in Scotland, and came to Australia for the purpose of searching out and fol-lowing the troubled life of our poet Adam Lindsay Gordon. In the course of this endeavour, he spent twelve years on outback stations, wrote poetry, admired our women and returned to Scotland. He took with him by all accounts a vision of "the shimmering Australian moonlight" and "the loveliness of (our) girls." Why then did he go back to the cold and the crags of Scotland?

Henry Lawson (1867–1922) who died at the age of fifty-five after a long battle with the alcohol and with depression spent time in Bourke in 1892 but unlike Ogilvie, he did not see the romance of the Darling and the outback. In fairness, he did an unusual amount of tramping or trudging while he was there. One of the odd things about Lawson is his appar-ent lack of sympathy with our fellow creatures: dogs, birds, horses, animals in general. You might argue that the itinerant, peripatetic Henry had no place to keep them and no money to buy animals of any kind let alone, for instance, a horse. But we do not even hear of a cat. Henry, if only you had had a dog, a German shepherd for example. Henry had other things that he did not want, like deafness from the age of nine or thereabouts. He also had women troubles — misunderstood by his mother and later on by his wife, beautifully and wonderfully in love with a girl to rival Dante's Beatrice who like Beatrice became an angel early in her life; the grog…yes, he had his disappointments and his crosses to bear.

Back to Bourke. My God, the Darling — what have we done to it? Much better to write about the town. I went down into what I supposed was the Aboriginal sector, not that there was any sign or any line of demarcation, but that sector comprised only Aboriginals as far as I could see. Houses ill-kept with no gardens, houses moderately well-kept and reasonable gardens and some, not a high percentage, but some houses well-kept and with good gardens and an Aboriginal girl wielding a lawn mower. So, in terms of our white standards, there was a degree of pride in many of the homes.

I went back to our "Poets Suite" to prepare for dinner. Unhappily my wife had been told that there was no dinner to be had at our establishment that night but dinner could no doubt be obtained at the nearby hotel. Really? Yes, of course — good food. Bloody unlikely we thought. But we walked to the hotel on a night that was crystal clear but, with a threat of rain, "highly likely by the morning", according to the local radio.

We went into what used to be called the Ladies Lounge and sat down. The place was two-thirds full and the smell of beer was strong. You had to go to the bar for your drinks and I soon saw that the barmaid was pulling schooners of beer (only) at a continuous and rapid pace. When I got the chance I quietly asked for two gin and tonics. She looked hard at me but after a moment's pause turned and made up the drinks very professionally and I gratefully took them to our table. Newly acquired friends from the motel at Moree were on the next table and recognizing us they suggested that we join them. They were going on to Lake Eyre. Good deep drinkers those blokes; they had somehow acquired big thirsts.

We left them eventually to go into dinner at the bistro. Yes, they even have a bistro in Bourke, and a well patronised one at that. After we placed our order I went back to the bar to get a bottle of wine and stood next to a tall and neatly dressed Aborigine. We had seen him earlier standing near the bar and talking to various white people as they came in. He held an empty glass in his hand. I asked him if he'd like a drink, but he declined. Those eyes — his hurt and haunted eyes. I gazed at him, and managed to make conversation until my bottle had been bought and paid for. I doubt that he had had any alcohol at all. Why was he in the bar and why was he talking to people so quietly and gently? I went back into the bistro and to our table and wondered about him.

After a while our blue ring began to flash and tremble and we went over to the counter to collect our chicken parma and some salad. The man still troubled me and I wished that I had asked him to join us for a meal. Our friends from Moree trooped into the bistro, collected their steaks and sat down with us. I didn't, I hadn't — but I regretted not asking him. An Aboriginal woman of about thirty-five sat at a table nearby and she was by herself. We *have* to do more. We have to reach out; it is very necessary.

Henry Lawson came to Bourke in 1892 after the spurious competition and ensuing publicity between him and Banjo Paterson. A competition in which Henry fared badly. Lawson had talked and written about some stark realities of "the bush" including fence lines of crows, haggard mothers, timid half-wild children, lone sundowners, snakes et cetera and the Banjo had hit back hard with his "In Defence of the Bush". Paterson asked him if he had never heard "the carol of the magpies" and he continued the attack with these lines:

> Did you hear no sweeter noises in the music of the bush
>> Than the roar of trains and buses, and the war-
> whoops of "the push"?

And then with a figurative shaking of his head —

>> You had better stick to Sydney and make merry with
> the "push",
> For the bush will never suit you, and you'll never suit
> the bush.

Jocular lines perhaps but they stung the man who defended the workers of the outback and when the *Bulletin* offered him a railway ticket to Bourke and back and money to spend (not much), he took up the offer and arrived at the Darling and Bourke on the 21 September 1892.

What was he doing in Bourke, and more importantly what would he do in Bourke? Well, there was his trade. He was a competent painter of houses, thanks to a boyhood apprenticeship with his father, and he could do some "outback jobs" and send articles on them back to the Bulletin, and he could gather material to dowse the little fire that Banjo Paterson had started. So he proceeded to do all those things, including a rouseabout job in a shearing shed. None of those occupations altered his view of the outback, but he began to be moulded by the countryside and its men, and gradually the concept of mateship took a hold on his mind and entered the very fibres of his body. He understood unionism, and loyalty and the outback workers' loathing of the scab. Lawson may have detested the outback and its heat and monotony but its principles had suffused his soul.

Some two months after reaching Bourke, and at the start of summer in the south, but the midst of summer in the far west of the western plains, Lawson persuaded two of his new mates to walk with him in a north-westerly direction to Hungerford on the Queensland border, some two hundred kilometres away. He was determined to experience the Outback.

They started on their journey at the end of November 1892: Lawson, de Guinney (a well educated Russian whose English was good enough to have articles published in the *Worker*) and Gordon (a wanderer who worked with Lawson for a while on a painting job). Lawson was twenty-five. Why did they go north-west where there were no nearby rivers, and in effect, little or no water, even to drink? No one seems to know why.

The Russian soon saw the error of the excursion and turned back. The other two ploughed on. Some forty kilometres from Bourke they would have gone across the beautifully named river, the Warrego at Fords Bridge, and then there was nothing in the way of streams until they came upon the Paroo at Hungerford, on the border. Lawson's mate, young Gordon, had life in his legs and decided to push on in a north-westerly direction to Thargomindah. Lawson said "enough" and turned back to tramp the red, hot dusty return journey to Bourke.

On his lonely ten days return trip he later recalled that he "wished that (he) was dead." But some romance and optimism entered his spirit during his nights under the sky and he wrote:

From the West the gold was driven:
I watched the death of day,
An' the distant stars in heaven
Seemed to draw my heart away.

He wrote more realistically to his Aunt Emma in Sydney:

"You can have no idea of the horrors of the country out here. Men tramp and beg and live like dogs." He wrote of dogs but as I have said it seems that he knew nothing of dogs or any animals.

So there you have it — the Darling, the town of Bourke and memories of Will Ogilvie and Henry Lawson in the poets' room in Bourke.

★ ★ ★ ★

We woke at five o'clock next morning to hear rain beating on the roof. Rain in Bourke? Surely not. I peeped outside. The local radio had been correct: there was a storm and the rain was drumming down. Not only that, but the toilet light was not working. We had lost power.

Breakfast was meagre: still no electrical power. We packed and left. The man at the petrol station shook his head. No power, therefore no petrol. "The power will be on in a couple of hours mate. You'll get petrol at Nyngan — no worries." We examined the gauge on our car with great care, and then took that ruler-straight road to Nyngan, two hundred kilometres away.

It continued to rain as we drove south-west. Water was lying on both sides of the road as if it had been pouring for a week and there were water birds paddling and wading beside the road, egrets mostly. We wondered where they had been yesterday and the day before and how it was that suddenly they were here. After driving for something over an hour I spied a simple petrol bowser outside a building that might well have been a store, or more correctly had been a store and which had now retired. A bare light bulb gave a dim orange glow through the rain. Nyngan was, what? Perhaps it was still some seventy kilometres or so away and the petrol gauge was shivering below the quarter line. We pulled in.

A bloke came out. Yes, he did have power and he did have petrol and he did take credit cards. I went inside to pay and put my card on the newspaper spread over the counter. I was sorry to have interrupted his day's activities. He had a property a few kilometres out and he had sowed his wheat yesterday.

"How was that," he said.

"Brilliant," I said.

He told me about his property and the season and what was happening locally and then he walked to the door with me.

"What's that tree about twenty metres along where the track re-joins the road?" I asked.

"A coolibah."

"Are you serious? Are you sure?"

"'Course I'm sure. Quite a few around here."

How wonderful! I had seen a coolibah tree.

"And," I ventured, "we saw a remarkable tree in the distance this morning. Just one. It was an amazing colour... almost iridescent grey with very black limbs and trunk. Quite beautiful."

"It'd be a brigalow. Pretty rare now — the brigalow scrub used to be mainly north-east of Bourke. Good soil but those trees were buggers to clear. Suckered, and thrived on burning. Then we got bulldozers and herbicides. Not many of them left now. Lovely tree."

I'd had a report on the local doings, some tree identification, a spot of history and a full tank of petrol. What did it matter that the price per litre was a bit more than yesterday and the day before. It had been a profitable fifteen minutes.

The rain was easing, the road ran straight and we resumed our trip along the Mitchell Highway through Nyngan, Nevertire, Trangie and Narromine to Dubbo. (Paterson mentions Nevertire somewhere. I thought he'd made up the name.)

Narromine is on or near the Macquarie River and although it is still in a dry part of the Western Plains, its main street is all gardens and parterres and flowers. They have water and they use some of it to beautify the town. In the midst of the island of gardens is an unusual sculpture by the rather remarkable Tom Bass — Tom Bass who was born in 1916 in Yass. His father was a baker and his grandfather was too. In fact his grandfather (born 1863, died 1913) was the baker of Narromine and he died just before Tom Bass's birth.

Tom's family was living in Gundagai in 1925 when Tom was nine years old, and he remembers his father showing him a loaf of freshly-baked bread and saying to him, "That is a beautiful loaf." This remark impressed the young boy and he looked carefully at the bread and its shape. The incident stuck in his memory and helped Tom to decide on his vocation as a sculptor and inspired him to produce the Narromine sculpture of his grandfather and the loaf of bread.

Tom Bass has done some wonderful work in Australia, for example, the superb Children's Tree (with owl and lizard) on the north-west corner of Elizabeth and Collins Streets in Melbourne and the famous or perhaps, the infamous, relief and fountain in Sydney (former P & O Building) at the corner of Hunter and Castlereagh Streets. And you might reasonably ask, what has happened to our sculptor, the son of baker Will. Tom Bass was still alive and at the age of ninety-three was active and continued to run his Tom Bass Sculpture

Studio School in Sydney at the time of writing but has subsequently died. A simple but a great man has left us.

We sat on after drinking our coffee in Narromine and then we drove back to the Shire Offices, not to see them, but just for the pleasure of being in a street called Dandaloo. What a name! Incidentally the spelling of Narromine has been refined. Originally it was a rough approximation of the Wiradjuri Aboriginal name and meant "the place of many lizards "or perhaps "the place of wild (Australian) bees." Reluctantly we took the road for Dubbo and its dozens of motels — Dubbo on the reasonably full Macquarie River. Dubbo has a branch, and a very important branch, of the Central West Catchment Management Authority and although I blew in, without any introduction or appointment they were very helpful. And after picking their brains I walked into the heart of the town to a bookshop which would be the pride of any of our capital cities. The stock of books is immense and the knowledge of the proprietor is just as large. I know that Dubbo has a population of some forty thousand, but the whole of Dubbo and the surrounding areas must be bookworms. The place would put a spring in the feet of any writer.

Dubbo has its somewhat remarkable Court House (where *did* the Justice Department get its money?) and rather a nice church — locked. It is a reflection on Australia that it apparently cannot leave its churches open as it once did. How can you pop in for a quick Our Father?

Before leaving the town let me mention an early morning group of galahs which were walking along the electric power wires in a residential street not far from our motel. Most of them were in pairs, and perhaps it was the cold of the morning, but they were smoodging and chatting and generally behaving in a very affectionate fashion. There were a few singles, however. I love the wonderful pink and silver-grey feathers of these birds and their swooping and daring flight. I often wonder how the old Australian saying originated and has been perpetuated: "Oh, he's a bloody galah." As far as I know it's a derogatory term: he's dense, stupid. How did they get this bad name?

Dubbo is more or less in the centre of New South Wales (more or less) and we could have gone in any of the three remaining directions. We chose Parkes and Forbes and all places south to Wagga Wagga after which we would head east and north up through Gundagai and Yass. We were late in leaving Dubbo — perhaps I had talked to the galahs for too long.

Finally we took the Newell Highway out of Dubbo and we wished that we had the time to go out to that place called Dandaloo on your right or into the Goobang National Park on your left. All these utterly Australian names which have grown out of the soil and rocks and have been natural and loved by the Aborigines for centuries, and yet we only half value them. And we have peppered the continent with Mansfields, and Adelaides and Brisbanes and Darlings…ah well.

Before you get to the town of Parkes the giant telescope (the dish) crowns the top of some distant hills, and you may think of its role in the moon landing, or you may think of the film "The Dish" or you may wonder about Australian/American relationships or, finally, if you have the time, you might take the turn and go in for a visit. We drove on.

Henry Parkes was an immigrant but like thousands of others very quickly became an ardent Australian. We have already met him at Tenterfield when he made his famous speech in favour of Federation. He wanted "a great national government for all Australia". He had an adventurous and a colourful life for a man who came out to Australia from England in 1839 at the age of twenty-four, married and a maker of ivory billiard balls. Yes, the call for thousands of billiard balls was not strong and the Parkes family lived very, very humbly in one room with boxes for furniture. He took jobs out in the country and they gradually got ahead. His initial doubts about Australia gave way to a love of the new continent and it is alleged that in one of his first speeches in Sydney he used these words: "Henceforth the country of my children shall be mine. Australia has afforded me a better home than my motherland and I will love her with a patriot's love." Whose bread I eat, his song I'll sing! Amen.

Well, a man who said that, a democrat, an orator, and, according to our splendid writer Vance Palmer, "lively, adaptable, with [at the time] a clean-shaven face and shrewd puckered eyes [with] natural intelligence", such a man would and did go far in his adopted country. He cut his teeth as a member of the New South Wales Legislative Assembly when he introduced the Public Schools Act in 1866. He died in 1896 after some forty years in both houses of the New South Wales parliament, many of them as premier. His business ventures were less successful than his political career and he died poor. At the end "his shrewd, satyr-like face [was] almost hidden in a tangle of grey hair and beard…was the delight of the cartoonists". And he had some women troubles along the way but his third wife was by his side when he died at Faulconbridge in the Blue Mountains, having first given the town his mother's maiden name. Not even the demagogue John Dunmore Lang could speak badly of him and on his death he summed him up as "a friend of the community".

And Parkes, the lively town of Parkes in the catchment of

the Bogan and Lachlan Rivers was re-named after Sir Henry. It was formerly known as Bushmans, according to Brittanica, and Currajong, according to another source. I suppose there is no chance of re-naming it yet again.

Anyhow, Sir Henry's bronze, by Terrance Plowright, gazes down and along the main street (renamed after his first wife Clarinda. All this renaming for two English immigrants!) and it is a very fine statue of an orator in full flight. It was unveiled by Professor Marie Bashir, the Governor of New South Wales, in 2008 to celebrate the one hundred and twenty-fifth anniversary of Parkes.

What with stopping for a picnic lunch, a moderately good cup of coffee and a tour of Parkes and the surrounding countryside we had frittered away a good part of the afternoon. We by-passed Forbes, took the Olympic Highway and made a dash to secure a room and a meal at Wagga Wagga on the Murrumbidgee. What a lovely name for a river and its town. There is a Jack O'Hagan song about the road to Gundagai which includes part of a line "Where the blue gums are growing the Murrumbidgee's flowing…" Maybe there are blue gums along the river near the mountains. I always associate the rivers, in this part of Australia, with red gums.

I knew something of Wagga some sixty years ago when I was based there doing a course with the RAAF. I knew something more of it forty years later when I did the short winemaking course at the Sturt University, but I was not prepared for the expanded, somewhat sophisticated Wagga of 2009. God, how things have changed: a restaurant which could rival many a first-class restaurant in our capital cities and a suite of rooms which left nothing more to be expected — and next morning a walk along the banks of the Murrumbidgee which *was* flowing, although a little slowly, I have to confess.

Burrinjuck, Wantadadgery, Wakool, Wagga Wagga… Just writing those names gives you a taste of rolling hills, grass, grain, gums, sunshine, and of course reminds you of the gentle, original inhabitants and their sensitive grasp of the essentials of the local ecology. We, the Europeans, exploited that ecology, but we have learnt or are learning, with the constant reminder that we should have learnt earlier and the fear that our wisdom comes too late.

Wagga in the local Aboriginal language is said to mean a crow, and Wagga Wagga is simply the plural. I cannot say that I have ever heard a crow crying "Wagga" as it flies overhead looking from side to side or sits high up on a dead branch watching you, but then it is fair to say that I am by no means a talented musician or linguist. Anyhow that is the only explanation we have for Wagga Wagga, apart from the suggestion that it might mean " drunken or reeling man".

Hume and Hovell, the queer couple or perhaps one should amend that adjective and write the curious couple, get most of the credit for "discovering" Wagga Wagga on the Murrumbidgee. It was they who corrected the dogmatic assertion of John Oxley, the Surveyor General, that the "southern region"— that great expanse of land between the roughly known area of New South Wales and Tasmania — was virtually barren and uninhabitable. Their expedition from Sydney to Westernport Bay was along a route that is roughly now the Hume Highway. Hamilton Hume was a currency boy, but only just, having been born at Parramatta in 1797. Even as an adolescent he took part in exploration around the general Sydney area and down as far as Goulburn. In 1821 at the age of only twenty-four he is said to have discovered the Yass plains and to have staked his claim to a sizeable area. As he rode or walked along, I'm sure he sang his songs and recited his poetry, almost one hundred years before the impractical Banjo rode his horse and recited his verse in and around Wee Jasper.

William Hinton Hovell, born 1786 and therefore Hume's senior by eleven years, was certainly *not* a currency lad; he was born in England, took to the sea, became a master of a ship and then at the age of twenty-seven migrated to Australia. He kept up his seafaring along the coast of Australia, made trips to New Zealand and then somehow managed to get a grant of land near Narellan (not far from the famous "Cowpastures" of John Macarthur.)

Hume, as an inveterate explorer, and Hovell, something of a new chum, were chosen by Governor Brisbane as the men to trek from Sydney in a general southerly direction to Port Phillip Bay, thus confirming or contradicting Surveyor General Oxley's view of the southern unknown. At the time of their commission, Hume was a mere twenty-seven years old and Hovell was thirty-eight — almost middle-aged. Hovell represented himself as the technical expert: able to take observations, determine latitude et cetera, and Hume was the practical experienced bushman. We speak today of "Hume and Hovell", but there is a suggestion that originally they were known as Hovell and Hume.

Definitely an odd pair who had more arguments than an ill-matched married couple. Nonetheless, they managed to cross the Murrumbidgee, but well upstream of Wagga Wagga some distance to the south-west of Yass. (The actual crossing is now under the waters of the Burrinjuck Dam).

The river was full at the time of their crossing and, apart from swimming, there was no way to get to the south of the Murrumbidgee or across any other Australian river except at the height of summer and at the end of a drought when, of course, it or they could be forded. Were all these explorers and convicts and the like competent swimmers and if so, where did they learn and why? I couldn't swim the Murray or the Murrumbidgee or even the Darling. Well, perhaps I could tackle the Darling at Bourke. But how to get the drays and equipment across? Someone devised a scheme for lashing a tarpaulin (tar as in tar: distillation from wood or coal, and pall as in pall, the cloth spread over a coffin) underneath and up the sides of the dray which was then loaded with an appropriate quantity of equipment and was hauled across by rope. The rope was taken across by a bloke who swam over with a light cord, or fishing line, which was then tied to the rope and the rope pulled across. Very ingenious.

Sadly, the two explorers each claimed the credit for the tarpaulin-boat scheme, the foresight in bringing the necessary ropes and tarps and the like, and its execution. And even some twenty-nine years after the event Hovell delivered a lecture at Mack's Hotel in Geelong where he was reported as having said: "That I should live [he was sixty-seven] to be among the children of the land of my adopting, and that these children should, with one accord meet and acknowledge me as the discoverer of their fine country..." Hume, on reading that report at his home known as Cooma Cottage at Yass came out of retirement, and his blood pressure soared. Yes, indeed it did.

Two brave men, two exceptional men, one an Australian, one an Englishman who had adopted Australia, but unable to become friends on a trek that would have welded together just about any other two men in the world.

And although Hume and Hovell are entitled to claim the discovery of the site on which Wagga Wagga is now built, it was perhaps Charles Sturt, the "Father of Australian exploration", who publicised the merits of the land around Wagga. It was he, the Indian-born Englishman, who waxed lyrical about the flat land to the west of the later township, calling those flats "extensive and rich" and "more fitted for agricultural purposes than the stiffer and purer soil amidst the mountains". Settlement in and about what is now the town of Wagga Wagga began at the time of Sturt's discoveries and accelerated thereafter. Wagga Wagga on the south bank (and later on the north) was away. The embryonic city almost half way between the capitals of Sydney and Melbourne had begun its expansion. And that expansion continued and will no doubt continue in the future.

We have to leave Wagga, captivating though it is, but before departing let us look briefly at its famous court case of 1921: a case that could only happen in a society where there were still bigots, that is, as the Oxford dictionary tells us, people "who hold obstinately to a belief…intolerantly of others."

A certain Bridget Partridge was born in Ireland at Kildare (south-west of Dublin) in 1890 to a Protestant father and a Catholic mother. At the age of fourteen she felt the call to a nunnery. She may have approached a convent in Ireland and they may have advised and assisted her, but eventually she migrated to Australia and she took some practical steps. In February 1909 she entered the convent at Mount Erin, Wagga Wagga run by the Presentation sisters and took the name Liguori, Sister Liguori. Now Liguori was an Italian and he founded the Redemptorist order in 1732 at Scala, Italy. Liguori viewed his religion seriously (and is now a saint) and he wrote extensively: "The True Spouse of Jesus Christ, The Glories of Mary" et cetera. He was undoubtedly a super successful author and his works have gone through 18,000 editions. Any modern author would mutter "Oh, my God" at those statistics and go green with envy. Sister Liguori, presumably modelled herself on his teaching and she, therefore, was a lady of some clout, or she wanted to become one.

Despite an auspicious and enthusiastic start, by 1920 Sister Liguori had grown tired of the religious life and finally in July she left the Wagga convent and went to live with the Burgess family in nearby Coleman Street. She telephoned the local bishop, Bishop Dwyer, and after that telephone conversation returned to the convent. A doctor was called who listened to her patiently and prescribed sedatives. Sister Liguori thought that she was being given poison and fled the convent barefooted and clad only in her nightdress. The convent became alarmed and called the police and they and Catholic (!) laymen searched for her, but then were told that she was safe and staying with another neighbour. Pickets were placed around the neighbour's house. She eluded the pickets, escaped, and with the assistance of the Reverend Touchell, a Congregational Minister she reached the southern Sydney suburb of Kogarah. Dr Leahy, the doctor who had seen her originally, a good Catholic, now sought from a Wagga Wagga magistrate a warrant for her arrest on the grounds of her insanity. The application was denied.

Bishop Dwyer was determined to be part of the farce and somehow persuaded a Sydney magistrate to issue a warrant. The good sister was arrested, deposited in a mental hospital but released after observation, and discharged as sane and of sound mind.

The newspapers had by now grasped the story and made a sensation of it. Why not? The Protestants in the guise of the Loyal Orange Lodge, not to be outdone, joyfully entered the fray and having guaranteed costs, they persuaded Sister

Liguori to sue the enthusiastic Bishop Dwyer for five thousand pounds for wrongful arrest and imprisonment. Now, at last, the Protestants and Catholics, the English and the Irish, had locked horns and the fight was on.

The case came up for hearing in Sydney on 30 June 1921 and ran until the thirteenth of the next month. The public gallery was packed, newspapers sold like wildfire and "every detail of convent life was exposed". Good stuff.

The action was heard by Justice (Sir) David Ferguson and a jury of four and they found for the bishop, Sir David remarked in his charge to the jury that "it is very unfortunate for the plaintiff that, at the time she left the convent she did not meet somebody (with) a little common horse-sense." Once again I am tempted to say "amen" — so be it.

Protestants and Catholics are somewhat relaxed about their religions today with the exception, perhaps, of the Evangelists, and it is hard to envisage the bigotry of less than one hundred years ago. My mother used to tell us rather humorously of her school days in Wangaratta where she as a girl in the uniform of the local Catholic convent was subject to taunts from the state school children: "Catholic dogs/Jump like frogs/Don't eat meat on Friday." The reply of the gentle convent girls was: "Catholics, Catholics ring the bell/Whilst the Prodos go to hell." Nice children.

Incidentally Bridget Partridge, Sister Liguori, was admitted to Rydalmere Mental Hospital in November 1962 and died there on 4 December 1966. What a wise man was Sir David, the judge.

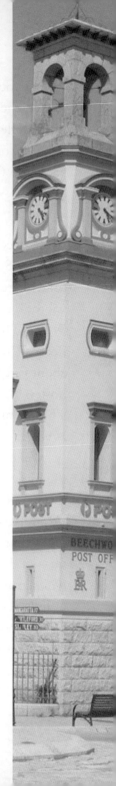

CHAPTER SEVEN

So, we left Wagga Wagga and the somewhat sad and somewhat stupid case of Sister Liguori and we returned to Melbourne because we had to. But on the way back we did manage an overnight stay at that wonderful town of Beechworth in north-east Victoria.

Beechworth, another gold mining town with architecture not dissimilar to that of the central and the central west of New South Wales and just as lovely. Beechworth is in the hills, with bush, and rocks and clear blue skies, and wines and good bookshops and restaurants. Ah yes, we are writing about New South Wales but it is hard to by-pass Beechworth in Victoria.

And might I say in passing that Beechworth also has a remarkable woman who runs a furniture, arts and crafts and small bookstore. I purchased from her a slim volume on Banjo Paterson. She put my money in the cash register and then she asked, "So you like his poetry?"

"Yes."

She took a couple of steps backwards and there and then recited the whole of *Mulga Bill's Bicycle*: "Twas Mulga Bill from Eaglehawk…"

Just wonderful. I shook my head, thanked her and walked back into the street.

★ ★ ★ ★

A few weeks later we managed to fit in another eight days in New South Wales, and to give ourselves the maximum time to see and re-see our chosen parts of the "senior" State, we took to the air from Tullamarine (Melbourne) to Wagga Wagga. The jet that transports you on that journey is fast, sleek, silent and altogether an absolute joy to be in. It takes about forty passengers and it just purrs along with a smiling hostess (flight attendant) who somehow manages to give you a biscuit and a hot drink before you glide along the tarmac at Wagga Wagga.

We drove north from busy Wagga on the Olympic Highway and stopped at a billabong for an early lunch. The first billabongs I ever saw were outside Wangaratta along the Ovens River and they fascinated me then, schoolboy though I was. This billabong just by Houlighans Creek was a classic — a deep and long basin half full of still water and reeds, wonderfully picturesque with craggy red gums overhanging it and giving the surface a dappled light. There was even a pair of kookaburras to welcome us. An excellent spot for the well-kept picnic reserve.

Wantabadgery of Captain Moonlite fame beckoned us on our right, but we had lingered too long by the billabong. About the only worthwhile thing Andrew Scott, the self-styled Captain Moonlite, did and the only sensible thing that he said was his plea at the murder trial of himself and his three accomplices: "...let me be the victim and spare these youths." The judge, considered Scott's plea and then obligingly ordered Scott to be hanged for the murder of the policeman. Two of the bushranger's mates were given life imprisonment. Incidentally, the story of the hold-up at the Wantabadgery Station and the subsequent trial was the lead story in the first issue of the *Bulletin* in 1880.

And on the subject of kookaburras: my Oxford dictionary defines the word "kookaburra" as a "large Australian kingfisher with a loud discordant cry" and the excellent Britannica is no better and describes the kookaburra's chortle as resembling "fiendish laughter". Well, I protest on behalf of that bird beloved of and named by our Aborigines. I would say that a kookaburra's cackle (usually two kookaburras and therefore their duet) resembles a joyful, carefree, Italian opera tenor greeting his beloved who has just returned to him pristine and pure after enduring and triumphing over the most tempting and salacious of ordeals. Discordant and fiendish? No, joyful and wondrous. There is no other duet from man, beast or bird more uplifting and carefree than that of a pair of Australian kookaburras on a dead branch of one of our gum trees in the late afternoon or early dusk, or even the early morning — if your head is refreshed and clear.

★ ★ ★ ★

Junee was known once as the "Rail Centre of the South" and a walk out on to its rather lengthy station confirms its reputation. The Refreshment Room is still in use and is largely intact, and it appears that the buildings are being repainted and we hope restored. True restoration will require a large expenditure but I believe it would be justified. The railway line cuts the town in two, always has, it seems, and this is a pity. There is the 1876 Junee Hotel on the "wrong" side of the line and as a writer from Lonely Planet observes: "The pub has not had a lot done to it over the years, but that means the original fittings are still intact." Yes, well, perhaps we could look at balance — the happy medium.

Junee is a dear old town but it needs a few enterprises such as say, a small but specialised flour mill, and an artisan baker (to free Junee and its surrounds from soft, white, sliced and plastic wrapped "bread"). Somehow the town has survived as a Victorian jewel but it really could do with something to jazz it up. It is a town of wide streets (country New South Wales learned from Sydney's mistakes), an ugly church or two, wonderful lacework verandas, and just to balance things, a rather attractive Presbyterian church in a back street and a reasonable Masonic Hall that has just been sold and which, no doubt, will be put to some worthwhile use.

Junee is in the grain belt and was looking superbly green and yellow when we saw it, but in need of that elusive thing called rain.

We journeyed to and through Cootamundra, famous as the birthplace of the ferny and fast growing blue and purple wattle (and the cricketer Donald Bradman) and on to Young, just in time for a cup of coffee before the excellent café closed.

Young is another gold mining town with gold mining architecture and is in a valley, as are many of the old gold mining towns. It was formerly known as Lambing Flat, and can claim a part in the early life of our talented Banjo

Paterson who in his youth "watched the fascinating sight of gold escorts passing by from Lambing Flat, guarded by mounted troopers". The golden days of Young are behind it but it seems prosperous and it has a couple of good restaurants — one, in which we enjoyed a meal, in the old Masonic Temple. Our grandchildren will have to find more and more uses for "temples" and churches.

Young has a lovely Victorian-era post office but oh my God, it has been vandalised. Australia Post, or its predecessor, has obliterated the classic façade of the old Victorian building with a couple of rooms in brick overhanging the footpath. They are a cross between a high ugly fence and a veranda. Please, please, pull the thing down.

Young is a town of creeks. They all meet here. I went for a walk to inspect the Burrangong Creek and then doubled back through the town and past the Anglican church which was preparing for morning service. I ventured in and glanced at the uninspiring stained glass. Outside on the surrounding fence were four currawongs hopping around and having a conversation. I eavesdropped. The birds tired of their talk and flew off in their controlled and swinging flight, and sang as they flew. What wise and graceful creatures.

I walked past last night's restaurant in its re-cycled temple, and then back to our motel. Just before I got to the motel I saw a neo-gothic church across the valley. It was artfully screened by nearby trees and I took a photo and showed it to the receptionist.

"Is that the Catholic church?" I asked.

"Don't know," she replied looking closely at the photo. "Could be."

"But you are here everyday and there it is, and…"

"Yes, but I live at Forbes."

She drove down from Forbes, only a hundred or so kilometres to the north! I wondered if girls from Young had jobs
at Forbes. It was only an hour's drive, she re-assured me, and
I suppose when one reflects on the commuters in our capital
cities… Why not?

We drove to Grenfell with the Weddin Mountains ever
present, ever visible and ever mysterious and beckoning. We
resisted the temptation to visit them and parked instead at
the bottom of the hill, outside the veranda of another nineteenth century hotel in the main street of Grenfell, Henry
Lawson's birthplace.

This meandering street is somehow both charming and
eccentric: it winds and twists its way over and around the hill
with Lawson by the footpath gazing dolefully at the sparse
traffic. A ute backed in (that is how you park in most of central New South Wales) next to us and I said "G'day" to its
driver and asked him the question.

"Because of George Street," he answered, looking at me
as if I was an imbecile.

"George Street?"

"Don't you know George Street?"

I soon knew all about George Street and Emu and the
creek and the days of the hopeful gold seekers. We took his
advice and drove around to George Street, historic deserted
track that it is and I parked outside the old Railway Hotel
(1879) and began an exploration. As I set out on my walk, lo
and behold, the ute pulled up and I was directed to "hop in".
Howard, the bloke, had been back to the Council buildings
and had collected all sorts of brochures and notes which he
presented to me.

We drove slowly along wandering George Street with its
"Oddfellows Hall" of 1878 and its neighbour of 1866 and

Howard showed me the original path of the Emu Creek and explained how the miners pitched their tents and how the track followed the course of the creek and how that track became George Street, the main street at the time, and then he recounted the story of the two fires and how the towns-people had started building on the adjoining street which ran exactly parallel to and followed all the windings of the creek and George Street and it all became clear. Apparently the little mining town was called "Emu" originally, hence Emu Creek, and then…and then Emu was not good enough and so the clever officials gave it the name of Grenfell.

In fairness Grenfell, the bloke, was a brave fellow, brave and foolhardy perhaps. He was the local Gold Commissioner and had the misfortune to be held up by two bushrangers. He drew his pistol and fired at them, and missed. They fired back and wounded him and he died a day or so later. Perhaps it is only right that the local gold town should have com-memorated him and yet…I still long for Emu.

What a generous man my guide was. We journeyed on to the Masonic Hall or Temple (shortly to be sold) and I had my first view of the sacred interior of this once exclusive club, called officially a lodge, a lodge for a fraternal society. Freemasons have lofty ideals: "high moral standards, kindness in the home, courtesy in society, honesty in business and fair-ness in all dealings." And yet they are on the decline. In fact it might be suggested that they are becoming as irrelevant as mainstream religions. It is not long since one saw serious, dinner-suited men hurrying along in the twilight clutching a moderate sized bag, intent apparently on participating in secret rituals inside a grand temple.

It was in these temples that the Worshipful Master pre-sided, seated in his canopied throne and assisted by his acolytes in theirs; it was there that the serious services took place around the geometric black and white tiled square (males only of course, and Protestant ones, at that); and there that the ceremony was performed, hallowed words were spoken and the procedure followed. But it is all disappearing, the era is nearly over. And yet it lasted for more than six hundred years. The buildings are being sold and can be used for any purpose but the thrones and the seats, the sacred floor tiles and the trappings are reverently going back to head office.

Freemasonry seems to be trying to shake off its reputation for slightly occult practices, but it is all too late. Oddly it has still retained the ceremonial aprons, the collars and gauntlets and there is still the knowing handclasp with the supposedly subtle pressure of the thumb.

Howard locked the door and took me in his ute back to my wife who had been wondering where I had got to and we drove into the now main street and up the hill to its group of existing shops set amongst a nest of nineteenth century buildings. Can we please have a couple of small and attractive industries for Grenfell too? It would not need much and the town has such a lot to offer.

Anthony Trollope (1815–1882), the London son of an "improvident barrister" (isn't that a flat contradiction?) was a full time postal employee but somehow managed to become a famous novelist (*Barchester Towers* et cetera) and to invent the pillar box. And Trollope came to the Grenfell district in 1871 to see his son Frederick who owned a nearby station.

Rolf Boldrewood (Thomas Browne) was not going to allow a prize like that to slip through his fingers and he arranged a literary lunch for the famous bearded Englishman. I would like to say that it took place at the top of the hill in the heart of Grenfell but unfortunately it was at Gulgong. At that luncheon Trollope muttered in his beard these famous words:"The idea that Englishmen are made of paste, whereas the Australian is [made of] steel, I found to be universal."

Well, old boy, you came, you observed, you heard and you went back to the Mother Country a wiser man than when you left. By the way Trollope wrote the whole of his novel *Lady Anna* on the voyage out to Australia. One has to take off the hat to this particular Englishman (tempting though it was to call him a pasty Pom).

William Holman (1871–1954) was the Labor member for Grenfell and became premier of New South Wales for seven years (1913–1920). Unfortunately he was not a dedicated party man and he ratted on the Labor party in 1916 but stayed on as premier for the remaining four years as leader of...the Nationalist Party — oh my God! He was a thinker (delivered the Macrossan lectures at the University of Queensland), but he was also a lawyer, and originally, an Englishman!

One should explain ever so briefly the origin of the Macrossan lectures. They were funded in 1925 by a gift from one John M. Macrossan, Secretary of Mines and Works and are given annually on an appointed day, on a wide range of academic topics. It is stipulated that they be free. One of the founder's sons became a Queensland Supreme Court Judge and he appears to have "topped up" father's endowment. He had this to say in an appeal from a case launched by the "Objectionable Literature Board of Queensland." The books, *Real Love, Romance Story*, et cetera emphasized "the thesis that an acceptable means of achieving (marriage) is a casual acquaintance made by a young girl with a man hitherto a complete stranger to her, the ardour of whose embraces and kisses provide the assurances of the constancy of his affection," and, he went on, this material did have "a tendency to corrupt members of an age group described as adolescents." Wow! The year of the case was 1955.

The matter went on appeal to the High Court and the judge's decision was overruled.

Holman, the member for Grenfell has led us off the track, or road, and we must return. We must leave this town with its undoubted and mysterious charm, which each June, hosts the Henry Lawson Festival of the Arts over a long weekend.

We continued on the Henry Lawson Highway to Forbes and the prospect of a picnic lunch. As we drove into the main street of Forbes our new rental car broke down, and it was a Sunday. Whilst waiting for a replacement machine we had ample time to have our lunch and stroll around the town. The place is remarkable: about a dozen splendid mid to late nineteenth century buildings grouped around a delightful square, with fountain, garden and memorial. The post office is outstanding, the town hall is opulent, Palmers Buildings are splendiferous, the churches are very good, the nineteenth century hotel (one burnt down) is wonderfully authentic, but the treasure of the square is not a Mechanic's Institute or library but…lo and behold, not another grand building, but, the 1920s Literary Institute. Yes, my friends, a literary building of modest demeanour but lofty aspirations.

After a wait of three hours (and I am not complaining for it was a Sunday and it was in the middle of New South Wales) we transferred our luggage to another vehicle and headed for our dinner appointment at Orange.

It was August and they needed rain but the crops were still a deep dark green and the canola the most brilliant yellow, and the hills and mountains were shades of lavender and purple. And we could not bear to drive any faster and we therefore arrived at Orange just on dusk.

The taxi driver who took us to the dinner was a former truckie. I have met some interesting and courteous drivers over the years but this bloke was amongst the best. It was a fare of twelve dollars but nothing was a trouble: he located the house, made certain of it and then drove us right up to their front door. May he continue to drive for many years and may he be showered with generous tips.

Banjo Paterson was born at "Narambla", a station property in the vicinity of Orange but soon after his birth, his parents moved to Illalong, north-west of Yass. His boyhood home was not far from the main Melbourne to Sydney Road, now the Hume Highway.

But the man who was actually born in Orange was the poet and writer Kenneth Slessor (1901–1971), and what a life he lead and what credit he has brought to this old hill town. His father was of German birth (Schloesser), but his mother was born in Australia although her parents were both Scottish immigrants.

After leaving school he took up journalism and lived and worked mainly in Sydney. The harbour features in much of his work including his poetry. The man from Orange is famous for a number of reasons: his poem "Five Bells" (which may have represented the apogee of his poetic powers), his reporting as a war correspondent with the Australian Infantry Force through Greece and the Middle East and back to New Guinea, and his hatred of "the delusions of grandeur of Field Marshall Sir Thomas Blamey" as represented or said to be represented in his poem "An Inscription for Dog River". His reporting of the war ended in 1944 when he resigned his army commission after disagreements with the boys of the military.

It is worthwhile taking a quick look at Slessor's friend Thomas Blamey, born at Lake Albert near Wagga Wagga, and the son of a butcher. Blamey was a Methodist and in his younger days was inspired to preach about God, as depicted by his religion. His earnest lay preaching lead him inevitably towards the ministry, which he almost embraced. The army though was also looking for instructors in its officer class at this crucial time and Blamey saw the financial and other advantages of the military over the church and accordingly seized the opportunity. At the age of twenty-five he married a thirty-four-year-old Melbourne girl, from Toorak, and shortly afterwards the couple went to India where he completed his officer's course. He graduated in 1913 with a pass of B standard and an accompanying report from the commandant which contained these words: "If he [Blamey] is not gifted with a large amount of tact he is not, in any way conspicuously devoid of that very necessary quality."

Blamey soldiered on throughout the First World War including a stint at Gallipoli, and at the end of the war was a Brigadier General. One of his colleagues General Birdwood, is said to have described Blamey thus: "An exceedingly able little man, though by no means of pleasing personality." Oh, those less than ringing endorsements, those qualifications.

Once more in civilian life Blamey applied for and obtained the position of Commissioner of Police for Victoria and once again the record was not quite perfect. His badge was allegedly found in a Melbourne brothel in 1925, but he was able to report that it had been stolen. Then, having once again soldiered on till 1936 he was forced to resign from the Police Force for issuing an untrue statement.

When he was fifty-five the Second World War arrived and Blamey was back into it. In the meantime he had made some good friends including Robert Menzies of Malvern (adjoining Toorak). Blamey served in the Middle East (with Slessor) and apparently his performance was…uneven.

It has been said that he was "rarely able to inspire their — the soldiers — complete loyalty and trust." It was also said that he, unlike Monash, "enjoyed life to the full." The ordinary soldier did not quite share that luxury.

He came back to Melbourne in 1942 and then served with General Macarthur in the Pacific. The General's view of his colleague was, one might say, ambivalent: "sensuously slothful and (of) doubtful character but a tough commander." He further alientated Australian troops in November 1942 when he addressed troops of the 21st Brigade who had survived the retreat along the Kokoda Track and was reported to have said: "It's the rabbit who runs who gets shot, not the man holding the gun."

In fairness to Blamey, one should mention that there were many people, politicians, ministers (of government) and top people in the military who thought well of him and his ability as a commander. It is apparent, however, that his popularity and perhaps, his talents fell short of those of our well-loved Monash.

Kenneth Slessor, the writer, philosopher and poet from Orange and, miles away from him and from near Wagga Wagga, the near Methodist minister, the soldier and policeman Thomas Blamey — Sir Thomas to be sure.

One imagines that Thomas Blamey would have been very proud of his knighthood, as were many other Australians, and yet it is odd: one might also think that a significant percentage of our new settlers came to Australia, *inter alia*, to get away from the suffocating English class, or should it be called, caste, system. We have already seen Wentworth's idiotic notion of a royal hierarchy for Australia and how it was laughed to scorn, and yet there were many Australians who crawled after Pommy honours. There was Blamey's mate Menzies who lifted his chin and announced, "I am British to my boot heels." He also simpered on a visit by Queen Elizabeth 11, "I did but see her passing by, and yet I love her till I die." Then with the prospect of decimal currency he made the suggestion that the denomination be called "Royals". Not Chocolate Royals, *bien sûr.* I dislike our currency being called dollars but perhaps it is a shade better than Royals.

Sir Thomas and Sir Robert (Warden of the Cinque Ports) — quite a pair when you come to reflect on it, and not surprising that they were friends.

We left the heights of Orange on a splendid morning and went due north along the Mitchell Highway. Rain, oh if only they had rain. At that point, it seemed rain was all this country needed to make it a part of paradise.

Molong is famous for the Fairbridge Farm School, which, from 1938 until 1974, held and "cared" for the discarded children from Britain. Hundreds of them. Perhaps one should use the word "infamous", which has a variety of meanings but in this case I would choose "notoriously vile". No matter which way you look at that exercise on the part of the British and the Australians it is hard to see why or how it happened. The fate of those children was in some ways similar to the fate of our Aborigines in the debacle which resulted in the stolen generation.

Banjo Paterson's grandparents (on his mother's side), lived, or perhaps squatted on the very large property known as Boree Nyrang but now known as Nyrang Homestead. The present attractive bluestone building was erected in 1901 and there is no trace of the rather humble dwelling of the Bartons, who were nonetheless quite well-to-do. The old property occupied several thousand acres and was adjacent to the road south from Molong through Boree and Cudal, on your left as you travel north towards Wellington.

It was coffee time when we arrived at Wellington and what splendid coffee we had at the newly renovated café opposite the park. Wellington is, once again, a town of creeks and rivers: Curra Creek, Bell River and, of course, the famous Macquarie River. It has a street called Nanima Crescent and it has a Nanima Reserve and we had missed out in seeing the "Nanima" homestead of the famous French writer Paul Wenz because of our car breakdown in Forbes. His property was and is in the Lachlan Valley, between Cowra and Forbes. I went into the Information Centre and enquired as to the meaning of the word nanima. I was told that it was Aboriginal in origin and that it meant "something that has been lost". It might also mean, the girl added, as an afterthought , "resting place". I prefer the latter.

Wellington has some lovely old buildings including the prominent nineteenth century bank. You need to leave the car and do some walking. We will do that on our next visit but once again we had to journey on. We took the road to our right which leads to Gulgong.

As we drove up a rise not far from the town of Wellington we saw a quite remarkable hill, and part way up the hill an equally remarkable house with a tower rising above the trees. We stopped and I employed the telephoto lens of the camera to have a closer look at the distant house, its garden and tower.

"That house is called 'Nanima'."

Surely not. Was I disoriented?

Was this the Frenchman's house on a hill overlooking

the Macquarie and not the Lachlan? I walked back to the mailbox and the gates. It was certainly "Nanima" and the drive-way and the kurrajongs and she-oaks lining it from the cattle grid and up the hill could be more than a hundred years old. Here was a puzzle. I returned to the car and made up my mind to go up to the house. Yes, I know that it was rude and I realised that it was right on lunch time but if I explained, and apologised, and begged pardons…I got into the car and despite constant protests I drove across the cattle grid. We had crossed the Rubicon. We had done a Caesar-like thing.

The driveway is rocky and steep and leads you into a garden with trees on the perimeter and shrubs and flowers, including roses, around the house. Verandas? Yes, extensive verandas and a large and lovely house of…what period? Certainly not traditional nineteenth century, a touch of the old, but a bold venture into the twentieth.

A dog greeted me barking loudly but not very aggressively. I waited. No one appeared but there was a ute just past the main entrance. I went on to the veranda and rang the bell. More barking but no footsteps. I rang again. No response. I was committed and I therefore walked past the ute, along the gravel path and through the garden and around the back. We had become friends, the dog and I, and he trotted along beside me. I rather wished that he would bark again. A bloke walked out of what I subsequently learned was the kitchen and greeted me with a puzzled and enquiring glance

"Reg Egan," I announced and put out my hand. He took my hand, but more from habit and politeness I thought.

"I'm making lemon syrup," he said and lead me to a huge kitchen with baskets of lemons and basins of citrus-smelling liquid and bottles. A large open pot was simmering and he took a oversized spoon and stirred it and then turned off the flame.

"I'm sorry," I said, "but I didn't quite catch your name."

"Nat Barton." He poured the pot of liquid into a huge jar.

"Nat Barton," I said, "But there's a Barton Street in Wellington and Emily Barton was Banjo Paterson's grandmother and those Bartons lived at Boree Nyrang until Robert died and Banjo went to live with Emily in Sydney when he was in secondary school and…Surely you're not related to that mob of…let me see, the Paterson brothers, of course, and Emily's tribe, the Darvalls, and the Katers and the Smiths and…God, what a tangle. And the properties: Boree Nyrang, Buckinbah, Illalong, Mumblebone, chateaus in the Medoc, your property here at Wellington. It's like a compressed history of grazing, cattle breeding, politics and public company directorships."

"Well, yes, I am more or less a descendant of that mob, as you call them, but I take it that Banjo is the man your want to know about. Am I right? Many's the time Banjo has been under this roof and dined at our table. Come on, I'll show you."

And so this generous and hospitable man showed me, and subsequently us, everything. The ballroom with its fantastic tower, the fireplace where Banjo's height is marked, the books in their hundreds, the amazingly lovely main bedroom, the dining room with its table and rows of chairs, the "private" sitting room and its intimate fireplace, the glorious verandas and the garden overlooking the Macquarie on one side and on the other, in the distance, the town of Wellington which we had just left. Oh, and the grapevine from the Medoc, near Bordeaux, for the Bartons still have relatives amongst the great chateaux of Bordeaux.

What an astonishing and fortuitous visit resulting in memories of Charles Barton, the bank manager of Wellington and builder of "Nanima" back at the turn of the twentieth century, the long-lived and intensely active Annie Barton, his wife (nee Smith), their children Nat Barton, the doctor, and Arthur Dunbar Barton (Dan) — the present Nat's father, the floods, the collapse of the Wellington Bridge, the good times, the droughts... Ah, there is such generosity and hospitality in the world and Nat showed us some that day and subsequently. It is true, people are people everywhere, and it does not take much to bring out those qualities. All you have to do is to speak the language and show your interest.

It was with great reluctance that we turned the car into the driveway, bore right, and resumed our journey to Gulgong at the top of the hill and at the intersection of the Castlereagh Highway.

CHAPTER EIGHT

Alluvial gold is, one need hardly write, gold "left by a flood or flow of water, especially in a river valley". And without having any background in geology I imagine that the gold ore has been gouged out of a reef higher up by rushing torrents of abrasive water and then carried a certain distance before its weight causes it to sink in some flatter part of the stream, be it creek or river.

Gulgong, however, unlike many gold rush towns is built in the hills. It came late in the era. It took off in 1870 and was said to be the last of the small man's gold rush. The town is none the worse for its rather humble beginnings; in fact it has a splendid democratic character about it. We had lunch in its gardens and were entertained by a heavily pregnant mother trying to control her small son. He had picked up a stick which he employed part of the time as a swashbuckling sword, part time as a horse and the rest of the time as a type of plough to be pushed in front of him where it was supposed to jump along in a staccato fashion but more often caught in the grass and speared him in the stomach.

Though our Henry Lawson was born in Grenfell, it was in and around Gulgong that he spent most of his childhood. His father Neils Larsen, a Norwegian sailor who anglicised his name to Peter Lawson, married Louisa Albury of Mudgee (or near Mudgee) and the young couple established themselves at New Pipeclay or Eurunderee well before the Gulgong gold rush. This was a locality well known to Henry's mother and her family.

Peter Lawson made a living by general farming (including vines) and by building. Henry's schooling was late in beginning and, hardly had it begun, when he was struck with deafness. His mother Louisa was, or thought of herself, as something of a "blue stocking", and she eventually tired of the bush life and left Peter and went to live in Sydney, where she became a feminist writer and activist. At the age of sixteen, Henry joined her. He had shaken off the physical presence of the bush, but its memories haunted, or enriched him for the rest of his short life. He died at the age of fifty-five.

It was here at Gulgong, in the sparsely settled and somewhat austere countryside (and the Blue Mountains) that the foundation for Henry's life was laid. And somehow that foundation never supported the uncertainties and difficulties that plagued him in his twenties and thirties. By the time he reached his forties it was all over or nearly so. Did he ever daydream as most children do? Did he laugh and joke and get up to mischief, as he should have done? Or was Henry always solitary, always serious and was he solitary in an anxious way? Tall, thin and in need of alcohol is how one thinks of the adolescent Lawson, the writer: bewildered by a mother who may have found him hard to love or who may have been occupied by her own thoughts. Henry, the adolescent Henry, may have been equally plagued by the cold genes of his northern European father and his fore-bears. And then the deafness. Beethoven was deaf too, and yet…And finally, what about those siblings? It is as if he was an only child.

You can go to the Lawson shelter (built beside the chimney of his old home at Eurunderee), if you wish, but I suggest that you don't. I recommend that you simply stop the car two or three times as you travel to Mudgee and look out across the valley and think of Lawson the writer, the poet and the battler. Likewise, when you go to Sydney you can go and look at Lambert's statue of Henry. George Lambert was a painter who became a sculptor, of moderate ability perhaps. Again I suggest that you do not make a special journey to see the statue. You might be puzzled by Lawson's companionship with the swagman (or sundowner) and you would be astonished by Henry's other companion — a dog. One of Lawsons's biographers Colin Roderick writes of the statue: "A symbolic design based on a concept of Lawson as an habitué of swagmen and — supreme irony! — a dog lover…" So far as I can recall the only dog Lawson wrote about was "The Loaded Dog." How you wish that he had had a dog, and that they had been companions, and how you wish that he had also had a close relationship with his siblings.

Lawson was a man of the city streets — his only outback experience as an adult was north-west of Bourke and that was damn near disastrous. He wrote competently about the working man and mateship and experiences with his father, but he was blind to the simple, though singular, beauty of the bush. He was one of those curious characters who write enthusiastically of their home country when they leave it: when he went to live in New Zealand, or West Australia or England he could hardly wait to get back to Sydney. But when he was back in Sydney he longed for London. "Go back of course I will, eventually, for London calls." London calls, Cambridge calls, Paris calls…but Henry was in Australia.

Henry's occasional mate, or his opposition perhaps, was the lucky, lucky Banjo Paterson and in 1902 Banjo wrote the poem "The Old Australian Ways" which sums up his attitude to foreigners such as the English. Here is a verse:

> The narrow ways of English folk
> Are not for such as we;
> They bear the long-accustomed yoke
> Of staid conservancy:
> But all our roads are new and strange
> And through our blood there runs
> The vagabonding love of change
> And westward of the suns.

It must be emphasised however, that Henry was not the first, or the last, to write nostalgically about his homeland from overseas. One could name at least three contemporary writers who indulge themselves in a similar way; and to be fair, it sometimes takes a trip or an enforced absence for us to realise the good fortune we enjoy at home. In Lawson's case, though, it seemed to occur and re-occur throughout his adult life. Perhaps a similar vein can be seen in his relationships with women.

Lawson's work is predominantly about Australia and it is written in the special language of the ordinary Australian

of the end of the nineteenth century. It was maybe, the apo-
theosis of the trend that started with the poets Harpur and
Kendall "to animate (their) country with speech and song".
And to do this they had to find Australian words for "English"
words like "dell and glade and field and village". All of these
words, and many more belonged and still belong to England
and its special Englishness. They do not have a place in the
glaring light of our southern land.

Henry Lawson was associated with numerous places and
towns in Australia — Mallacoota, Mudgee, Leeton, Sydney,
Melbourne and Grenfell of course — but to me Gulgong and
its surrounds were and always remain the town and the locality that best express his philosophy, his life and his writing.

We did as we should and we stopped from time to time
on our journey to Mudgee in the south, and looked out
across the hills and saw the lower slopes of the Great Dividing
Range and the Wollemi National Park and once or twice as
in a mirage I thought I saw that tall thin and troubled writer
with his uncomprehending eyes. Henry…to have come so
close, and to see it all turn to ashes. And your commemorative statue…Oh dear, oh dear.

Mudgee is worth a look, my God it is. I have heard it said
that Mudgee is overdone with its ridiculously wide streets
(avenues), laid out by Robert Hoddle incidentally, and its
grandiose historical buildings and its pretention. No, I cannot agree. I think Mudgee is a delight.

Mudgee has a "Camping Tree" — camped under by some
of the town's first white settlers, George and Henry Cox in
1822, sons of the famous road builder William Cox. It also
has the Cudgegong River which flows to the Burrendong
Dam and it has, or rather had, the Shires of Meroo and
Cudgegong and the Malakoff Reservoir. All in all a pretty

good start. What else? Well, William Lawson the explorer was in and about the district, and Adolphus George Taylor, who was born there in 1857 and died at age of forty-three.

Adolphus may have been a mere teacher and a journalist and his roots may have been in Mudgee and Bathurst but by the time he was thirty-four he was editor of the famous (or infamous) rag called *Truth*, then a Sydney weekly. He was best known as "The Mudgee Camel". But when he was only in his early twenties he was in the New South Wales parliament, the Legislative Assembly, as the senior member for Mudgee. Prior to being a Member of Parliament he had been in the army and had been gaoled for six months for insubordination (and yet he got into parliament). It has been said by the provocative writer Cyril Pearl that Adolphus was "a rowdy, alcoholic radical, anti-squatter, and anti-monarchist and sometimes an admirable champion of the poor and friendless…"

Taylor was frequently ejected from the New South Wales parliament and on one occasion the Speaker, the exasperated Edmund Barton (who went on to become the first Prime Minister of Australia and later, a High Court Judge) suspended him for a week "for persistently and wilfully obstructing the business of the House". Before his suspension had expired Taylor re-appeared in the House and asserted that he had "a right to speak". Barton had him ejected by the Sergeant-at-Arms. Taylor then issued a writ against Barton in the Supreme Court, claiming wrongful expulsion, damages for assault et cetera. And he won, and was awarded one thousand pounds and costs.

Barton appealed the decision to the Privy Council and Taylor then announced that he would journey to England and put his case himself. He raised the expenses of the trip to London by lecturing in New South Wales on "The Iron Hand in Politics". Taylor was accompanied on this trip, it was said, by the missus, his mother and his favourite cocka-too, "Billings". The remarkable thing is that their lordships listened to Taylor with respect and that Barton's appeal was rejected and Taylor was awarded costs, and even more re-markable, that he refused to enforce the claim for his one thousand pounds: "I will not take it out of the pockets of the people of New South Wales."

Taylor was a "lean gangling fellow, over six feet tall". I cannot quite see the connection with a camel but there it is. Taylor was succeeded in due course by John Norton, as editor and proprietor of Truth and in some way Adolphus may have influenced the stylish (!) prose and the alliterations of his notorious successor. Here is a sample of Taylor's ef-fort: "In religion cant reigns supreme, in politics, self seeking, cloaked by patriotic platitudes and even science is perverted and prostituted by plausible quackery." And to think that this man once represented the elegant, nineteenth century town and the famous twenty-first century wine town of Mudgee.

You can start your buildings tour of Mudgee anywhere — up on the hill outside the "Mudgee Public School and residence" 1876, for example. What an absolutely striking pair of buildings these are and what credit they do to the education department of those days. I do not know if they are as functional as today's buildings but their exterior does something for the heart and soul.

Or you can go down Perry Street past the gardens and shake your head in wonder at the monumental and no doubt very costly post office. Why spend so much on a mere post office? The Catholic church dominates (yet again) the main street, Market Street, and beside it is the impeccable 1850s presbytery. The Anglican church (1860) is not as striking as St Mary's but it has a charm and a homeliness which is appealing. The façade of the shops on one side of Market Street is most impressive and…well, you can stroll and explore and wander around Mudgee and you can look and ruminate and wonder whether "The Camel" once walked and pondered as you are doing. Mudgee has a Byron Lane Place, a Lawson Street, of course, a Flirtation Hill Lookout and a bloody good spot or spots, perhaps, for breakfast.

CHAPTER NINE

Lithgow is famous for its coal, no doubt, and for the Olympic runner Marjorie Jackson, who won two gold medals in the 1952 Olympics and was known as the Lithgow Flash. She went on to become Governor of South Australia from 2001 to 2007. Marjorie was actually born at Coffs Harbour in 1931 but her family moved south to Lithgow when she was a child and naturally, Lithgow has claimed her.

It is also famous for John Whitton's Zig Zag railway, which was developed from 1857–1890 but this picturesque marvel was made redundant by the new line and its extensive tunnels which were completed by 1910. The old Zig Zag is now a tourist attraction. We confined ourselves to a picnic lunch in a park looking down on the rooftops in the valley and up towards Mt Victoria.

The Blue Mountains are spectacular whether viewed from the west or the east and on the road up you must resist the temptation to drive on to get there. Instead you should stop and look. The once thriving town of Hartley is on your right and is almost deserted, and it is a place to stop for. The buildings that are left are graceful, although somewhat humble reminders of our past, and the pity is that their age is beginning to weary them. I think that we should re-double our efforts to look after these interesting and historic structures.

We arrived at Mt Victoria in time for coffee and found a spot to park outside the Imperial Hotel (1875), a very imposing and impressive building with furniture to match its age. The parapets are unusual as is the wing to the side, added later I would think.

We had booked two night's accommodation at Katoomba and although the afternoon was beginning to slip away we thought that there would be no harm in a little detour, or two — as it turned out. As we drove through Blackheath we could not resist a sign on our left which directed us to go to Evans Falls. Naturally we would have to tread in the footsteps of the man who went the whole distance, the man really who opened up the west.

We parked the car by the lookout and I reread the sign. It was not *the* Evans, no, it was a local solicitor by that name. Disappointed I trudged down to the guard rails, gripped the iron piping and looked out. I have heard often enough that such and such is "breathtaking". I tell you that this was the first time I have experienced the literal meaning of that overused word: your stomach draws in until it meets your backbone and for a split second you feel that you are being sucked over the guard rail and into the abyss. But what an abyss. Perhaps it was the time of day, late afternoon. Perhaps it was the subtle smoky blue haze, but either way it was quite wonderful. Certainly one of the most startlingly beautiful views I have ever seen.

You can go for walks from here along rough but adequate bush tracks and I think one of those walks goes to Govett's Leap, and you can, I believe, ride your horse somewhere as well. The bush…how is it that some of the newcomers to Australia take a while to see the bush? Ah, it is diverse, colourful, angular, stark. It is full of character. I spent a long time leaning on that railing and thanking God for what he (or it) had achieved. And reluctantly thanking that local solicitor for his acumen.

Oh, yes there certainly is something about this escarpment and its creeks and the Grose River in the broad valley, and all the Lookouts: Victoria Falls and Pulpit Rock and Cripps and Govetts. And I knew quite a lot about two blokes connected with Govetts. So I wondered as I began walking to the north along a rough and rocky bush track, I wondered if I had time to walk to Govetts and back. It is about six kilometres, all told; roughly the same distance as a tramp around a golf course.

The track veered away from the cliffs and up a small hill. At the top of the hill there was a pile of huge rocks artistically placed and surrounded by banksia; and so I sat down. Instead of walking I would think.

William Romaine Govett was born in 1807 at Tiverton, an inland town in one of England's largest counties, Devon. The county was famous for its tin, its wool and to an extent for its bleakness. William's father was a surgeon, and one assumes, quite well off. William, the third child, went to a local school until he was thirteen, but did not go on to any tertiary studies. Presumably William's parents knew or obtained some sort of introduction to Thomas Mitchell, the former Scott who came to Australia in 1826 and achieved fame here as an explorer (best known in Victoria as Major Mitchell) and, to an extent, as Surveyor-General of New South Wales. They, therefore, secured for William, the unqualified young man, a surveyor's job with Mitchell and William arrived here in December 1826.

Mitchell, in a report done some time after William had worked in his department for a few years, described him as "a wild young man who needed control" but who was nonetheless "perhaps the ablest delineator of ground in the department and…was remarkably clever at dealing with unexplored country". Pretty high praise. One of William's assignments was to produce a plan of the country around and in the vicinity of the Bells Line of Road, the wonderfully named major road than runs from North Richmond to Bell in the Blue Mountains, and in his report to Mitchell he was lyrical about "the bold broken nature of the country (and the streams that) arrive at the cliffs of the main channel where they fall in cascades…"

William's love of the bush, his enthusiasm and his descriptions in his reports impressed Mitchell so much that he insisted on naming that particular part of the escarpment in the young William Romaine Govett's honour. Mitchell, one assumes added the word "Leap" (Scottish for waterfall) as a touch of nostalgia for his birthplace.

Sadly, the department had to institute some cuts in its activities in 1833 and William was made redundant. He returned to Tiverton where he wrote, and had published, some articles on New South Wales and he supported those articles with very competent paintings. He died in London in 1848 aged only forty-one. I would like to know more about this talented young man. You cannot help but wonder. Was he a remittance man?

And the other man connected with Govett's Leap was an Australian, Vere Gordon Childe, born in Sydney in 1892.

Gordon Childe, as he was known, did post-graduate studies in Oxford and obtained a B.Litt. and a B.A. in 1916 and 1917. He returned to Australia and was appointed a senior resident tutor at Sydney University's St. Andrew's College. He made the mistake of speaking at a pacifist meeting in 1918 and was told he must resign his post. He did so and was then refused an Ancient History position. It sounds extraordinary but it happened.

Gordon Childe was as man of exceptional abilities even on the world stage, especially in history and archaeology and he lectured at Edinburgh University for just on twenty years. He was also a linguist and a writer: *The Dawn of European Civilization* (1925), *Man Makes Himself* (1951) and others.

In 1957 at the age of sixty-five Childe, fearing the diminution of his mental faculties, went over Govett's Leap, and of course, fell to his death. One hopes that his mind was flooded for an instant with the sensation of effortless flight and that he was suffused with the beauty of this wonderful corner of the Blue Mountains.

As I walked back towards the car park, I also thought of a relatively unknown writer who was born in this general area in 1903 and became famous for things other than literature. His name was Bernard O'Reilly and he is best remembered firstly as the man who lone-handed found a lost and crashed single-engine passenger plane in the Lamington Plateau in Queensland in 1937 and saved two survivors, and secondly, as one of the O'Reilly family who founded and ran the O'Reilly's Guest House at the Green Mountains not far from the plateau and roughly of the same latitude as Coolangatta.

Bernard was born in a "slab house on Long Swamp Creek", not far from, and to the east of Jenolan Caves and within hearing distance of Cox's River, especially when it was in flood. The O'Reillys lived very much in the bush and even the Blackheath of the early 1900s was a strange and exotic place to the family. By today's standards they were isolated and poor and yet Bernard had nothing but love for his life there in the bush. Despite his subsequent fame and despite the success of the family in its Queensland ventures, it was often that his dreams returned to this remote high, cold, wet and sometimes hot part of the wild Blue Mountains. Bernard loved everything about the area but he had a particular affection for our Australian birds.

"Wild birds," Bernard wrote, "were the greatest joy of my boyhood. Wild birds… are I think the most beautiful of living things; the most sweet voiced and the gentlest of creatures."

We returned to the Western Highway and continued on towards Katoomba with the extensively and expensively "being renovated" Hydro Majestic Medlow Bath on our right and then the Explorer's Tree, also on our right. When we arrived at our destination in Katoomba, they took our bags and they took our car keys and our car (and later our money) and we warmed our bums in front of a welcoming open fire before we went up to our room.

There was just time to dash down to The Three Sisters before the dusk began to obscure the view. Near our hotel there was rather a good bronze of convicts making supervisor Cox's road, the road that opened the minds and hearts of thousands of immigrants: the road to Bathurst and beyond.

The Blue Mountains can lay claim to many writers, artists and poets — more than thirty according to John Low, an erudite historian. There is the famous Eleanor Dark (1901–85) who although born in Sydney spent most of her life in the Mountains and whose home is now the Varuna Writers' Retreat, Sumner Elliott, 1917–1991 (he became an American citizen though), Colleen McCulloch, born in the little river town of Wellington in 1937, who apparently set her *The Ladies of Missalonghi* (1987) in the "Upper mountains", and there is the multi-talented Norman Lindsay.

Norman was born at Creswick in Victoria in 1879 and despite ill health lived to the venerable age of ninety. All of his nine siblings also seem to have been talented in one way or another and it did not take long until Norman's was realized: when he was only nineteen J. F. Archibald of the Bulletin gave him a job as a cartoonist. Sydney seemed to be where the action was and so Norman moved there. Within a few years the very young Lindsay and his equally young wife had separated, were divorced and the artist Norman was heavily involved with his erstwhile model Rose Soady.

In 1911 the new couple moved to Leura in the Blue Mountains and then to the house now known as "Springwood" at Faulconbridge (next to the locality known as Springwood). Norman lived out there on the edge of the bush for the rest of his long life. Norman was certainly the most commercially successful of the Lindsay artist tribe and yet there is a lot to be said for his brother Lionel and his artistic sister Ruby who married cartoonist Will Dyson and who died tragically in the influenza epidemic which followed the First World War.

I went to "Springwood" and walked its grounds to look at Norman's cement statues, the photographs of which I had seen in books. I found it hard to be excited about them and I regret to write that my long held assessment of the man returned to haunt me — he was ambivalent towards women. He had a tendency to draw women as muscular harlots.

As to his *Magic Pudding* (1918) — superb, wonderful and without doubt one of the great Australian books. Had I been his editor, however, I would have cut it down a bit — 171 pages for a bedtime story, now really. Certainly it would have lasted most sleepy children right through the winter months.

We drove to Glenbrook (almost, well vaguely, overlooking Sydney) and then we did a u-turn and re-traversed the road to lovely Bathurst. There is no doubt about those three blokes and Evans the fourth: they chose the best possible route across the chasms and cliffs of the Blue Mountains. If you had gone up in a helicopter and inspected the area you could not have done better. Compare, for instance, this rather gentle drive with the winding, tortuous but spectacular route along the King's Highway from Batemans Bay to Canberra. No wonder the Canberrans entertain themselves in the capital or in the two historic towns of Bungendore and Braidwood.

CHAPTER TEN

We arrived at Bathurst just in time to dump the luggage in our room and get down to the shopping area for a stroll in central park: Machattie Park. We had a glimpse of the astonishing Court House and we also had time to stop outside our restaurant for a quick inspection. While we were waiting to cross the road on our way back, we were privileged to receive advice from two local…Christians, I suppose, one of whom gazed intently at me, wagged his finger and said, "Repent, and turn to God." We turned in the direction of our motel and its hot shower.

Bathurst, named after Earl of Bathurst, Secretary for the Colonies, even today is a town of moderate size (37,000 odd), but its 1880 court house is stupendous. When I first viewed it I was impressed but the next morning when I saw it clearly, I was staggered. Were they attempting to outdo Versailles? Oh, it is magnificent. Without

doubt it is "neo-classical in style" and I would also agree with the guidebooks that it has "Renaissance elements". Why? Why? Why this magnificent building erected here one hundred and thirty years ago in the days of bullocks and horses and wagons. Good luck and congratulations to Bathurst and its citizens and their brick and stone building in the park.

Also in the park is that westward facing statue of the renowned George Evans (1775–1852). George was born in England but in 1802 at the age of twenty-seven he showed his innate wisdom and came to Australia. He did go "home" after he retired as a surveyor but once again returned to Australia, to Tasmania, where he remained until his death at the age of seventy-seven. Now, we all know about the famous trio of Blaxland, Lawson and Wentworth (son of D'Arcy) and how they crossed the Blue Mountains in 1813 but, really, the job was only half done. It was the young Evans and his party who did the whole job. Evans was the first white man to gaze across and marvel at, the expanse of the western plains. And what his gaze encompassed: tall grass, trees, hills, valleys, parkland without limit.

Evans later familiarized himself with much of this western part of New South Wales including, of course, the Lachlan and Macquarie Rivers and it is to the credit of the people of Bathurst that they should have erected this delightful statue, and that the mere names of the famous three are acknowledged at the base of the statue in small letters. Evans has his head up but his companion is shading his eyes and both of them are looking into the western sun. There is also a bloke with a sheaf of hay and a lass with her top off, but they are placed one each side and in the background, as it were. Evans and his Aboriginal mate are the stars, as they deserve to be.

There are other things in this excellent park including All

Saints Cathedral, built in 1848 and designed by the famous architect Edmund Blackett. The cathedral is not actually in the park but it overlooks it, and it has a full complement of bells, and when they ring or even chime those bells, the sound floats through the park and its gardens and paths. So… the bells make the cathedral part of the park. The bells were expensive in the first place and were cast in London. Their frequent ringing and vibrations were blamed for cracks in the tower of the cathedral. In 1970 the tower had to be demolished, and the bells which had been stored, were then sent back to England for re-tuning. They (and some new ones) have now been returned and are in place in the renovated tower. I am pleased to report, they have again been rung, and there are not yet any cracks in the new tower.

Bells have been around for thousands of years and although I had heard them rung in Australia, it was not until we first went to France that I really fell in love with their marvellous and complex music. Bells and cathedrals, bread and cheese, wine and olive oil… The Chinese, my Brittanica says, "rang bells to communicate directly with the spirits," and in Catholicism "bells have symbolized paradise and the voice of God".

There is one final statue in the gardens near William Street and it is a memorial to those New South Welshmen and Australians who fought in the cruel and largely unjust Boer Wars (1880–1881 and 1899–1902). I found it ironic that the controversial Kitchener (1850–1916), the somewhat callous conqueror of the Sudan, did not unveil the statue until 1910. Did it take that long for Australians to get the sour taste of the man out of their mouths?

Alan Moorehead, the prolific Australian writer, has cast some doubts on the British hero Kitchener, Horatio Herbert,

First Earl of Khartoum, the man whose moustachioed image appeared in the recruiting posters in the First World War above the caption, "Your country needs you!"

He writes of Kitchener: "In Cairo he was regarded as a snob…He showed no interest in the welfare of his soldiers… His attitude to the wounded Arabs was to say the least, one of indifference: they were left on the battlefield to die…The Mahdi himself was dug up…the head was severed and this was purloined by Kitchener as a trophy of war… (A Mahdi (in) Muslim belief is a spiritual and temporal leader who will rule before the end of the world and restore religion and justice.)" One Muhammad Ahmad had claimed this title and had lead the revolutionary armies a few years prior to Kitchener's little foray on behalf of the British.

The Mahdi and his forces had captured Khartoum in 1885 and had killed and then beheaded the much loved British General Charlie Gordon. Kitchener might have had this in mind when he had the Mahdi's head severed and brought to him. The Mahdi, to complete the picture, had not died in battle but of typhus late in 1885.

Kitchener himself had an easy death when a warship taking him to Russia was sunk by a mine during the First World War.

Australia's vision of that Great War owes much to Charles (or Charlie) Bean, who was born in Bathurst in 1879 but went "home" as a child of ten. He was educated in England and then studied law and classics at Oxford at the turn of the twentieth century. We thought we had lost him to the English but he came back to Australia and was admitted to the New South Wales Bar. Then, remarkable though it was, he joined the *Sydney Morning Herald* as a journalist in 1908 and he became a wandering outback reporter, and more importantly he re-became an Australian.

In 1910 he had his *On the Wool Track* published and in 1911 *The Dreadnought of the Darling*, and both books are still classics today. He was an official war correspondent with the Australian Infantry Force throughout the First World War and later became our war historian with twelve volumes produced over a period of twenty-three years (six by Bean personally). His *History of Australia at War 1914–1918* has played a substantial part in propagating the Anzac legend.

Bean could have remained in England but he was drawn back to his homeland and its dry and hot plains, "the back country" as he called it. He maintained that "out-back hospitality sets the ideal for the Australian". He goes on to assert that "the strongest article in the out-back is that of loyalty to a mate." That article has lasted for a hundred years and one hopes that it is now ineradicable.

Bean, the war correspondent, faced some trenchant criticism from the diggers when they were training, and misbehaving, in Egypt prior to going into action, but in the end he earned their respect and their admiration. He was indeed a loyal and true Australian.

Bean was to a large extent the driving force behind our Australian War Memorial at Canberra but of war itself he had this to say: " it [war] should not be glorified but these who died fighting for their country should be remembered."

William Cox, although born in England in 1764, is worth a mention as a Bathurst boy. He was the man who built, or rather supervised, the building of the road over the Blue Mountains in 1814, and was, therefore, responsible for the opening of the great expanses to the west of the ranges. Cox and a team of twenty-eight convict labourers put through that road in six months and earned their freedom along with that incomparable view.

Cox was given a grant of land near Bathurst for his skill and dedication, but lived most of his life near Windsor. He died in 1837 and his narrative of the background of the famous road was published in 1888.

★ ★ ★ ★

On the morning we were due to depart from Bathurst I left the comfort of our apartment on the flat ground not far from the well-kept railway station and I climbed the wonderful hill that allows you to look down on the city.

Near the top of the hill is a magnificent school with large grounds securely fenced in black wrought iron. A private school no doubt, built with the money of rich Bathurstites. I walked one boundary, turned and went up the equally long side boundary to a pair of heavy gates — locked. I did want to get in. It was only seven-thirty. No one would be around. I took my camera off my shoulder and stood there tapping one foot and wondering. From the corner of my eye I saw a small truck pull up and park.

A youngish and athletic man came up to me and said, "What's the trouble mate?"

"I want to get in and take some photos of this lovely building."

"Why?"

"I'm a writer from Melbourne…"

"All right," he said and put out his hand, "I'm Rocky the caretaker. Come with me."

He told me, as we walked around the grounds and then explored the main building finishing in the hall on the third floor, that he had been born in Wilcannia. Now we know that Wilcannia is one hundred and ninety-five kilometres east of Broken Hill and well to the south-west of Bourke and that it is definitely in the outback.

"I used to be a boxer. You've got to be tough to live at Wilcannia," he said.

Rocky was proud of his school and his responsibilities and remarkably…it was not a rich man's school. It was the Bathurst High School built in 1923 and a credit to the people of New South Wales and Bathurst. It needs money spent on the building and the grounds but it is a great complex.

Bathurst was also the home of Ben Chifley, Prime Minister from 1945 to 1949 and one of Australia's best-loved Prime Ministers.

Bathurst has history and a certain elegance, despite its annual motor racing event. It is situated on, or just off, the good old Macquarie River and it hosted the 1896 People's Convention for the proposed federation of Australia. Oh, and it was also the national head office for Cobb and Co. What more could you want?

Cowra is on the Mid-Western Highway and the Lachlan River and perhaps its modern claim to fame is the quelling of the breakout of the Japanese prisoners of war in 1944. The camp held some one thousand prisoners and in a well-planned mass breakout, two hundred and thirty-one were killed along with four Australian soldiers. It was unfortunate but what would I have done, what would any of us done had we been a soldier on guard at that time? What a massacre. But, that was almost seventy years ago and in the years since the most wonderful memorial Japanese Garden has been created. It is open to the public and you simply *must* go and walk through it. I have admired gardens in Japan, including one or two famous ones in Tokyo, but have seen nothing to touch this marvellous creation.

The trees, shrubs and plants in this heavenly garden are just right for the area and underline the superb classical design, but the use of the existing rocks and trees was inspirational. There are many parts of New South Wales where the tops of the hills are crowned with the most wonderful rocks and trees and the architects here have made perfect use of these features, and have brought in a few truckloads of boulders and rocks as well. There is water, pebbly streams, ponds, rushes, fish and there is a small but very good café. Well done and doubly well done in terms of healing old wounds and fostering understanding and friendship between two very different countries.

Cowra is not large but it is worth a one-day stay and a walk along the serene banks of the Lachlan in the dappled shade of the river red gums. And if you are continuing south, as we were, you should also stop and linger over Evans the surveyor's garden by the river.

It is hard not to wax lyrical about so much of this Central West area in New South Wales and perhaps we saw it as its best: no floods, no drought, and no scorching heat. But it is a beautiful drive between Cowra and Yass, with the Lachlan away on your left across the flats, the tree lined creeks in the foreground, the rolling hills with their cluster of rocks and trees on top, the merino sheep, the grain crops, and the relative scarcity of traffic. Altogether a memorable one hundred and thirty kilometre meander down to the town of Yass.

CHAPTER ELEVEN

Yet again we were late in arriving at our destination, due in part to a very informative and lengthy conversation with a bloke, a stranger, we met by chance at Boorowa, but there was still time to walk along the main street as far as the Court House and then to the bridge over the strongly flowing Yass River. I turned and looked at the Court House and I wondered for the hundredth time how it was that so much money was spent on the administration of justice. The court houses of the gold rush era vie with the churches and cathedrals in their splendour. Was it for the same reason: to dominate and cower the people? A most impressive building for a town of some twelve or thirteen thousand people today.

There are a number of graceful verandas in Comur Street, the main street, but the building to warm the heart of any Australian is the 1869 Mechanics Institute guarded by its two kangaroos mounted on sturdy columns on each side of the pediments. You can travel around Australia and see all sorts of decorations on Victorian era buildings including urns, griffins, dragons, classical busts, et cetera but when did you last see two kangaroos? Good on the Mechanics Institute and its altruistic aims — the roos are still admired today and are, I am told, the delight of visiting schoolchildren. The building is very well maintained and is now a doctor's surgery.

When we returned to Melbourne I made some telephone enquiries about our sentinel marsupials and a very obliging lady from the Yass Historical Society gave me some more information, courtesy of the bloke who recently painted the building. He was a European from Canberra and he went to some trouble to restore the 'roos. He maintains that they are metal models encased in a concrete shell. It seems that some of the concrete had cracked off one of the ears. He first carefully repaired the beasts, filled the crack and then painted them. I am impressed by a tradesman of that calibre.

There is a Memorial Park in Yass not far from the main street and there is a statue in memory of that local boy Banjo Paterson. It has been very well done with his poems in raised bronze plaques — expensive and impressive. There is also a concrete bust of the poet which looked out of place and on enquiry I was told that the original bronze had to be removed to the library because of vandalism. I hang my head in shame that that is so. When you walk around Yass you know that you are walking where our great balladist once strolled, or I suppose more realistically rode either on his horse or in his car, for Banjo died only in 1941.

The staff in the dining room of our motel, last night and again this morning, could not have been friendlier or more obliging but the size of dinner was intimidating.

The man on the table next to us on receiving his meal

looked desperately at the waitress and said, "God, I can't eat all that — please…"

"Yes, you can," she replied, touching him on the arm and moving off towards the kitchen.

He squared his shoulders and he attacked the formidable mountain of rump steak and prawns and potatoes and salad and… Brave man, brave man.

"Appetite comes with eating", as I was told firmly by a Brunhilde Lufthansa flight attendant on our first overseas trip. It may, but it could not successfully grapple with the task set out for our gallant companion that night.

The next morning we journeyed to Wee Jasper — Man From Snowy River country. Well, the Monaro Tablelands and the Snowy River are only over the hill. It happened to be a morning that was absolutely perfect for our trip: cool to cold, a heavy dew, a few clouds, the faintest of breezes and a promise of sun later in the day. I stopped the car some distance to the west of the Murrumbidgee. Well away on my right was the Burrinjuck Dam and there ahead to my left was Mount Narrangullen and again in the distance was the Brindabella National Park. Great country - rolling hills, river flats and the freshness and the mauve of the mystery of the mountains.

A breeze I said, no, it was a little wind and it carried to me from the sky the song of a lark. I looked up and finally saw him. You could just discern the rapid fluttering of its tiny wings and then he fell silent as he dropped like a stone, arrested his fall, circled and landed out in the paddock. The carolling of a magpie reached me from some hidden tree and then I saw high above a nearby hill a hawk circling slowly, its wings stretched out tight. The only animals were two horses down towards a creek. There were no cars, for the moment, just space, countryside and those few sounds. Banjo Paterson may not have made a commercial success of his large grazing property out here, but he must have had some wonderful moments. That man, he had everything — the city, the country, overseas travel, a profession, talent, horses and…a grandmother, who was well-to-do and a poet, and — he had a dog! Oh, and a wife and children.

I started to walk back to the car and then stopped. If you shielded your eyes and then looked far into the distance across the Burrinjuck Dam, slightly west of north, you might almost see "Illalong", Banjo's childhood home. I determined to go there despite the fact that we would be crossing and re-crossing our tracks two or three times. We would take in Bookham too, where Banjo had won a couple of horse races.

Bookham is now just off the busy Hume Highway and when we arrived there we saw that it was…derelict. Oh, the disappointment. It has a worm farm, to be sure, a classic Australian homestead which someone is trying to restore, a type of milk bar cum café, a church on the hill and hundreds of rusting steam engines and farm machinery, but no racecourse.

Sorrowfully we took the rather lovely road to Binalong and stopped at the Royal Tara Motel to enquire about the locals, the historic racecourses and the exact location of the pastoral property of Illalong.

Binalong is worth a long and a leisurely walk. It is scattered now and I suppose it will never be a bustling town again but… Canberrans must, or should come here for a weekend. It certainly has a good food reputation. You wish you could compress it: move all the buildings together in the old part near the historic railway station. The Catholic church sits remotely and forlornly up on the hill and Banjo's father lies quietly in the nearby cemetery. What industry could we suggest for Binalong?

We turned around and went back to the side road and through the loveliest gum trees along a quiet road that leads to the Illalong Station on the Illalong Creek. The property is just short of the bridge on your left and the old quarry is up on the hill on your right. The very welcoming Grogans now own the somewhat smaller acreage that the property once encompassed in Banjo's time and the house is set in a lovely garden where a wisteria planted by Banjo's mother still blooms in the early spring. Alas the present house was built in 1929 beside where the old house of stringybark slabs and timber used to be. Michael Grogan, incidentally, described to me the use of stringybark as a roofing material. You skin or de-bark a good size tree, cut the bark to size, soak it well and then put in on the roof with heavy weights on it to flatten the bark.

Michael says the creek, the Illalong Creek is magical — it was to him, it has been to his children and it was to Paterson. The creek meanders through gums of yellow box, white box and the occasional red box and the creek itself and the coarse grass, the bushes and the trees would not have changed since Banjo's days.

As we passed through Yass (yet again) on our way to Goulburn I thought about another poet, a man whose po-etry, according to the Oxford Companion to Australian Literature, is "simple…centred on the Irish-Australian-Catholic rural communities", poetry which was very much favoured by my non-Irish mother and read to us religiously (!) on the winter evenings around a roaring open fire such as only my father could make and maintain.

The poetry collected in a volume called *Around the Boree*

Log and other Verses was the work of a Catholic priest Patrick Hartigan (pen name John O'Brien) born in Yass in 1878, fourteen years after Banjo's birth. Hartigan's ballads are not dissimilar to Paterson's and whilst they may not be of a high literary calibre they held some wonderful memories for me. The school described in the poem "The Old Bush School" was in many respects quite similar to the one I attended in Tolmie in the 1940s. I recollect that the average number of students to crowd into that sumptuous weatherboard and galvanized iron edifice was about sixteen. The school had been built in the early 1900s, and was shifted in the thirties by a bullock team to Mahaikah, which is often thought of as being part of Tolmie.

Great memories of the "simple" poetry, the bush school and the quite wonderful teachers, many of them having just graduated. When I look back and reflect that some were girls of twenty or so yet they were content to board in an old farmhouse, walked to the school, supervised children from four to fifteen, chopped wood, lit fires, treated sick students…and seemed always to be smiling.

★ ★ ★ ★

We got to Goulburn in time for afternoon coffee. I always think of Goulburn as a sister city to Bathurst, I don't know why. It was founded before Bathurst because they did not have to cross the dreaded cliffs of the Blue Mountains but its population is about twenty-five per cent less.   It has a court house which resembles that of Bathurst but it is not within coo-ee of the palace of the north. On the other hand, I would think that it has always been adequate for Goulburn's peaceful and law-abiding citizens. It is situated by a park, a small and charming park called Belmore Park. The park is a touch unusual in as much as it has an attractive fountain built and donated by the Temperance Society and — the fountain was dry. And it may not be relevant but there is a very good bakery nearby which sells excellent croissants. Goulburn has a stunning post office in the main street, and once again you marvel at the resources, the money that was available for such a building: the clock tower is quite magnificent. The 1870s Town Hall is cumbersome but the churches, that is a story.

The Catholics built their green stone cathedral on the hill but despite the exclusiveness of their material they were definitely trumped by the Anglicans: there the magnificent structure of St Saviour stands (St Saviour?), dominating the hill and plainly visible along a wide avenue leading up from the main street, and designed by none other than the famous Edmund Blackett. Well done Anglicans, and well done also in raising the money to complete the tower.

Unfortunately all was not plain sailing in the new cathedral because of a little fracas between its sole trustee a Mr. Rossi, or M. Rossi or Captain Rossi and the Archdeacon Puddicombe and Bishop Thomas and some of the more notable parishioners. Matters came to a head in 1884 and involved "court actions, newspaper controversies and synod debates". Captain Rossi had a bit of clout; son-in-law of the local minister Parson Sowerby (an Englishman from Cumberland who was said "to have an honest face"). Rossi was also Registrar of the District Court of Goulburn and... captain of the Goulburn Volunteer Rifles. And his wife (Sowerby's daughter) laid the cornerstone of the cathedral in 1870, "for the glory of God and the benefit of His church".

Despite his prestige and power Captain Rossi was told by Bishop Thomas and his supporters to remove a Rossi family tablet that he had erected in the cathedral. He refused and furthermore he stayed in the cathedral and mounted guard over his tablet. Thomas's supporters blockaded the doors of the cathedral in an attempt to starve him out but Rossi's supporters poked a siphon through the keyhole of the back door (and was there holy water, one wonders?). The battle ebbed and flowed whilst God stood to one side and watched with amusement as did Livingstone Hopkins (Hop) of the redoubtable *Bulletin*, that lovely old pink covered Australian weekly. The dispute and court cases over it were not resolved until 1891.

You may think that Rossi rather over-emphasized his importance: Captain of the Goulburn Volunteer Rifles, et cetera, but the bloke had an impressive background. He was born in 1823 at Port Louis, Mauritius, came to New South Wales with his parents in 1825, lived at "Rossiville," a country estate acquired by his family, was educated at The Kings School, Parramatta and was a descendant of a noble Corsican family — in fact he became Comte Rossi in 1896 on the death of an uncle. Unfortunately the church dispute was the first in a long line of disputes and court cases, which ultimately ruined him. On his downward journey he lost the family property "Rossiville", lost the wife who divorced him in 1892 and he died in 1903 childless, friendless (except for the second wife) and broke. *C'est la vie, peut être*.

When you stroll through the park in Goulburn you should spare a few thoughts for our friend that wonderful Australian who was born here in 1865, Mary Jean Cameron. She was a thinker, a poet, a writer, a teacher, a democrat and she is better known by her married name of Gilmore: Dame Mary Gilmore. And why she accepted that spurious honour is quite beyond me. She was seventy-two years old when it was conferred on her, and who knows, it may have been a low point in her life, yet it is said that she cherished the award. All I can say is that we cherish Mary.

She was born near Goulburn of Celtic parents, her father a native of Inverness on the east coast of Scotland and her mother from County Armagh in the north of Ireland. Armagh was the seat of the kings of Ulster and had Saint Patrick as its archbishop (AD 445), so Mary had some historic blood in her veins, and some wandering blood too, as demonstrated in her childhood when the family moved back and forth across south-western New South Wales. She completed her peripatetic education and somehow passed the teacher's examination. This enabled her to get an appointment as assistant teacher at the Silverton School near Broken Hill in the valley of the Darling. The two years she spent there formed an important part of her experience of outback Australia.

Mary returned to teach in Sydney in 1890 and her association with the writer Henry Lawson dates from there. It appears there was a romance and even, perhaps, an intention to marry, but Lawson's wanderings were even worse than her father's.

Mary became politically involved as a supporter of the maritime and shearers' strikes and then a few years later her altruism caused her to endorse William Lane's romantic New Australia movement. She resigned from the department and, along with fellow hopefuls, she sailed for the Paraguay settlement in 1895. There she met an Australian shearer from Casterton, Victoria, and they married. Their first and only child, a son, was born in 1898.

The Gilmore family left the Paraguayan settlement in 1899 and eventually returned to Australia via London.

The Lawson family was also in London (somewhat briefly) and they stayed with them. The Gilmores then returned to Sydney where Mary resumed her literary and political interests. But her husband wanted to return home, so the family packed and moved to Casterton in 1907 where they stayed until 1912. Mary then went back to Sydney with their son, and her husband went to join his brother on a property in Cloncurry, Queensland.

Back in Sydney, Mary was once again in her milieu, and although she had kept up a correspondence with A.G. Stephens of the "Red Page" of the *Bulletin*, now she was able to see him and to see other people, talk to them and participate at meetings. The First World War appalled her and she gave the royalties of her second book of poetry to a fund for blinded soldiers. She managed to make a living as a full time writer of prose and poetry, and continued her political activities. She became, too, an even more ardent supporter of Aborigines and their traditions. Mary was appointed a Dame Commander of the British Empire in 1937. The Australasian Book Society commissioned the artist William Dobell to paint her, in honor of ninety-second birthday in 1957.

Dame Mary Gilmore was a remarkable person who died at the age of ninety-seven in 1962. We have already quoted from one of her poems, but here, from "Nationality", is more:

I see the world as one;
Yet, though I can no longer hate,
My son is still my son.
…this loaf is my son's bread.

I am not in favour of eulogizing bushrangers but let us make an exception for another currency lad born near

Goulburn in about 1830, some seven years before Queen Victoria succeeded to the throne — Frank Gardiner. He began his apprenticeship with a bit of horse stealing and trading in the Yass-Gundagai area and then in 1862 with the smell of gold in his nostrils he and his gang held up the Forbes gold escort near Eugowra and stole some fourteen thousand pounds. He was captured two years later and sent to prison. After being imprisoned for ten years or so, someone got up a public petition for his release on the grounds that his behaviour had been exemplary and lo, yes indeed lo and behold the Parkes-led government pardoned him and he was released. Parkes was censured by parliament, went to an election and lost. Bloody bushrangers.

Gardiner wisely took ship to San Francisco where he was welcomed and with his background, ran a successful bar known as the Twilight Saloon. He even learnt to speak with an American accent thus setting the pattern for Australian sportsmen (did someone mention the name Greg Norman?) and others who come back to their homeland with a similar accretion.

Apparently Goulburn was designated as the appropriate spot for a town by the affable Hamilton Hume in 1818, and why not choose such a site at the confluence of the Wollondilly and Mulwaree Rivers? I think I could live anywhere along the sweetly flowing Wollondilly. Henry Goulburn was the under Secretary for the Colonies when we Australians had the inspiration to name the town after him Well, honestly "Goulburn" is not too bad. Not half as good as Gubbata, or Thulloo or Binya, but…well, it is alright.

Bungendore is worth a visit, if only to roll the name around on your tongue. It is not large but it has a gallery which also features some splendid things in Australian wood and there are some well maintained old buildings and there is Molonglo Street. What more could you want?

But Canberra was our objective and as we drove across the huge plain or valley towards the Capital the temperature dropped and dropped and it began to rain. Fine gentle rain at first and heavier and heavier as we came into the weekday home of our hardworking parliamentary representatives. Canberra continues to grow, and to grow with a touch of grace.

Our car negotiated a couple of circles and we found ourselves in Commonwealth Avenue with the new Parliament House towering over us but beckoning us on. We decided to leave the House for the following day and went down to the edge of Lake Burley Griffin and so to Kingston, our destination. Everyone knows about Burley Griffin, the American architect who won the town planning design circulated worldwide in 1911, and his spider webs and swirls, and I must say that it all works rather well. Once you get the hang of it, it is easy to find your way around.

The name of our capital city derives, thank the Lord, from an Aboriginal word meaning "meeting place", and the original white settlers spelt it and pronounced it Canbery (or sometimes Canberry). There is also a claim that the original spelling may have been Kanbarra . What does seem fairly certain is that a Joshua Moore had land there in 1826 and that he called his property Canberry.

Canberra has quite an old Anglican church, St John the Baptist in the Reid area (1845). Our capital is rather hard done by for old churches. Old anything for that matter, but Burley Griffin tried to retain as much native flora as possible and it has been known as the bush capital, for that reason... alone. Sadly bush and gum trees burn, as people in the capital found to their cost in January 2003 when bushfires killed four people, injured some hundreds and burnt down nearly five hundred houses. I keep going back to the conversation I had with the farmer at Yamba where in effect he was saying — you have Europeanised Australia but you have done little to minimize the natural fire hazard. Plant swathes of *non-volatile* trees and shrubs. I wonder…

I do like Molonglo as a word and of course Canberra is on the river of that name, the river that fills the good old Lake Burley Griffin. And when the lake is full the Molonglo generously flows on and into the Murrumbidgee.

We did have some great tucker at Kingston. We even had lunch in a restaurant but in fairness it was raining heavily. Then we had a splendid dinner and a wonderful breakfast next morning. There was a breakfast place that turned out baguettes and bread of all kinds and delicious croissants and good coffee and really… everything. Canberra is worth another visit, it most decidedly is, despite its lack or comparative lack of nineteenth century history.

Before leaving our capital we drove down to the old parliament and inspected the house from the outside. We also viewed the Aboriginal tent embassy, which seemed rather tired, and we strolled over to the composite statue in Parkes Place known as the King George V Memorial. What does one say to such a nonsensical monument unveiled some fifty-three years after the largely republican sentiments of the Australia of the nineteenth century?

I suppose one could say that it is cumbersome and anachronistic and that it elevates a "royal" Englishman and belittles some Australians.

As royals go George V (1865-1936) was really not a bad sort of a bloke. He was the second son of Edward V11 and would not have expected to reign, except if his brother were to die. Oddly enough that event happened in 1892 when George was twenty-seven years old and he was thereupon created Duke of York. The duke believed in simplifying matters and in a slightly curious fashion he married the dead brother's fiancée, Princess Mary of Teck. He visited Australia in 1901 and opened the first Federal Parliament with Edmund Barton, the Prime Minister. He succeeded to the throne in 1911 and acquitted himself with credit during World War 1. His wife was prolific and bore him five sons and one daughter.

And that life entitled him and entitles him to hog the pride of place on this composite memorial statue. His allegory, St. George slaying the dragon is on the other side. I cannot complain that Australians are utterly neglected for there are some ten bronze plaques around the base of the statue celebrating the Duke of York (as he was in 1901), the Duchess, Edmund Barton, our first Prime Minister, a sailor, an airman, a soldier, a nurse, Henry Parkes, a crown (!) and Samuel Griffith.

We already know something about Edmund Barton but let us look at the Queenslander Samuel Griffith, born 1845 in Wales and died 1920 in Australia.

Samuel, or Sam as he seemed to be known, was a good student, a scholar in fact and he had no trouble in getting his law degree. He travelled to Italy as a young man and was entranced by that country. He must have been more than competent in the Italian language for after he returned from Italy he translated Dante into English, which is no mean feat. He practised law but also became a Queensland parliamentarian and the premier.

Surprisingly for a man in his position in those times he

had distinctly democratic views and he made them known. Then in 1891 as Queensland Premier he deemed it necessary to break the Shearers' Strike and this was done with the assistance of the military — not an endearing act as far as the union boys were concerned. They named him — "Oily Sam." Well, maybe they did but he has a suburb of Canberra named after him and a university and he is one of the ten placquists to adorn the imposing memorial statue of George V and his mate St. George, and he was the principal draughtsman of our Federal Constitution and the first Chief Justice of our Australian High Court. A man of talent and a hard working bloke, as you might expect the son of a Congregational Minister to be.

★ ★ ★ ★

Canberra has outgrown its callow youth and in the autumn in particular it is full of colour and falling leaves and beauty, a balance between buildings and transport and people and their surrounds. Canberra even has pedestrian laneways between buildings and those laneways are lined with trees interspersed with appropriate shrubs, and they are all cared for.

In the parks frequently there are deciduous trees in the valleys, and old creek beds, and Australian trees on the higher ground.

It is a city of politicians and a city for politicians and all their no doubt excellent habits and ethics, and yet it is developing a warmth and a spirit.

We took a plane for Sydney.

CHAPTER TWELVE

Sydney taxis can be excellent, but anyhow, this one got us from the airport to our hotel. By luck we were given a room overlooking Hyde Park, which was in the foreground, St.Mary's in the middle ground and Woolloomooloo, wonderful euphonious Woolloomooloo (but why not two double Ls in the last syllable?) and sinful Kings Cross in the background. Sydney has a raffishness about it, in fact it is a ragamuffin city and because it has and is both of those things, it is interesting and lovable.

As I stood there in our hotel room looking out towards Hyde Park with its fountain, and with St. Mary's in the distance I thought of all the people who had brought me back to walk again the streets of the City of Sydney — the people and their lives and their buildings.

I had held a copy of the weekly *Bulletin* newspaper in my hands when I was a teenager and marvelled then at its colourful pink cover and its "Red Page". In fact, for some reason no longer apparent, I have an even more distinct memory of the *Age's* companion the weekly *Leader*, which came into existence in 1862 but died in 1957. The *Leader* had its literary section and I suppose could have been, but never was, a national rival of the *Bulletin*. Did it have a green back and front page? All these colours: pink for the *Bulletin*, green for the *Leader* and of course a sort of dirty orange for the Victorian rural newspaper, the *Weekly Times*.

Then there were the people who owned, produced or contributed to those papers and not forgetting booksellers and publishers like Archibald, George Robertson, John Norton, Sydney Ure Smith and poets and writers like Lawson and Paterson, Charles Harpur, Mary Gilmore, Christopher Brennan, Charmian Clift, Adam Gordon, Henry Kendall…

The rain had stopped, my reminiscing had ceased and, grabbing an umbrella, I found the lift and was soon down the steps of the hotel and out into Elizabeth Street. I crossed the street and went into Hyde Park and up to Archibald's fountain by the excellent French sculptor François Sicard. The fountain was unveiled in 1932 and is in the classical tradition, complete with Diana and her bow and Apollo and his pool, and prancing horses and spouting tortoises, and is very popular and much photographed and … it deserves to be. It is not perhaps, original, nor is it Australian, but it is grand and it connects its donor Jules François Archibald with his beloved France and Europe and the First World War despite the fact that he was an Australian to his shoe leather. Perhaps Jules was right and Australia and its capital cities could do with a soupçon of the Tuileries Garden.

And who better to walk with you through the streets of Sydney town than Archibald, the famous editor and part owner of the truly historic Australian weekly newspaper or journal, the "Bushman's Bible" known as the *Bulletin*. I wonder if this man would indeed have walked or rather strolled with me. I promise you I would not have said anything. I would merely have kept my head down except to glance at him from time to time and occasionally nod in agreement with anything he said.

Archibald was born in 1856, two years after the Eureka Stockade, to a policeman father Joseph and, according to Sylvia Lawson in the Australian Dictionary of Biography, an "impulsive and sunny-natured mother", nee Charlotte Madden, and his place of birth was Kildare, now known as West Geelong, Victoria. His mother died when he was only four, and it seems that her death left a gap in his life and that he never quite got over his loss. You get the impression that he was, at least in his early days, searching for his identity and searching for *sa mere*. Oh these mothers.

Archibald's first venture after he left school was an apprenticeship to the local paper the *Warrnambool Examiner*. Then at the age of eighteen after his country apprenticeship, he decided to go to Melbourne where he was confident that he would become a reporter for the *Argus* newspaper (long since defunct). The Argus did not recognize his talents and he took a job as a clerk in the Victorian Education Department. He boarded in Emerald Hill (South Melbourne) with a French couple from Brittany and this, and perhaps a liaison with a French actress, inspired him with a love of France and things French. His passion for France caused him to discard his given names John Feltham and to recreate himself as Jules François, born in France of a Jewish mother. His identity was secured and the new man had started his life.

Jules Archibald went to Maryborough in Queensland in

1878 to work there as a clerk but soon found himself away up north at his employer's gold mine or quarry, well inland from Cooktown at a place called Maytown, on the Palmer River. Maytown is on the Cape York Peninsula and was hot but not always dry. It is written that he "lived in a hut…and survived a food shortage, snakebite and an outbreak of fever". There was a pub of sorts because he wrote about the "pub-keeper and the pub-keeper's daughter, a drunken bush parson and argumentative miners who spent their nights writing letters to the newspapers". Archibald stayed there long enough to become imbued with the spirit of the outback: loneliness, mateship, stoicism, hardship. In other words he realized the extent to which each person, if he was to survive, had to play a lone hand.

Eventually he got back to Sydney and took a job as a reporter on the *Evening News*. He had met up with another journalist John Haynes and they hatched up the idea of the very Australian weekly to be called the *Bulletin*. They had almost no capital but somehow they rented premises in the run-down Scandinavian Hall at 107 Castlereagh Street and they were off. I searched in vain for any evidence that the *Bulletin* had ever existed there near the corner of Market Street. All trace of these two men and their wonderful enterprise has been buried by one of Sydney's plainest structures. Jules François, you and your business have gone, and yet you are there and in Pitt Street more prominently than ever.

I looked too for the nineteenth century Angus and Robertson, booksellers and publishers of 110½ (yes ½) Market Street and then of 89 Castlereagh Street, but I found them not.

But once again that George Robertson, the Scot who became an Australian, haunts the City of Sydney as surely as the cries of the convicts under the lash or the tinkle of the Tank Stream. Robertson, of all people grasped the flavour of the new country and depicted and fostered it. We owe him a great deal. Would "G.R." have walked with me? I doubt that he would have had the time, he was too busy knocking writers' manuscripts into shape including those of the rather careless solicitor — poet Banjo Paterson.

Not many people today will remember the Sunday weekly *Truth*, started in Sydney in 1890, mentioned earlier in connection with its originator Adolphus Taylor of Mudgee. *Truth* expanded to Melbourne and Brisbane and made a fortune for its Napoleon loving long time owner John Norton who came from England to Australia in 1884 as "a brilliant, impudent, radical, undersized English journalist in search of a job". During his ownership of *Truth*, Norton was, according to Cyril Pearl, "publicly denounced many times as a thief, a blackmailer, a wife-beater and an obscene drunkard (and more)", and it was maintained, he never refuted those allegations. And yet the fellow had, and still has, a certain appeal not least of which is his lampooning of the idiotic notion of royalty.

When the sycophantic Sydney paper the *Daily Telegraph* suggested in 1896 yet another royal celebration to mark Queen Victoria's long reign, a reign in excess of George 111's, he wrote and printed in *Truth*, inter alia, the following: "the podgy figured, sulky faced little German whose ugly statue at the top of King Street sagaciously keeps one eye on the Mint while with the other she ogles the still uglier statue of Albert the Good (yes, believe it or not those words are chiseled beneath the bust)…in the garb and posture that is suggestive neither of decency in attire…" and: "God Save the Queen, if only to keep her rascal of a turf-swindling, cardsharping, wife debauching, boozy, rowdy of a son Albert Edward, Prince of Wales, off the throne." And that was only part of his fulminations against the crown.

As a result of those words, Norton was charged with sedition — "conduct or speech inciting to rebellion". As writer and proprietor of *Truth*, he had become somewhat experienced in court battles and when the case came on for hearing he refused to brief a barrister or consult a solicitor. He appeared in person and at the end of a long and some-times relevant diatribe, he was congratulated by Mr Justice Stephen on his "very able speech".

The jury failed to agree about those words being sedi-tious and were discharged. The Crown (and the people of New South Wales it seems) had had enough, and Norton and his *Truth* were also discharged and Norton went off to celebrate and to drink himself into blissful oblivion.

The offices of *Truth* no longer grace the streets of Sydney. The muck-racking rag has gone and John Norton who became its owner in 1896 or thereabouts in somewhat clouded circumstances, has been in his grave for almost one hundred years, but by God, he left his mark. He probably invented the word "wowser" and without doubt was the most addicted of any other turn of the century public fig-ure to the disease of alliteration.

Here is part of his attack on our own dear international soprano Nellie Melba: "You are…a harrowing handful to harassed hotelkeepers, (and) a terrorism termagant to trem-bling timeservers." Nellie ignored the nonsense and went on singing her opera and sipping her champagne.

Would John of the *Truth* have walked with me? Or would I have walked with him? I wonder. Maybe, maybe.

Further down, and following roughly the course of the

OF RIVERS, BAGUETTES & BILLABONGS

Tank Stream, I came to a street that, in business hours, housed an Australian whose gift for popular bush and country poetry — ballads — has never been surpassed. Banjo Paterson, born and raised in the plains and rolling country west of the Great Dividing Range but within sight and smell of the Snowy River country, practiced as a solicitor in Bond Street for some ten years in partnership with a bloke called Street. Street and Paterson. You cannot help but wonder about his expertise in the law and his concentration on the business and legal affairs of his clients.

> I am sitting in my dingy little office, where a stringy
> Ray of sunlight struggles feebly down between the
> houses tall
> And the hurrying people daunt me, and their pallid faces
> haunt me
> As they shoulder one another in their rush and nervous
> haste.

Banjo, instead of thinking those thoughts, you should have been looking up the latest Full Court decision and reading it right through, instead of just glancing at the head-note; you should have been bringing yourself up to date with the latest Acts of Parliament and amendments to Statutes. You should not have been gazing and dreaming.

I would have proposed to Banjo a long walk, up Pitt Street and along Bridge Street. During the course of that walk he would have explained to me that Bridge Street had nothing to do with the proposed and much talked about Harbour Bridge but had everything to do with the little bridge over that famous Tank Stream.

I can fantasise that we would have strolled in a general

easterly direction along the northern footpath and that Banjo would have stopped opposite the Burns Philp building and he would have said, "One of the most original buildings in Sydney — just look at it." And I would have said that too, and even today I would still say the same.

Further along he might have paused opposite what is, I believe, one of the most remarkable public buildings of nineteenth century Sydney, the Lands Department Building. Isn't it superb: four stories of glorious sandstone topped by a turret or dome facing Bridge Street and a wonderful clock tower and a sort of minaret overlooking Farrer Place. It was designed by our friend the famous James Barnet and the style was nominated as "Italian Renaissance of the Venetian type". As we continued our walk up the hill he might also have pointed to the Loftus Street façade and explained, "Really that is the front."

Further along he would have shown me the site of the first Government House on the corner of Phillip Street and pausing to catch our breath he could have, would have, muttered the first two lines of his latest poem: "Twas Mulga Bill from Eaglehawk that caught the cycling craze/He turned away the good old horse that served him many days."

Soon we would be at the corner of Macquarie Street outside the excellent Treasury Office building (now incorporated rather nicely into the Intercontinental Hotel), but Banjo would, I think, be looking across the road at the Colonial Secretary's office designed earlier in the century in 1879 by the somewhat younger Barnet and I am sure he would have told me this:

"Barnet was a Scot — yes, another Scot and he was born at Arbroath where they produce the most wonderful smoked kippers. He came to Australia in the fifties and first worked for Edmund Blacket. Later he joined the Colonial Architects Office and then he became the Colonial Architect in the mid-sixties. The work done by and under that bloke is amazing. Court Houses in places like Bathurst, Yass, Boorowa, and so on, our General Post Office, these buildings here in Bridge Street, Goulburn Post Office… The man is brilliant and I was sad when he resigned. We had a bit to do with that damned Royal Commission…Great man, say what you like, great man. See that dome and the rather odd offices up there? They were added this year by the current architect bloke, Walter Vernon. I hear Barnet calls him Vernon the Vandal. Rather good isn't it?"

And at that point Banjo might have pulled his hat down and told me that he had better get back to the office. As he walked back down to Bond Street I am sure he would have been mumbling the next couple of lines of his new poem: "He dressed himself in cycling clothes, resplendent to be seen;/He hurried off…hurried off, he hurried off…"

And as he strode away from me down the hill I would have kicked myself for not having asked him about what really happened to cause him (or her) to break his long engagement of eight years to Sarah Riley. Was it really his collaboration with Christina Macpherson, Sarah's friend, in the writing of the lyrics and music for "Waltzing Matilda" that caused the breach between him and Sarah? "Waltzing Matilda" was written and composed at Winton, Queensland in 1895 when he was thirty-one and he had been engaged to be married since he was twenty-three. Paterson and his ghost would perhaps have told me to mind my own business and fair enough too.

Banjo would be appalled by the change to Bond Street today: no dust, no dingy office, only palatial air-conditioned offices, no sunlight, indeed only second hand air pumped in and recycled and no horses and their droppings, no gigs or wagons or buggies but if you listen carefully you might still hear the now subterranean murmur of the Tank Stream as it winds its way through the rock tanks or pits down to Sydney Cove. That stream not only supplied Sydney with water for the first thirty years of its existence, it also performed the very necessary task of separating the elite from the plebeians: the governor and the better people lived on the right bank (as in Paris) and the…rest inhabited the left. In Melbourne the faithful blue waters of the Yarra separate the Toorakians from the commoners of Richmond, and the elite inhabit the left bank. But then Melbourne has always been more democratic than Sydney.

So many interesting nineteenth century and early twentieth century Australians lived and loved and wrote in Sydney but we cannot write about all of them. There is one in particular who I would liked to have known and would have loved to have listened to over a long lunch with his mates of Les Compliqués, the club that met in a little restaurant called Paris House in Phillip Street.

And I realize it is nonsense but I imagine that two contemporaries of this bloke would also, somehow, have been present on the day that I was invited. Never mind, well mind a bit, the food and the wine — at the very least potatoes and cheese and bread, good bread — but here is the company that might have gathered at Paris House in: say 1910. There would have been the currency man and host Christopher Brennan, Robert Frost from America and England, and Hilaire Belloc from France and England, and I hope myself. Christopher Brennan would have opened proceedings by standing there and reading in his sonorous voice from his

"The Wanderer" and he would have declaimed the whole of his first verse:

> When window-lamps had dwindled, then I rose
> and left the town behind me; and on my way
> passing a certain door I stopt, remembering
> how once I stood on its threshold, and my life
> was offer'd to me, a road how different
> from that of the years since gone! And I had but
> to rejoin an olden path, once dear, since left.

And knowing, or substantially knowing, what happened to the rest of his life I would quietly have wept.

Robert Frost would then have got to his feet, but with some diffidence I think, and he might have read the whole of his little poem "Mending Wall" and I would have concentrated on these two lines:

> There where it is we do not need the wall…
> He only says, "Good fences make good neighbour's.

And he could have followed that with the even shorter poem "The Road Not Taken" and I would have repeated again and again in my head the last three lines:

> Two roads diverged in a wood, and I
> I took the one least travelled by,
> And that has made all the difference.

It would have been difficult to restrain Hilaire Belloc, the writer of all sorts of poetry and prose and in many ways most famous for his little book *The Path to Rome*. That book, he described as "the only book I ever wrote for love". Belloc might have recited any of his poetry from children's verses to lines in favour of wine (and cheese and bread) but I would have asked him to paraphrase his reasons for attending morning Mass in out of the way little churches on the path that he walked from Toul, near Nancy in France, to Rome. He would have enumerated them as follows:

1. For half an hour just at the opening of the day you are silent and recollected.
2. The Mass is a careful and rapid ritual. Now it is the function of all ritual…to relieve the mind by so much of responsibility, and initiative and to catch you up (as it were) into itself…"
3. The surroundings incline you to good and reasonable thoughts. [It] is like a short repose in a deep and well-built library, into which no sounds come, and where you feel yourself secure against the outer world.

Rather like the sentiments of that son of a Unitarian minister, the redoubtable Ralph Waldo Emerson and his remark: "I like the silent church before the service begins better than any preaching."

Churches! Beautiful churches all over the world, and what do we do with them? Houses, offices, libraries? Two things are certain, they must be preserved and they must be used — for something.

But back to our lunch with the Les Compliqués at Paris House in Phillip Street, just a block away from the Governor Macquarie's Rum Hospital, and back to Christopher Brennan, the big tall man, the Celt, the son of an Irish brewer who lived in Darling Harbour. What a boon and what a curse to have Celtic blood in your veins. The blood of a people of the Indo-European category whose origins go back at least to the thirteenth century BC and who left their mark in the Upper Danube countries and who practised the religion of the Druids and who loved beer and wine and anything alcoholic and who also loved farming and creating works of art the like of which are not excelled even today. Such people!

And those people, it seemed, had an inbuilt leaning towards the west. They rolled forever westward across Europe, across France, across the Channel, across the British Isles to end in Ireland. They left settlements behind them all the way: in Europe, in Brittany, in Wales, Scotland and Ireland but they largely eschewed England and frustrated at last by the rocky west coast of Ireland, they nonetheless once more took up their belongings, and in the nineteenth century continued westward to the United States of America and Australia. Christopher Brennan was one of those "craytures" and a brilliant and at the same time a tortured man he was. Could have been great, oh yes, he could have been great.

"Christopher Brennan's life was a tragic one. His scholarship was so wide that he could well have graced a university chair in any one of the schools of classics…" So, writes Kenneth Slessor and his mates in the splendid but little *The Penguin Book of Australian Verse.*

He died in poverty at the age of sixty-two, leaving a wife and four children and leaving too a longing for his companion Violet Singer who died in a tram accident three years after they started their affair, although we might also call it a relationship. Immensely gifted, Christopher was afflicted with the soul of an ancient Celt. Towards the end of his life he wrote: "I feel a peace fall in the heart of the winds and a clear dusk settle, somewhere, far in me."

I turned into Phillip Street from Hunter Street and walked slowly along it to King Street and then I turned again and walked back. He was not there, he had gone. I suppose I was almost exactly one hundred years too late. Ah, how I would have liked to walk with him. Indeed, with that trio.

Hunter Street boasts a wall fountain or fountains by that great Australian sculptor Tom Bass and there were two reasons for me to go and linger by it or them: one because of its creator and the other to marvel that just over fifty years ago two Australian avant garde writers were prosecuted for obscenity for pretending to pee into its sculptured basins. I must say it does look a bit like a urinal. In 1964, Richard Neville and Richard Walsh of *Oz* magazine had themselves photographed from the back standing in front of the fountain and they labelled the photograph P and O-ing in the Tom Bass fountain. They were convicted and sentenced to imprisonment but as one would hope and expect, the conviction was quashed on appeal. It is a most unusual "fountain" or indented creek and may well have been inspired by the historical Tank Stream which originated in the swamp near Hyde Park and flowed down the hill across where Hunter Street now is. How puritanical to prosecute those two wags and prosecute in those circumstances. When we first went to France in the seventies, the truckies simply stood by the side of the road and peed in the general direction of the *forêt*.

I was determined to see the much-criticised statue of Henry Lawson which, according to guidebooks, apparently stands in the Botanic Gardens "somewhere near the road to Mrs. Macquarie's Chair". My books on Lawson gave no better directions, nor was the internet any more specific. So, I set out on a day of 100% humidity, 27° C and frequent downpours.

The Art Gallery would be able to help me, for the statue would be within a ten-minute walk of that sophisticated establishment. But — they had no idea. They would look it up on their screen. I tried to explain but to no avail. She looked at me in a puzzled way and admitted that she could not help. I went outside, put up my umbrella and walked towards that famous chair: Woolloomooloo Gates on my left, Lawson Park further along and again on my left, but no statue. I accosted a bus driver and encountered a shake of the head. A Frenchman from Angoulême stopped and asked directions of me and I explained I was from Melbourne. We discussed France and the Hostellerie du Maine Brun and we talked about the cépages of Cognac and Marguerite of Angoulême and other things French but I had made no progress with my search for my Australian. I continued on until I could see Bennelong Point across the water and then I turned for home — well, the hotel. When I had despaired and had accelerated my step because of the sniff of lunch carried to me by the wind, suddenly there on a little hill on my right and almost obscured by trees was the much maligned bronze. There was Henry gazing back towards the city with an almost cross-eyed intensity and there on his right was the dog and on his left the swagman.

★ ★ ★ ★

Lunch. I was a long way from lunch and my shirt was wet through from rain or sweat or both but I was reluctant to hurry. Did we have the capacity to share of bottle or should we confine ourselves to a glass? A winemaker ordering a glass of wine — no, I could not sink so low. A bottle of Vernaccia di San Gimignano is what I would have liked, to remind me of the carafe that we had for lunch that day… How is it that wine can taste so utterly different on various occasions? How can a flask wine taste so wonderful at a modest *ristorante* in the countryside outside Siena and yet an expensive bottle of the same variety be so disappointing a few nights later at Ristorante Il Pozzo in Monteriggioni.

I puzzled over this and other problems as I traipsed through the rain in the general direction of the Archibald Fountain and, finding no answer, I for some reason began to think of another precious gift that gives pleasure to the human heart and mind and soul. Music. Not marching music, although at this moment, perhaps it was the appropriate kind, but piano music. And if piano music then of course it would have to be played by Eileen Joyce.

It is no use my pretending that Eileen Joyce was a Sydney girl, no, no, it is quite clear that she was born at Zeehan in Tasmania in 1912, but she almost adopted Sydney and it her, and I am therefore justified in writing about her and thinking of her as at last I stand here before the fountain.

I first heard her playing in the middle 1940s when I was completing my secondary education and boarding privately in Wangaratta, and although she was only on the radio I was immediately smitten. She played Schumann's Devotion and on hearing it, and her playing, I became *her* devotee. Somehow I managed to save the price of a vinyl record and to get the permission of my landlady to play it on their His Master's Voice radiogram. I played it almost every night to soothe my path to the evening's study. Eileen, you were wonderful but at that time, of course, I knew nothing about you. Now, I know a little more.

Our own Percy Grainger, who sadly but also gladly deserted us for the United States of America in 1914, on hearing her play during a tour in 1926 wrote this: "she is in every way the most transcendentally gifted young piano student I have heard in the last twenty-five years. Her playing has that *melt* of tone, that elasticity of expression that is, I find, typical of young Australian talents, and is so rare elsewhere." Percy disapproved of her continued coaching by anyone but an Australian. He feared, otherwise, that her expression would be "Europeanised".

She had a reputation as a beauty "with chestnut hair and green eyes" and she developed a style of dressing and arranging that chestnut hair. She also had a style in clothes: blue for Beethoven with hair up, green for Chopin with hair back, et cetera. As a music student in Sydney, Richard Bonynge used to flock to her concerts along with his mates, "not least because of the extraordinary amount of cleavage she used to show!" I did not know about that, *malheursement*, but I loved her.

And there is another person that I have always loved (but not in the way I loved Eileen) and that person is Jack Mundey (nothing to do with music as far as I know), who was born on the Atherton Tableland in Queensland in 1929, came to Sydney to play Rugby League and stayed on. He is now identified with Sydney. When not playing football he was a builder's labourer and became secretary of the Builders Labourer's Federation in the 1970s. He influenced or initiated "green bans" on many of Sydney's historic and heritage buildings and open spaces and in many cases secured their preservation. Our Nobel Prize writer Patrick White admired Jack and referred to him as "the wasted great Australian". But Patrick was wrong and Jack was usually right and did some wonderful things for the history of our eighteenth and nineteenth century city of Sydney. He has been rewarded and his name commemorated by "Jack Mundey Place" in (or just off, I am not sure which) Argyle Street in the Rocks. And there is not a better locality in Sydney to celebrate his deeds.

Jack's personal life has had its tragedies but he has fought on and so far as I know is still fighting. In his interview of 2009 with the ABC's Peter Thompson, his concluding words were to the effect that he hoped the modern era of rationalism and corporatisation would not overlook the values of fairness and compassion.

I left the fountain.

Sydney on one of the most beautiful harbours, historical Sydney, vibrant Sydney which absorbed, sorted and culled the workers, writers and artists of the West and the outback, Sydney which was itself made and modified by the rural population. Sydney our oldest state capital, we could dream and stroll through your streets for days and days and in the process absorb the essence of this unusual and wonderful country. But it is lunchtime.

CHAPTER THIRTEEN

No, we did not have a bottle of Vernaccia di Gimignano but we did have a very good five-year-old Hunter Semillon, and we left some wine in the bottle for the kitchen, or anyone else who could get their hands on it. Our time in Sydney had expired but I wanted one more walk. I rechecked the hour of our flight to Melbourne and calculated the taxi trip and the queues or more appropriately "pig tails" for security, et cetera, and yes, I did have time for one last meander. It was to be down King Street to George Street, to Alfred Street, to Macquarie Street (and a glance in the direction of Bennelong's hut) and then back along Macquarie Street to Hyde Park. Out of our window I viewed the weather — definitely it would be wise once again to beg an umbrella from the hotel.

That bloke Bennelong was the man who oc-cupied my thoughts as I walked to the north, a direction he must often have taken to get to the hut built for him by Governor Phillip.

Bennelong, the Aborigine, was born about 1764, and was therefore in his mid- twenties when he was persuaded somewhat forcefully to come over to the enemy. Phillip's plan in capturing him was "to learn the language and the customs of the local people". And to use Bennelong as an informer? To turn him into a collaborator? It is hard to say. There is some evidence for that proposition. Perhaps the great warrior Pemulwuy who "lead a guerrilla war against the British settlement" between 1788 and 1802 may have thought so. Pemulwuy was shot dead in 1802 and his head was sent to England! Pemulwuy was known as the "Rainbow Warrior hero" to the Aboriginal Eora people. There is, after all, a sort of parallel between Caesar's treatment of the leader of the Gauls and our treatment of this leader of the Aborigines, isn't there?

Bennelong had curly hair and wore it rather as barristers wear their wigs. He is said to have had a "love–hate relationship" with the British intruders and Governor Phillip, but on his return from his much publicised trip to London, he adopted more and more the dress and manners of the invaders.

I put up my umbrella yet again as the rain fell gently but heavily. Was Bennelong a collaborator or an informer? And what about the spearing of Phillip at Manly that day in 1790 in Bennelong's presence? Perhaps he started out as an informer *for* his Aboriginal mates but was won over as Petain was won over by the German occupiers. In any event he had his hut and he entertained the Governor there — pretty heady stuff. I wondered afresh if we should not think of calling the Opera House, Bennelong's Hut. More Australian in many ways — "Let us go to the Hut tonight, dear."

Somehow I had traversed Alfred Street and had begun my return journey. The rain had stopped, and I was in

George Street across the road from Australia Square when a remarkable event took place: I was spoken to by a charming young lady.

"*Excusez moi…*Oh I am sorry, excuse me I meant. I am looking for the old Post Office in Martin Place. Can you 'elp me?"

She did not have a map and she lamented the fact that the sun travelled across the northern sky here in the southern hemisphere (when it shone), and that the sun rose on your right and that generally directions seemed confusing. I sympathised with her, and naturally I was going down to Martin Place and I would show her the way.

She was from Bordeaux and knew the Médoc well and had dined at restaurants where we had and she came to Australia often because her mother lived and worked in Bordeaux and her father for some years lived and worked in Melbourne. I told her she was the second French person I had spoken to that day and I asked her how she liked coming to Australia.

"I love it," she replied.

I ventured that there were great similarities between the two countries.

"Not at all," she said, "I do not agree. They are such different countries. As different as male and female but…complementary — in the same way. You think so too?"

Well, no, I had not thought of it in that fashion at all. The rain began again and I put the umbrella up. She moved under its cover naturally and without false modesty. She continued to explain her analogy to me as we continued down Martin Place and then, too soon, the façade of the old GPO came into view. It had stopped raining and so I closed the umbrella. As we walked towards the steps I saw a very tall young man raise his arm. She waved back, shook my hand and said *"Au revoir"*.

I walked back to Macquarie Street past the State Library, and Parliament House and the Sydney Hospital. Hadn't I intended to go in and over to the Nightingale Wing and to look once again at the most unusual fountain? Yes, I had but my head was full of that analogy. How appropriate it was and why hadn't I thought of it? Male and female — so different, but so alike in many respects and so…complementary, so complete when they were a pair in harmony. There was no better word than complementary. And if one country was male, it was not hard to identify which one, and certainly there was no doubt as to the female of the couple. How simple and how brilliant of her. Australia might well have been a French colony, the French certainly had a good look at us. What then?

There on my left was "Albert the Good" gazing into the western infinity. Albert, time you made way for an Australian; yes, time for you to be stored away in some musty cellar. Go underground Albert — get out of the Australian sun.

★ ★ ★ ★

So many poets and writers and artists who lived or congregated in Sydney: Charles Harpur the man whose father was from County Cork and whose mother was a convict from Somerset, Charles who died young and in sorrow after the accidental death of his second son; A. D. Hope the boy from Cooma and Bathurst, the republican whose writing was said to be on a par with that of the rather wonderful French poet of the 19th century, Leconte de Lisle; Rex Ingamells, founder of the Jindyworobak Club (Aboriginality and country) which endorsed Spengler's suggestion "that continents shape everything within their shores to a special, almost demiurgic blueprint", seconded by Max Dunn who wrote, "And the people grow/Into the likeness of the country…"; and Douglas Stewart, the Kiwi who abandoned the law and who, amongst other things, edited for a while the *Bulletin*'s "Red Page" and who wrote some lovely poetry including these lines:

> Australia's the violent country; the earth itself
> Suffers, cries out in anger against the sunlight.
> From the cracked lips of the plains,
> I have come to understand it in love and pity;
> Not horror now…

And expatriate author Ray Mathew born in Sydney in 1929 and…yes, and we could go on for page after page about all those Australians and their interpretation of their country.

But it was the city of Sydney and the publisher George Robertson and the newspaper proprietor J. F. Archibald who, at the end of the nineteenth and the beginning of the twentieth century, drew all our writers together, collated their works and re-issued them to Australians from Cape York to Hobart, from Port Hedland to Brisbane. I sometimes think of all these people, these writers and poets and dreamers and of their ideas and writing, as so many creeks and rivers and streams forming a gossamer network from the west to the east of New South Wales and flowing not to the south-west as our waterways do, but to the east where they converge on this mighty reservoir of Sydney, and then, having been processed and digested by the men of the capital, they are flung back through New South Wales and indeed throughout the whole of Australia.

East of the Darling! Well, Australia now encompasses east, west, north and south of that enigmatic stream, but perhaps this part of our continent, the old state of New South Wales has done, at least in the early days, most to shape both old and modern Australia.

New South Wales, I, a Victorian, I bow to you, I salute you, yes indeed, I take off my hat — in fact I love you for your contribution to the country that we have become.

★ ★ ★ ★

I think it was our first open zoo in Victoria and they had put up the appropriate notice warning people of the wild, ferocious and dangerous animals, and forbidding you to open your car doors, and directing you to keep your windows up; and some Aussie had written in black texta underneath, the following simple sentence — "Poms on pushbikes are welcome".

I hasten to write that Australians have always made a sharp distinction between poms and Englishmen.

CHAPTER FOURTEEN

I repeat an earlier refrain — you do not own the country, it owns you. Or you could say that each human generation acts or should act as caretakers of that country. Get rid of that proprietorship attitude and concentrate on the role of carers.

In France, the Celts may have been passive exploiters in their earliest days but they quickly became farmers and conservationists and, from my observations, the caring attitude to their country is today well established and practised, for example, their wonderful forests, especially their oak forests.

England, despite its loving care of its own countryside, when it travelled the seas of this planet and grabbed and held in its possession land all round the world — the Colonies, the Empire — it may have done so for one principal reason: to enrich itself. And England did become rich, although towards the end of the Empire which then became the Commonwealth, there

was an aggravating tendency for the milch heifers (alright, cows) to ask for something in return. And then after the last war there was the inconvenient problem of some of the children of the Commonwealth wanting to come home and live with mother.

It all amounts to this. We are a relatively small planet and that planet is getting more crowded, humans are, it might be argued, entitled to live on any part of it. No particular race is entitled to claim outright and absolute ownership of any country on this globe. However, all people in all countries have an obligation to manage and care for the country in which they live and to regulate its affairs in such a way as to preserve its essential integrity. They can only do this successfully if they develop a great love and loyalty to their country and its spirit and traditions. They need to be local patriots and then world patriots. If you do not love your immediate surrounds and then by degrees, your greater surrounds and then your country, how can you pretend to love the world? Loyalty — what a word and what an ideal. Loyalty is the stone dropped in the billabong: it starts in the centre and its ripples go out and out and become stronger and stronger till they reach the shore.

The loyalty of people to their country can be shown and manifested in many ways. Two of the most obvious are the national anthem and the national flag.

Flags have been around for many centuries, and their original use was perhaps to identify an army and provide an insignia for the troops to rally around and become attached to. Over the years they have become symbols of the country and of one's loyalty to the country; they are of almost religious significance — for example America and its flag.

Since the Revolution of 1789, the French flag has been

the tricolour, but with an interregnum of fifteen years from 1815, when the French for some reason permitted a Bourbon to lord it over them. The "Royal" French flag was usually plain blue with its gold fleurs-de-lis and a lovely flag it was too, but it was swept aside by the Jacobins and their mates who wore the colours red and blue in their caps. (These were the colours of Paris — blue for Saint Martin and red for Saint Denis.) White, however, had a symbolic meaning in France and the revolutionary flag, as a measure of reconciliation eventually became the tricolour: red for the nobility, white for the clergy and blue for the bourgeoisie. Just to confuse you, red was, of course, the colour favoured by the Jacobins and later the Socialists.

The point, the real point of the above, is that France has had the tricolour for just on two hundred years and is likely to have it for the next two thousand years. The flag of France is settled and unchallengeable. Not so the flag of Australia — our lovely Southern Cross but with the anachronistic Union Jack in one corner.

If our present flag is unacceptable for the Australia of today, a de facto republic, then what are we to do about it? One simple solution is to leave the flag as it is and simply remove the Union Jack. Another is to use the flag of Eureka Stockade fame, and a great flag it is, but perhaps too radical for some of our traditional Australians.

There is a third remedy and that is to adopt the Aboriginal flag with its colours that harmonize with the colours of this sunburnt (and green) land; the flag that our lovely Olympic champion draped over her athletic body as she did her lap of honour a few years ago. It is truly a flag that blends with our country. It does not have the Southern Cross, it is true, but it does not need it. This is an inspired piece of bunting and I would gladly salute it.

In my primary school days in the bush we lined up every Monday morning and when the line was straight and our faces suitably composed we sang "God Save the King" and we saluted the flag. Our father mumbled and muttered about this little ceremony and to please him I merely mouthed the words. One of the last acts of our former Prime Minister John Howard was to allocate a large sum of money for the erection of flag poles in Australian schoolyards, with the idea of the children lining up in a similar fashion and, I suppose, singing "Advance Australia Fair". I do not know if the poles are all up and the flags issued and venerated, nor do I know if any particular form of obeisance was stipulated. If so I sincerely hope that the American habit of placing your hand over your heart was not and is not a part of the ritual. The French are pretty fond of their flag and it certainly flies over every *Marie* (Town Hall) on every day of the year. As to its place in their schools, I know not.

Another symbol of our loyalty to our country, our patch of earth, is our National Anthem. Now there is a subject!

Let us deal first with the French national anthem. It is now, after two hundred years, accepted and settled. The song was composed by and written by Claude-Joseph Rouget de Lisle on the evening of 24 April and the morning of 25 April (auspicious days for Australians — the night before Anzac Day with our troops in their ships off the coast of Gallipoli and then the first morning of the bloody battle), but his music was composed and his words written in 1792. De Lisle was a captain in the Engineering Corps of the French Army which was garrisoned in Strasbourg. It is said that it was requested by the Mayor Baron de Dietrich, oddly enough, and it became known as the *Chante de Guerre pour l'Armée du*

Rhin. The song was quickly adopted in other sections of the army but in particular by the National Guard of Marseille, and as it was in marching time, they sang it as they swung into Paris on 30 July 1792. The Parisians heard it, loved it, adopted it and called it "La Marseillaise". It had a slightly checkered history in the nineteen century but survived in popularity and official circles until, in 1958, it became part of the French Constitution.

In 1974 the conservative President Valéry Giscard d'Estaing found the tempo too sprightly and…er, unseemly, and had it slowed down. It did not stay slow for long — wasn't it a march and a march composed after rather a rousing revolution? In 1981 the tempo returned and no doubt will not be tampered with again. Attempts have also been made, from time to time, to modify its eulogizing of blood and battles and things martial, but once again without success. The fact is the whole thing is exciting and invigorating and is just so damn good. I love it.

And that brings us, naturally, to the Australian national anthem. It was, once again, composed by and written by the one man: a Scot by the name of Peter Dodds McCormick (1834–1916). Peter was a stonemason by trade but a natural musician. He had enthusiastically adopted Australia (and the Presbyterian church, naturally, but that is by the way), and one night after a concert which included many national anthems of the world, he reflected on the fact that there was no Australian anthem — only "God Save…" He roughed out the words and then over the following days he set them to music. His song (or anthem) was performed publicly in Sydney in 1878 on Saint Andrew's Day and then, to his great pleasure, it was sung by a choir of ten thousand on 1 January 1901 at the inauguration of the Commonwealth of Australia.

In 1907 our then government purchased the song for one hundred pounds or two hundred dollars and the song was played intermittently thereafter along with "God Save . . . " and our very own Australian "Waltzing Matilda".

In 1974 there was a mini-poll as to our anthem initiated by the Whitlam Government, and then in 1977 the Fraser government conducted a national poll — there were seven million ballot papers issued. The results were: "Advance Australia Fair", 43.2%; "Waltzing Matilda", 28.3%; and then with some 18% and 10% came "God Save the Queen" and "Song of Australia". In April 1984 the Governor General issued a proclamation designating "God Save the Queen" as the Royal Anthem to be played if members of Royalty were present but declaring "Advance Australia Fair" the official Australian national anthem.

The question that must be asked is whether "Advance..." is really what Australians want having regard to the tumultuous reception always given to "Matilda" whenever it is deliberately or accidentally played. With the greatest respect to our very patriotic Scot, I find "Advance" anaemic and dull. Its rhythm is dreary and the words are general, mundane, and uninspiring — they might relate to any country. There is no hint of our climate, our history, or our philosophy of individuality. It is good but it is tame.

"Matilda", on the other hand is stirring (it is a march as is the "Marseillaise"), and encapsulates our history; it is poetic, allusive and elusive and it is recognized world- wide as Australia's anthem. And it was written and composed in the outback by two outstanding Australians — Banjo Paterson and Christina McPherson and later knocked further into shape by Marie Cowan (whose version was used to advertise Billy Tea) and Thomas Wood, a relatively famous English musicologist and musician and an Australiaphile.

"Waltzing Matilda" is truly poetic, especially in its original state: its story is short and to the point but that story and its characters and its setting allow for many different interpretations which, in my view are the essential features of all good poetry. Any Australian song which contains words like billabong, swagman, troopers, jumbuck is more than just a song, it is the distillation of our country and our history and it *must* become our national anthem. Away with the Queen, excellent woman that she no doubt is, away with our loyal but pedestrian Scottish stonemason — bring on the outback and Banjo and Chris and stir Australia to its depths with "Matilda", as France is stirred to its depths by the "Marseillaise". Ah, if only.

The story surrounding the composition of "Matilda" is quite fascinating and has been much written about. It concerns romance, a broken engagement (perhaps), two pre-existing tunes and songs, a zither (loved by Strauss amongst others), a commercial promotion of billy tea, a swagman, policeman (troopers), station properties and their owners in and around Winton and Kynuna and the Diamentina River and the Oondooroo and the Wakingham Creek and of course the Como Waterhole and buggies and the intervals when gates are swung open and horse drawn vehicles passed through, and... And, yes, there is so much about the origin of this song, this wonderful national anthem of ours, and so little known about Christina McPherson's later life and even that of Sarah Riley after the breaking of her eight-year-old engagement to Banjo. It is all there. It is just as fascinating and romantic as the French Revolution. Let us bring ourselves abreast of the frogs — let us hear the sounds of "Matilda" filling the *Tuileries* from the fountain to the *Musée de l'Orangerie.*

Banjo Paterson may not have been a "great" poet in the sophisticated and international definition of poets and poetry, but, by God, he loved Australia, he wrote about what he loved and he was at home in any part of our country including outback Queensland, the Northern Territory and of course New South Wales generally and Sydney, and he travelled to some extent outside Australia. "Matilda" as our national anthem would be a fitting memorial to him and Christina and Marie, and even Sarah and Thomas.

★ ★ ★ ★

Australia and France are so different but complementary — that is what she said, or something like that, and I keep turning it over in my mind.

What about the languages?

When we first drove west across the Rhine into France I was enchanted — the villages, the Citroën *deux chevaux*, the countryside and, of course, the language. Not that I have ever been able to grasp their language. In fact when I do speak in my best French the locals wince and reply in their excellent English, "Monsieur, while you are staying with us we will speak only in English." In those circumstances how will my French ever improve?

French is one of the romance languages and has grown substantially out of Latin and Italian (and perhaps a little Greek) and a substratum of Celtic, and its hybrid purity is jealously and officially guarded by the French. It is true that foreign words are now part of the language but the French are proud of their tongue and it is taught in schools very seriously. Without doubt it is beautiful, as are Spanish and Italian, and, of course English and German and others. I sometimes think that Italian errs on the side of being just too sweet, German can be very romantic but can also have a certain authoritarian character and English is perhaps the most comprehensive of any language.

On that first stay in France I had to take our car into a nearby dealer's garage for a service and in the taxi back to our hotel I basked in the language and accents of the girl at the depot speaking to her crew of drivers. It was wonderful just to sit and listen.

And what does Australia do with its language? Do we speak with the appropriate BBC accent? Do we sound our vowels or round our vowels, sound our consonants or even open our mouths properly? We are lazy layabouts who need a veranda post to lean against. Yes, that is us and perhaps none the worse for it; that is the way we are.

I do, however, have an objection to the Americanisation of our speech and our writing, although what you can or could do about it is another matter. There is a terrible tendency to tautology (sorry about that John Norton alliteration) in America, for example, apple cider, free gift et cetera — they have to explain the words to you.

And then there is the lapse into picture language on the premise that people can no longer understand abstract terms; for example they render "future" as "down the track", "equal opportunity" becomes "the level playing field" and you "ramp it up" instead of increasing it. Then there are dates which have been reversed and have become December 25 instead of 25 December. Why, one asks, why? I hardly dare mention "guys" instead of people and "gays" instead of homosexuals, "passing away" in lieu of dying and on and on it goes. I can understand people who prefer to be optimists and I approve of calling some things by a less offensive name but out and out euphemisms such as "killed by friendly fire" are simply insulting to one's intellect. Please say the thing honestly and directly — we shot him accidently.

But let us leave these peripheral comparisons of two lovely and distinct languages and the way in which they are articulated and move on to a comparison of the respective countrysides and their buildings — the architecture of Australia and that of France.

I am still amazed at how quickly the nineteenth-century Australians adapted their houses both small and large to the hotter, sunnier climate: awnings over windows, ventilation in deliberately high gables and of course verandas. And I am equally amazed at how we then abandoned this wonderfully practical method of keeping our houses a little cooler. I love the stone houses of Australia, I like those in brick and I am reasonably fond of weatherboards. The feature of Australian buildings which stands out though is their utilitarian character and the attitude that "she'll do — for the time being", this on the basis that the building can or will almost certainly be pulled down in a few year's time and re-built in the then fashion. And throughout the suburbs of the capital cities of Australia we are at this very moment ripping down thousands of thirty and forty year-old houses and replacing them with larger, often unseemly large, so- called McMansions. These "mansions" must have a separate room for the children and their electronic entertainment as well as a "home" theatre for the parents. Once again we are, I fear, aping the fashions of the mighty United States of America.

What about renovating, repairing and, if appropriate,

extending those older houses, thereby saving their bricks, their timber, their roofs, their…everything? What about the wasteful production of a new house and new materials and global warming? Eh, what about it? I cannot say much about city office buildings because I cannot distinguish those in our Central Business District from those in the CBD of any other city in the world, except Dubai. And I do not want to write anything at all about Dubai.

Stone is my great love, because it is quarried in the vicinity of the building and its colours and textures, therefore, harmonize with the locality. Furthermore, it is eminently recyclable and in fact is recycled whether it is a modern building or an old building. Stone, mud bricks, pise — they are all from the earth and are in their natural state, and how they suit. As for the roof: well, slates are superb, tiles of all kinds, especially terra cotta are lovely but the old corrugated iron has a charm. If I lived overseas for a year or two, I think I would suffer a bout of homesickness if I were shown a picture of a painted corrugated iron roof — rather like the waft of a scorched gum leaf.

Hills, rivers, mountains, streams, forests and architecture — they frame the appeal and the beauty of France. For instance, the architecture of the houses in the villages and towns along the Dordogne. Think of a village like Carenac. Why would you want to change that architecture ever? The son of the owner of the Pont de l'Ouysee had just started building his house when we stayed there and the exterior of the new house was only somewhat different to the old and the ancient houses of the area. The interior was quite different but the exterior paid deference to harmony and tradition and in my view that was as it should have been. Sameness and similarity do not for a moment mean boring architecture: you have only to think of the classic terraces of Bath, in England, to scotch that one. A country rich in building stone is a country that has been blessed by God, and its inhabitants should be aware of that blessing and should quarry it and build with it, under pain of being sent to Purgatory, or even Hell.

Complementary? Yes, maybe, but here is a straight out difference between Australia and La Belle France — the bird life in the respective countrysides. There are so many birds in Australia and so few in France — with the exception perhaps of in and around the Pyrenees and in and around the mountains of the Auvergne.

Let me mention a few widespread Australian birds whose flight patterns will entrance you and whose music will not only thrill you but send you into a blissful reverie: the handsome Butcher Bird whose song is amongst the most enthralling music you will hear (never mind his rather uncouth way of feeding himself); the Magpie whose vigorous flight surpasses the rowing stroke of an Olympic sculler and whose warbling is just wonderful; the Currawong whose flight pattern is so swingingly effortless and who turns his head from side to side as he flies and beguiles you with his varied and melodious calls; the Shrike (or grey bush) Thrush with the most velvet soft eyes and some of the most beautiful song you will ever hear; the Eastern Rosella parrot whose colour will dazzle you, whose graceful, looping flight will entrance you and who charms you with his brief fluting music; the Fantail…

I am not exaggerating when I say that you could go on for pages describing Australian birds.

As to why there are not more birds in France, I cannot say. When we went to France in the 1970s it was not hard to tell which day of the week was Sunday because you always woke in your country hotel to the sound of shot guns. And when you drove on from your hotel you would see cars pulled to the side of the road and plenty of hunters walking near the road with guns over their arms. I do not know whether they were after game or birds or both but it is fair to say that I did not see anything much being carried and their shoulder bags looked rather floppy.

We have talked about trees and the glorious foliage of those of France but I want to write just a little bit more on the trunks and barks of our native gums — how colourful, varied and dazzling they are. You can start with the plain old Ironbark with its blackened bark and go then to the White Gum as an interesting contrast; then think about the classical majesty of the Flooded Gum — oh, but it is superb; the colourful and oddly named Monkey Gum; the ubiquitous but lovely Spotted Gum which we have already mentioned; the Ribbon Gum with its carelessly but so artistically arranged hanging ribbons of bark; the Snow Gum which enchants in winter or summer; the Blue Mountain Ash and of course the common but reliably beautiful River Red Gum. I have listed only a few of our eucalypts — there are dozens more and they all have trunks that are unexcelled in their variety and casual beauty. And we have not even mentioned the wattles, the acacias and the shy orchids of the poor and stony hills. We have a remarkable variety of vegetation throughout the whole of Australia.

★ ★ ★ ★ ★

There are people of many backgrounds and nationalities who have come to know and love Australia but let me conclude with a short note on a Frenchman who became an Australian, almost, (at least he died here) and an Englishman who went back to England after two years but who carried a love of Australia in his heart, even though he died in his homeland.

The Frenchman Paul Wenz was born in 1869 at Reims, the capital of the Champagne region, and therefore somewhat to the north of France. His parents (Wenz and Dertinger) were natives of Würtenberg but they decided to make France their home and settled there eleven years before the birth of Paul. His father owned spinning mills and branched out into wool buying, with agencies in Melbourne, Sydney and Perth. It was a successful business and Paul went to an excellent private school in Paris where he met and became friends with the (afterwards) prominent writer André Gide. During his compulsory French military service he was also wise enough to become friends with Joseph Krug of Champagne. Then and now Krug made and still make one of the greatest, if not the greatest, champagne of France.

In 1892 at the age of twenty-three Paul began his "gap" year, or in his case, years. He sailed to Australia, fell in love with the place and did two years jackarooing, going as far north as the Gulf country. He went back to France, after one or two detours along the way, and then in 1898 he again sailed for Australia. On board the ship he met an Australian girl Hettie Dunne, the daughter of a pastoralist, and they married later that year.

The rolling country of New South Wales west of the Great Dividing Range appealed to Paul and Hettie and they bought several thousand acres near Gooloogong in the beautiful Lachlan Valley, almost half way between Cowra and Forbes.

They built a house to their liking and specifications (with verandas) and called it "Nanima". That house although modified over the years, still stands, and is undergoing sensitive restoration in the hands of the Moxey family.

Paul Wenz was a big man (six feet four inches) and was described by our writer Nettie Palmer thus: "with his Norman blue eyes from Rheims (Germany actually), his fresh colouring under white hair, his broad shoulders that make you wonder how the man had ever found a horse strong enough to carry him." Big and strong though he was, he died of pneumonia in August 1939 and is buried in the Forbes cemetery. Wenz and his family (and his wife) had money — there was no doubt about that. And they did not spend all their time living on the property in the tranquillity of the Lachlan Valley. No, indeed, they were often in France and Europe, and to some that would make it all the more remarkable that his love of Australia and things Australian never wavered. Paul Wenz was a man of many interests and one of them was writing and he became imbued with the character of Australia in a similar way to native-born writers like Lawson and Paterson. He was proud to submit his work (in French) to publishers in France and in 1900 his short stories began to appear in the Paris magazine *L'Illustration*. He wrote under the pen name "Paul Warrego". The Warrego River is, of course, an outback stream which joins the Darling just to the north of Louth (south-west of Bourke).

Paul was not a famous writer, despite a considerable output of short stories and books. Frank Moorhouse says of him: "[he] was a good writer, not a great writer…But Wenz's stories such 'The Waggoner' should be in our standard anthologies."

The thing that interests me about Paul Wenz is the way in

which he immersed himself in the Australian ethos whilst being bombarded constantly by the sophistication and history of Europe and with the opportunity at any time in his life to rejoin that history and sophistication. He was one of a relatively small group: a Frenchman, educated in Paris, and wealthy, who chose to live in Australia and, in his case, to write extensively about his new but adopted homeland.

★ ★ ★ ★ ★

Thomas Wood (1892–1950) was a remarkable Englishman and was both talented and courageous. He was born with severe eye problems — cataracts in both eyes. His right eye was virtually sightless and he could see only tolerably well from his left with the help of a powerful lens. And yet he became a prominent composer, a Doctor of Music (Oxford), was chairman of the Royal Philharmonic Society and Arts Council's Music Panel and was a member of the British Broadcasting Commission's Music Advisory Committee; and to top it all off he came to Australia by himself for two years in 1930 on an assignment as an examiner in music — with his eyesight! Thomas left behind him a wife whom he had married in 1924 when he was thirty-two and her maiden name was St. Osyth Mahala Eustace-Smith, and with a name like that you would expect her to get an OBE which she duly did. They lived the whole of their lives in the historic Parsonage Hall, in Bures, in the Stour Valley north-east of London and not that far from Cambridge.

Thomas Wood disembarked at Fremantle on his Australian trip and proceeded to travel round most of West Australia before tackling every other state and making copious notes as his journey progressed. When he got back to England he wrote a book and called it *Cobbers*. It was first printed in 1934 and ran through many re-printings.

Thomas fell in love with Australia but it was not an uncritical love and his affection for his home in the Stour Valley was not decreased by that of his new love. He dedicated his book to his wife with these few simple words: "To Osyth, who waited", and he defined the word "Cobbers" as "Australian Slang — Companion, Mate". And that word "Cobber", is one of the most moving words Australians have invented.

Here is an extract of his thoughts on the evening that he left on his two-year trip:

When I came back everything would be just the same — the old house, a treasury of beams and panelling; the red roofs of the village sloping down to the bridge; the Stour banked with reeds, a mill in the crook of its arm; rooks in the elms and dusk on the Suffolk hills. [I] threw on [the fire] apple logs to burn, since it was an occasion, and lavender sticks, because they smell sweet.

And he also thought about a recent conversation he had had in the local pub and about how he had told his friend the Admiral that he was going to Australia. The Admiral had spent time here and the Admiral was not without his criticisms of Australians and the importance they attached to money:

"And money! That sets the standard of taste…" but then he went on to add, "But there is something which balances all this."

"What is that?"

"Friendship. They will do anything for you if you meet them halfway …They are the most hospitable people I have ever some across in the whole of my life. And you will find good cobbers wherever you go."

"What's a cobber?"

He told me.

Well, as I say, Thomas Wood toured the whole of Australia but perhaps the highlight of his trip was his outback adventure in Queensland. He went inland from Rockhampton and through Blackwater and Emerald to Barcaldine, thence to Longreach and finally to Winton and Kynuna — in other words, deep into the cattle stations of the outback. He had booked into the Gregory Hotel at Winton but he was exhausted from his long and hazardous rail journey and instead of pursuing his letters of introduction to notable locals he "dozed in the lounge". In fact he did no calling in and around Winton because he made the acquaintance of Mr. Shanahan the hotel manager, the local magistrate and the mayor, and Shanahan was a mine of information on a local folk song much admired by Thomas — "Waltzing Matilda". Thomas Wood, having listened to Shanahan's description of the origin of the song waxed enthusiastic about it and said to Shanahan, "(It is) good enough to be the unofficial national anthem of Australia…"

And then Thomas Wood in his enthusiasm and heedless of any copyright problems set out in his manuscript the music, "Harmonized by Thomas Wood", and the words, both as amended by Marie Cowan.

Thomas Wood enjoyed quite a measure of fame in England, not least because of his promulgation of the lovely "Waltzing Matilda". He has been described as "The man who arranged the music to the Aussies' National Anthem — Waltzing Matilda". Well, that may not be quite accurate but through his highly successful book which contained the music and the words he certainly did much to boost the worldwide popularity of our "National Anthem".

Thomas Wood, courageous and sunny man that he was, should have the final say on the merits of the capital city of the State we have been writing about. Here then is his assessment of Sydney.

"An exotic: a lovely and petulant spendthrift, going its own wilful headstrong vivid way, self centred, yet open hearted, absurdly vain, yet very likeable."

POSTSCRIPT

Food plays such a central role in French culture that it is impossible to think of France and not think, too, of the food and the wine and the pride the people take in them. A meal is a celebration of life itself. Traditionally France closed for lunch, and in many towns and villages we visited, it still does. A meal takes time. Food is something to be thought about, meditated upon, and thoroughly enjoyed. So it seems only fair to share with you the food and wine we enjoyed during our trip.

Given the importance the French place on food, French restaurateurs should be different from restaurateurs in the rest of the world. They should be utterly sophisticated and devoted heart and soul to the traditional and regional dishes. They should not be swayed by fashion, but sadly some are, especially at the occasional "great" place, where they ought to know better.

Those of us who are somewhat long in the tooth will remember cuisine minceur and the way it swept around and through La Belle France in the 1970s, like a fitful dust storm. And now, sadly it is the turn of the froth and foam and deconstructed, with artful architectural structures to accommodate and show off the cleverness of the kitchen. Spare me, please, from these artists of the hotplate and give me back simple food, simply cooked — food of the region which has stood the test of one or two generations of cooks and diners. I don't say that food should not evolve, of course not, but I do say that it should evolve thoughtfully and that it ought to have regard for what is and can be produced within a reasonable distance of the establishment.

On our trips we have tended to go from one known place to

another — there are few unpleasant surprises and the path is easy to find and follow. The comfort of such places is gratifying and we have ceased to be adventurous. May I suggest that you sprinkle your next trip with some adventure: bed and breakfasts perhaps. Bed and breakfasts are obtainable throughout France and appear to range from the great to the humble. Then you can wander around and choose your bistro or restaurant. For example, one night after a few sophisticated meals we deliberately chose a humble but busy bistro which served (God be praised) in the middle of the table with your main course…*a bowl of pommes frites!* There was no froth on those hot and aromatic potatoes, no foam whatsoever, not a scintilla of a garnish, nothing at all but golden brown potatoes proudly giving off their vapours there in their shining oil. And the previous course had been a plate of crudités.

Gourmets may scoff at my adoration of the ubiquitous tuber but let me tell you that it had the approval of Raymond Oliver, master of Le Grand Véfor from 1948 to 1983, and of the horticulturalist August Parmentier (1737–1813), and the great, well moderately great, reasonably good, well…fondly remembered Louis XV1 who wore a potato flower in his buttonhole. Raymond in his book "The French at Table" writes: "We owe a great deal to them [potatoes]. It was they, who above all others, created modern French cookery." Some people may maintain the "they" that Oliver is referring to are "the plain people of bourgeois families" but I think that he is praising the potato.

The last word on the value of those bistro pommes frites comes from the redoubtable Encyclopaedia. "Potatoes, containing (as they do) starch, are highly digestible. They also supply vitamin C, amino acids, protein, thiamine and nicotine acid." I need say no more.

But to return to the point, the word classic would sum up what we expect from French restaurateurs: "of acknowl-edged excellence, remarkably typical, serious, conventional, outstandingly important." Yes, that is the sort of food one anticipates in the good places of France.

Here are details of some of the food and wine we enjoyed during our exploration of the Dordogne.

★ ★ ★

HOTEL: LE PUY FERRAND at PUY de SANCY

Le Mont Dore, Puy de Dôme, Auvergne

www.auvergne-alc.com

Aperitif: Gentiane Salers — bright yellow, very acidic and bitter, and made from gentian flowers growing everywhere in this area. Served with ice.

Entrée: Soupe de Champignons; Le Pounti Maison, as a terrine with beautifully fresh oakleaf lettuce with hazelnut dressing (a traditional speciality of the region — cake with onions, prunes, herbs).

Main course: Sandre, beurre blanc sauce, tiny boiled potatoes.

Fromage: Fourme d'Albert (blue-vein), Cantal and Saint Nectaire.

White wine: Chateau Gay (local).

Red wine: Côte d'Auvergne

★ ★ ★

HOSTELLERIE de la MARONNE

Le Theil, St. Martin Valmeroux, Cantal

www.chateauxhotels.com

Amuse bouche: Boudin Noir and apple puree.

Aperitif: Lillet blanc (from Bordeaux region).

Entrée: Local asparagus, sauce vierge; Ravioli of langoustine, basil sauce.

Main Course: Sandre with fresh spring vegetables (primeurs) from their own vegetable garden.

Fromage: Cantal, Saint Nectaire, Bleu d'Auvergne, le Rocamadour.

Dessert: Strawberries done three ways; Tarte de Thomas (chef) — apples, bananas and glace.

Wine: Louis Latour 2006 Fleurie.

SECOND NIGHT

Amuse bouche: Very delicate scrambled egg, tomato and bacon, served in tiny cups.

Aperitif: Lillet Blanc and Campari soda, with tiny muffins of Pounti.

Main Course: (No entrée for us tonight!) Filet de boeuf Salers, served with braised shallot and red wine sauce, accompanied by La Truffade

(very traditional: potatoes pureed, with cream and cantal cheese).
Fromage: Cantal, Le Rocamadour, Gaperon from St. Flour (an onion-shaped fresh cow milk cheese).
Wine: Le Chablisienne — Chablis 2003. Beaune-Perrieres 2003.

★ ★ ★

LE MANOIR DE BEAULIEU

Beaulieu-sur-Dordogne (Auvergne Limousin)
www.chateauxhotels.com
Aperitif: Walnut liqueur with white wine, a speciality of region
Menus Degustation: Some in molecular style: Presse de morue et fondant,lait de morue en espume et lard seche; L'Oeuf a la Truffe ,L'Oeuf coque, Emulsion de truffes madeire, Le Jaune (of egg) Beignet, Le thon et le Radis Noir braisee a la orange et en dive etuvee;Le Cabillaud et la Basilico.
Wine: Alsace, 2005 Sylvaner

★ ★ ★

LE PONT DE L'OUYSSE

Lacave near Souillac
www.chateauxhotels.com
Aperitif: Lillet blanc with tiny pastries.
Entrée: Foie de canard, chutney de pommes et La Mique; Risotto de legumes de printemps.
Main Course: Poularde rotie et pochee, legumes de printemps; Dos de cabillaude rôti, piperade piquillas farci et pâtés fraiches.
White Wine: St.Veran
Red Wine: Domaine St. Andre de Figuiere 2006 Vielles Vignes Les Maures (Provence)
Dessert: Tarte fin aux pommes au glace cannelle.

SECOND NIGHT
Aperitif: Lillet Blanc with delicious morsels.
Entrée: Gratiné d'huitres aux epinards, beurre blanc d'estragon; Risotto de legumes du printemps, un bon jus de barigoule.
Main Course: Sole rôtie aux cepes, sauce crème; St. Jacques et langous-

tines aux artichauts violet et asperges vertes.

Fromage: Cantal with a petite salade, walnut vinaigrette.

Dessert: Croquant au Café; Glace Café.

White Wine: Viognier 2007

Red Wine: Château de la Selve, St. Regis, Ardèche

THIRD NIGHT

Aperitif: Lillet Rouge, Campari soda, with amuse bouche.

Entrée: Terrine de foie gras with spicy apple in quenelle shape; Duo des aperges vertes et blanches, oeuf en longue cuisson, sauce du grand pere Maury.

Main Course: Ventriche de thon poelèe, une pipérade aux olives, queues de langoustines rôties, pommes de terre Charlotte, ecrivisses a la four chette, jus deglace truffe.

Fromage: Le Rocamadour et petite salade.

Wine: Bourgeuil

FOURTH NIGHT

Aperitif: Lillet blanc, with amuse bouche.

Entrée: Millefeuille des legumes, presse foie gras, asperges vertes et truffes noir; Risotto, artichauts violets, girolle, sauce queue de boeuf.

Main Course: Ris de veau, epinards a la créme et ecrivisses; Piece de boeuf, puree de pommes de terre, cepes.

Fromage: Le rocamadour et petite salade. Café Noisette and beautiful petites fours.

Wine: Château Tour des Gendres Bergerac 2003. Delightful touch on back label — "Le Gloire de mon Pere".

★   ★   ★

LE MOULIN DE L'ABBAYE,

Brantôme-en-Périgord (Dordogne)

www.relaischateaux.com

Aperitif: Lillet blanc

Entrée: Thon rouge marine, caviar d'aubergine, fin ratatouilles du basilic, fromage frais des Terres Vielles, et coulis de poivron; Cannellonis de petits pois et d'asperges, avec ses legumes de saison.

Main Course: Filet et côte d'agneau du Perigord en croute de noix et d'herbes, pommes Grenailles a l'huile d'olive, navet et carrotte glace du jus; St. Pierre pique au romarin, gnocchis de pommes de terre a la Salardaise, supreme de blanc de poireaux, jus vert pre.

Fromage: Several from the cheese trolley.

Dessert: La tarte de chocolat noir, glace a la crème brulee, espresso en emulsion.

Wine: Chablis — Gilbert Picquet et ses Fils Château de Tiregand *Pécharmant* 2005

★ ★ ★

LE VIEUX LOGIS
Trémolat (Dordogne)
www.relaischateaux.com
Aperitif: Lillet with delicious tidbits.

Degustation Menu: Balade Printanier.

Wine: Selected for each course by sommelier: Château de la Robertie 2005 – Bergerac sec Château Haut Perthus 2003 Côtes de Bergerac Rouge

Dessert: La Noix comme un Tiramisu.. Wine served with Dessert: Château de Rooy 2007 – Rosette

SECOND NIGHT
LE BISTRO EN FACE
Owned by Le Vieux Logis and in street opposite.
Aoeritif: Lillet blanc served with Duck rillettes and delicious bread from their oven.

Entrèe: Assiette de crudités (grated carrot, small diced oven roasted beetroot, celeriac remoulade, oeuf dur with chilli mayonnaise.

Main Course: Dos de Cabillaud; Omelette aux truffes , both served with pommes frits and salade verte.

Dessert: La Tarte Tatin.

Wine: A Kameleon Semillon

★ ★ ★

CHATEAU de SANSE

Ste Radegonde, Aquitaine

www.guidesdecharme.com

Café noisette served with petits fours on terrace on arrival.

Aperitif: Lillet and Campari Soda.

Before entrée: A tiny bowl of soupe de langoustine.

Entrée: Duo asperges tiedes, huile de noix, croustillade foie gras, confit d'oignon.

Main Course: Fondant de volaille fourèe saumon frais, epices Cajun, petites legumes printanier.

Fromage: Of the region — goats, washed rind.

Wine: Tapon Rose, local area (Cabernet Sauvignon, Cabernet Franc)

SECOND NIGHT

Aperitif: Lillet and Pineau de Charente.

Ameuse bouche: Tiny cup rich tomatoey-cream soup with tiny clams.

Entrée: Terrine de foie canard, layered with coco beans and with a superb chutney of plum and apple; Filigree of parmesan and noix, fresh goat's cheese with herbs and small slices of duck breast with mesclun salad.

Main Course: Roasted bass, tiny spring vegetables, quenelles of aubergine caviar; Salmon with tapenade.

Dessert: Vanille parfait, framboises, fruit coulis (orange, passionfruit).

Wine: Tapon Rose 2006

★ ★ ★

CHÂTEAU MEYRE - LE CLOS DE CHÂTEAU MEYRE,

Avensan, Medoc

Bed and breakfast only — on a wine estate

www.chateauxhotels.com

BISTRO 'LE LION D'OR',

Margaux, Medoc

Aperitif: Lillet Blanc

Entrée: Terrine de foies de Volaille served with Cornichons and toast.

Main Course: Gigot d'agneau, Grosses d'ail and flageolets; Medaillon de lotte au legumes printantier. Both dishes served with a dish of buttery oven- roasted potato slices.

Dessert: Dessert omelette stuffed with strawberries and Grand Marnier.

★ ★ ★

RESTAURANT 'LE PLAISANCE'
Bourg
Aperitif: Lillet blanc, Campari soda.
Entrée: Salade Nicoise; Moules a la Plancha.
Main Course: Turbot sauvage a la plancha, pommes frites, salade verte.
Wine: Bassereau Château de la Grave — "Homage de la Grave" 2006

SECOND NIGHT
Aperitif: Lillet blanc
Main Course: Turbot a la plancha; Moules et pommes frites.
Fromage: Assiette de fromage - various local cheeses plus a little plate with Brebis from Pyrenees served with melon jam.
Red Wine: Bassereau Château de la Grave
White Wine: Grains Fin 2006 (Semillon 70%, Columbard 30%, fermented and left on lees in barriques)

★ ★ ★

ACKNOWLEDGEMENTS

Everyone should be able to operate the keyboard of a computer — I can, no doubt, but I don't.

Were it not for the skilful and willing fingers of my wife Bertina, this book and the previous ones would not have been printed. Thank you Tina for your hard work and your patience with alterations and revisions, and thank you too for all your research.

Editors. What would we do without editors? My editor is first and foremost a writer, but for some reason she consents to edit my manuscripts. Once I thought that editors were the opposition. I have changed my mind. Thank you Margaret Geddes for all of your suggestions, your graceful persistence and for giving my effort a continuity that it lacked. You are a true professional.

Oddly enough it is also appropriate to thank my two daughters and our four grandchildren whose support is consistent and quite wonderful when and if the spirit lags. *Merçi beaucoup,* Elizabeth, Maryann, Isabella, Lily, Amelia and Hannah.

Reg Egan

OF RIVERS, BAGUETTES & BILLABONGS

Reg Egan

		Qty
ISBN 9781922036599		
RRP	AU$26.99	.....
Postage within Australia	AU$5.00	.....
	TOTAL★ $_____	

★ All prices include GST

Name:..

Address: ....

....

Phone:...

Email: ....

Payment: ❑ Money Order ❑ Cheque ❑ Amex ❑ MasterCard ❑ Visa

Cardholders Name:..

Credit Card Number: ....

Signature:...

Expiry Date: ....

Allow 7 days for delivery.

Payment to: Marzocco Consultancy (ABN 14 067 257 390)
PO Box 12544
A'Beckett Street, Melbourne, 8006
Victoria, Australia
Fax: +61 3 9671 4730
markzocchi@brolgapublishing.com.au

Be Published

Publishing through a successful Australian publisher. Brolga provides:

- Editorial appraisal
- Cover design
- Typesetting
- Printing
- Author promotion
  - National book trade distribution, including sales, marketing and distribution through Macmillan Australia.
  - International book trade distribution
  - Worldwide e-Book distribution

For details and inquiries, contact:
Brolga Publishing Pty Ltd
PO Box 12544
A'Beckett St VIC 8006

Phone: 0414 608 494
admin@brolgapublishing.com.au
markzocchi@brolgapublishing.com.au
ABN: 46 063 962 443